Gardening Made Easy for Seniors

Secrets the Experts Never Tell You

Publisher's Note

This book is intended for general information only. It does not constitute medical, legal, or financial advice or practice. The editors of FC&A have taken careful measures to ensure the accuracy and usefulness of the information in this book. While every attempt has been made to assure accuracy, errors may occur. Some websites, addresses, and telephone numbers may have changed since printing. We cannot guarantee the safety or effectiveness of any advice or treatments mentioned. Readers are urged to consult with their professional financial advisors, lawyers, and health care professionals before making any changes.

Any health information in this book is for information only and is not intended to be a medical guide for self-treatment. It does not constitute medical advice and should not be construed as such or used in place of your doctor's medical advice. Readers are urged to consult with their health care professionals before undertaking therapies suggested by the information in this book, keeping in mind that errors in the text may occur as in all publications and that new findings may supersede older information.

The publisher and editors disclaim all liability (including any injuries, damages, or losses) resulting from the use of the information in this book.

But the fruit of the Spirit is love, joy, peace, forbearance, kindness,
goodness, faithfulness, gentleness and self-control.
Against such things there is no law.

Galatians 5:22-23

FC&A Publishing®
103 Clover Green
Peachtree City, GA 30269

Produced by the staff of FC&A

ISBN 978-1935574675

Table of Contents

Yard and garden design: plan like a pro

7 smart ways to beautify your yard. One key to a beautiful yard or garden is a good landscaping plan. There are several ways you can get a quality plan for little or no cost.

- Thumb through gardening books and magazines, and save articles and pictures of things that might work for your particular layout.

- Look for ideas and instructions on internet websites like *diynet.com*. You can find millions of other possibilities with a search engine hunt for "landscaping."

- Sketch out your own ideas. Hire a landscape designer to look over them and make suggestions or corrections. You'll spend a fraction of the cost of having a whole plan drawn from scratch.

- Check with your state or county extension office. They can give you advice or set you up with a trained Master Gardener volunteer.

- Talk with an expert at your local nursery or garden center, which might offer formal planning services in addition to in-store advice. Fees may be discounted if you buy your plants from them.

- Inquire at a nearby college or university with a landscape design or horticulture program. You might find a student who will take on your project for free or at a reduced cost.

- Snag free landscape designs from the Arbor Day Foundation at *arborday.org/trees/landscapedesign*. Plans range from a traditional knot garden to a flowering woods edge.

Sometimes — particularly in complex situations involving structures or earthmoving — you can save money by hiring a trained and certified professional. Get recommendations from garden centers or friends and neighbors with yards you admire. Look up members of the American Society of Landscape Architects at *asla.org* or the Association of Professional Landscape Designers at *apld.org*.

Get professional landscaping for less. You have always wanted to add raised beds, solve that drainage problem, or even landscape the yard for low maintenance. But landscaping can be tricky, and you may want professional advice.

Expect to spend $1,000 to $3,000 for a landscape plan from a landscape architect, while the cost of a plan from a certified landscape designer may cost between $375 and $1,350.

Landscape architects are college-educated, trained, and licensed professionals who understand all aspects of landscape planning, drainage correction, grading and erosion issues, and landscape-related construction. Certified landscape designers do not have the licensing and construction training of landscape architects, but they have expertise in designing with plants and can create a customized plan for your yard.

Your local garden nursery can also design you a landscape plan that may cost from $240 to $400. You could even get a plan for free if you buy the plants from their nursery, or get discounts or rebates on their plants and supplies. You may receive a wonderful plan that works well for years or end up with a cookie-cutter plan that does not fully adapt to your yard's characteristics. Still, it can be a fairly inexpensive way to create a yard you can be proud of.

> Decide how much money you can spend and the time span of your project. Don't try to do too much at once. You might try a five-year development plan.

Be a better planter with a plan. You might be tempted just to go to the garden center and pick out what you like. But you'll make expensive mistakes if you mix and match plants that don't grow well together, or aren't suited for your soil. A little knowledge goes a long way. These sources can make your planning — and your planting — a lot easier.

- Guidebook. A simple guide for your geographical area will help you identify plants that will thrive. If your local garden center doesn't have a knowledgeable salesperson available, take your guidebook with you. When you see something you like, check its requirements. And look at the pictures, too, because sometimes plants get mislabeled.

- Experts. If you aren't sure what flowers to plant, visiting garden shows will give you a lot of good ideas. You may be able to get advice about your specific needs and even buy plants you like on the spot. Garden tours can be even better. You'll get to meet people in your area who will be happy to share tips about their gardening successes.

- Neighbors. You don't have to take a tour to take a peek at the garden next door. A quick, reliable way to choose plants for your own garden is to see what's growing well in a neighbor's yard.

Reap more benefits with raised beds. "Raised beds don't have to be expensive," says consumer horticulturist Robert Westerfield, who has taught many programs on the subject. People balk at the idea when they consider the price tag — you could easily spend over $100 on a raised bed kit. But you don't need to splurge on pricey materials or pre-made sets. In fact, you can purchase low-cost supplies at your local home improvement store and build a 4-foot by 4-foot raised bed for under $20.

And think of it as a long-term investment. "When you build a raised bed," Westerfield says, "you're looking at getting 10 to 12 years out of it." That means your expenses come out to just $2 or less a year.

Even if you do end up investing a little more in your raised beds, these elevated plots have many benefits that outweigh the initial cost of getting your garden off the ground.

- They make planting simple and weeding easier. "With raised beds, a couple of hand tools is about all you need for maintenance," says Westerfield. Plus, they're convenient for gardeners who have a hard time getting around.

- "By bringing your garden off the ground, you've improved the drainage," he adds. In places where waterlogged roots are common, raised beds can literally save your crops.

- Get a head start on the season, and grow more produce. "The soil in a raised bed typically warms up quicker," Westerfield explains, "so you can get the crop in the ground a little bit sooner."

Use a garden hose to mark landscape design. Planning a new flower bed? Do like the pros and work with curved shapes instead of straight lines. Lay a garden hose out on your lawn and experiment with gentle curves and arcs. When you're happy with the design, secure the hose temporarily and use a spade to mark the edge of your new border. Remove the hose and get to work digging.

Plot the perfect garden layout every year. Find an empty squeezable ketchup or mustard bottle or an empty drink bottle that has a pull-up "sipper." Clean it out, let it dry, and fill it two-thirds full with flour.

Now go out to your garden bed and use this squeezable marker to mark where each plant should go. For best results, "draw" a shape that matches the plant's mature size and leave a gardener-size working space between plants. You can even mark spaces for walking paths or garden art.

When you're done, you'll have the perfect garden layout for your space. This clever trick also saves money because you'll never buy more plants than your garden can hold.

10 tricks for jaw-dropping borders

Create incredible borders with endless eye appeal using these 10 tips.

- Divide the border into sections when planning it. Design one section, then repeat that design in each of the others.

- Plan a few large, bold curves in your border rather than many small curves.

- Design borders to curve in at corners.

- Choose flower colors next to each other on the color wheel for a serene, calm feeling.

- Combine opposite colors on the color wheel for bright, striking contrast.

- Add variety to one-color flower borders with a mixture of foliage and textures.

- Interplant bulbs among perennials to hide bulbs' dying foliage.

- Lay strips of cardboard around bed edges and cover with mulch to eliminate weed eating.

- Edge borders with creative materials like seashells.

- Mass containers together to create a potted plant border if you have poor or no ground to grow in.

Design a maintenance-free yard. You can have the best-looking yard in town without all the watering and chemicals. Here's how to start.

Notice which plants in your yard, including grass, require the most watering, pesticides, herbicides, or fertilizer. These contribute the most dollars to your yard-care costs. Consider trading away these high-cost plants in exchange for plants that grow better and need less maintenance. Go native.

Native plants are tough but beautiful. They have survived your climate for hundreds, even thousands, of years without being babied. Put them in your landscape, and they'll do the same. Once established, they will rarely need watering or fertilizing. Plus, they're naturally resistant to local pests. You'll have a beautiful garden and spend less in the long run.

To find out which plants are native to your area, check with your state or local native plant society, visit your area cooperative extension website, contact your cooperative extension agent, or visit *plantnative.org*.

As you replace your high-maintenance plants with less costly substitutes, keep these five other tricks for a low-maintenance landscape in mind.

- When you cannot use a native plant, choose plants like daylilies that are famous for being tough to kill.

- Opt for little or no lawn. The average suburban lawn gets 10 times as much pesticide per acre as farmland and accounts for at least 30 percent of water used, the National Wildlife Federation reports. Unfortunately, the cost of all that pesticide and water comes right out of your wallet. Replace grass with ground cover, low maintenance native or ornamental grasses, or hardscaping like gravel.

- Choose drought-tolerant plants for parts of the yard that dry out quickly, such as unshaded areas in the southern or western sides of the yard.

- Emphasize trees and shrubs in your landscape. Most of them require less care than other plants.

- Fill beds and borders with perennials and shrubs instead of annuals. And avoid fast-growing plants. They need pruning more often.

Make a small yard look bigger. A small yard will seem to expand like magic if you plant cool-colored plants at its far end and warm-colored plants at the front and entry. Warm colors include red, orange, and yellow, whereas blue, purple, and pastel pink are cool colors.

Plant a tree to enhance property value. Greenery in front of your house not only beautifies it for your enjoyment, it increases your property's value. And while flowers may increase curb appeal and attract a buyer when you're ready to sell, hardier shrubs and trees are more likely to raise the selling price.

Best plants to protect your home. Want thieves to steer clear of your property? Burglar-proof your home with beautiful but unwelcoming plants. Think thorns, dense branches, and razor-edged leaves. These plants, in particular, will make thieves think twice about breaking into your home.

- berberis — with some of the sharpest spines around

- acanthus — with its spiny flower heads

- pyracantha — perfect under windows

- climbing roses — ideal for training up drainpipes and walls that thieves might try to climb

- pampas grass — whose knifelike leaves make it perfect for dark corners where intruders might try to hide

Hardy plant choices for hard-to-grow areas. You can find plants that grow in any sort of garden — whether shady, salty, or dry. Don't give up hope of having the garden of your dreams. Look for plants that thrive in these tough environments. Call your local extension office and ask them to recommend more plants. They'll know what grows best in your area.

Land is	Try growing		
	flowers	shrubs	trees
Dry	lavender, artemisia, coneflower	juniper, Japanese barberry	eucalyptus, Eastern red cedar
Shady	geranium, impatiens, columbine	hydrangea, barberry, mountain laurel	flowering dog-woods, Western red cedar, many types of maples
Salty	dianthus, iris, salvia, sedum	rosa rugosa, bayberry, sumac	Southern red cedar, white oak

Get the facts before you plant. Don't risk a size surprise when you're picking plants for your landscape. A cute little sprig of rosemary can turn into a shrub that's 4 feet high and 5 feet wide in just a few years. Before you buy any plant for your yard or garden, find out how high and how wide it can get. Then you can be sure to place it where it will grow well and look its best.

Spotlight entryway with a specimen

Put a "specimen plant" near your front door, and you'll highlight your home's main entrance. A specimen plant is landscapers' lingo for any plant with eye-catching and attractive features. Enchanting flowers, bright berries, or an interesting shape can grab visitors' attention — and guide them straight to your front door.

Shrubs shrink heating and cooling costs. Azaleas with their springtime color, sweet-smelling gardenias, or even a formal hedge of boxwoods — shrubs are the mainstay of any landscape. Make sure you include some in your design, and with careful planning, you can trim some bucks off your energy bill.

- Plant shrubs 3 feet away from your air conditioning unit to shade it and improve its efficiency by 10 percent.

- Line dark, paved surfaces with shrubs to keep the concrete cooler, and you may lower the temperature of your yard and home, as well.

- Add insulation to your home without packing it into the walls. Plant shrubs 1 foot away from your exterior to create a cushion of still air that insulates your home and prevents heat from escaping.

Divine vines offer cooling cover. Take a stroll around your yard and inside your home during a hot summer day. Which windows are really baking in the sun? Notice that along with direct sunlight, they are letting in a lot of heat. Now build a temporary or permanent trellis around each one and plant deciduous vines. This simple step can reduce air conditioning costs by up to 50 percent.

Some utility companies may offer free trees or a home energy audit that includes ideas for landscaping. Call your gas or electric company, or visit their website to see what's available.

Trees can grow your energy savings. A 6- to 8-foot tree begins shading your home the very first year, and could grow to protect your simmering roof within five to 10 years. In fact, just one shade tree can pack the cooling power of 15 air conditioners. The best news is a tree "runs" for free.

If this sounds like an energy-saving solution you'd be interested in, plant some trees on the sides of your house that receive the most sunlight — usually the west, east, or south sides. Choose deciduous varieties that will block summer rays, yet still allow sunlight to help heat your home in winter.

To save even more heating dollars, experts say to plant a line of trees where they can block the chilling winds of winter, most often along the north and northwest sides of your house. A windbreak like this can protect an area that is 10 times its height. So trees just

Tree-shaded neighborhoods can be 3 to 6 degrees cooler in summer than treeless areas. Plan your home's landscape with this in mind and slash your air-conditioning costs by 15 to 50 percent.

30 feet high can shield a 300-foot-wide area. A row of ever-green trees can cut heating costs by 10 to 50 percent a year.

Light the night for less with a DIY kit. Hire a professional and he can design and install a full package of quality lighting that includes path lights, accent lighting for trees and house features, and other specialty lighting. But that could cost between $3,000 and $4,000. Throw in motion detector lights and other accents, and the price tag could skyrocket to $5,000.

The good news is you truly do not have to turn landscape lighting into a major production to get stunning effects, says Warren Elwell, Registered Landscape Architect for All South Lawnscapes, Inc. in Georgia. In fact, Elwell empha-sizes that just a few fixtures can make a big impact. "Lighting should be an accent to the landscape, not a run-way for planes to land," he says.

With that in mind, consider a DIY path lighting kit that will let you "test drive" outdoor lighting without spending tons of cash. These kits can range from $80 to $150, and usually include a selection of lights, a length of cable, and a trans-former. Besides that, they are a cinch to install.

"Lighting systems can also be planned to expand over a period of time," Elwell adds, "which can make it very economical." If you install lighting in stages, you'll spread the cost out over months or years. At each stage you can make new cost-saving adjustments.

Smart tips help you roll back the darkness. Here's how you can light up your night, but still save money, time, and trouble.

- If you plan to add extra lights to your design later, you may need a more powerful transformer or an extra one to support the new lights. Decide if starting out with a larger transformer is more cost-efficient than replacing it down the road.

- DIY won't work for everyone, so read the directions very carefully before attempting to install your lighting kit. For example, you may want help from a pro if you need to run wiring under a concrete driveway, or if you don't have an outdoor GFCI receptacle or GFCI breaker at the circuit panel.

- Unlike halogen or LED lights with replaceable bulbs, integrated LED lights are a single unit. These may be easier on your power bill, but they can be more expensive to repair or replace than other lighting.

- Solar lights may not require wiring, but they also may not last all night or be as bright as LED or halogen lights.

Whether you have simple path lights to welcome you home or a dramatic nighttime display, you can expect great benefits like these.

- A well-lit home is a safer home. Deter intruders by giving them fewer places to hide.

- Prevent accidents and falls with illuminated steps, driveways, and paths.

- Boost your curb appeal — and perhaps your home's value — with lights that accent your property's best features and add visual interest.

Harvest free gardening advice. Love gardening? If this is your favorite hobby, your computer can dig up all sorts of tips for you. The internet is fertile ground for all things gardening.

One great resource and starting point is the National Gardening Association's website at *garden.org*. Landscape your yard for the cost of materials with their how-to projects. Get free landscaping and gardening advice from experts, regional reports, and helpful tips. You can look through reference materials and connect with others on message boards.

Learn how to grow anything, inside or out, with the help of these great gardening sites.

Aggie Horticulture Texas A&M AgriLife Extension Service	*aggie-horticulture.tamu.edu*
Clemson University Cooperative Extension Service Home and Garden Information Center	*clemson.edu/extension/hgic*
Garden Guides	*gardenguides.com*
GardenWeb	*gardenweb.com*
The United States National Arboretum	*usna.usda.gov*
University of Illinois Extension Watch Your Garden Grow	*urbanext.illinois.edu/veggies*

As usual, a search engine can come in handy for gardening tips. Just enter a keyword, like "perennials," to get more information on any garden-related topic. Search engines are also a good way to look for cooperative extension programs and Master Gardener classes in your area.

Pick a perfect plant. Want to learn more about plants? Which ones fare best in your climate zone or soil type? Get all the answers at these searchable online plant databases and encyclopedias.

USDA Plant Database	plants.usda.gov
The National Gardening Association Plants Database	garden.org/plants
Audobon Native Plants Database	audubon.org/native-plants

Insiders' secrets to nabbing free stuff. Gardening shouldn't cost a fortune, and if you have access to a computer, it won't. Little-known websites like the ones below are packed with advice on getting free plants, mulch, pots, tools, and more.

- For tips on snagging free plants, mulch, and pots, head to *frugalgardening.com*.

- Find a tool lending library near you at *localtools.org/find*.

Call on the experts. You can always go to names you know and trust, like corporations and national or local nurseries, for a wealth of gardening information. Here are just a few examples.

Pike Nurseries	pikenursery.com
Better Homes & Gardens	bhg.com
The Old Farmer's Almanac	almanac.com
Home & Garden Television	hgtv.com

Know what's below — call before you dig. "We thought the backyard was safe," admits one homeowner. "Oh, we knew digging could cut a cable in the front yard, because pipes and wiring come in to the house from the street. But we nearly cut the wiring buried in our backyard because we forgot the previous homeowner had run electrical wiring to the backyard shed."

Digging without knowing the approximate location of underground utilities can result in damage to gas, electric, communications, water, and sewer lines. In fact, an underground utility line is damaged once every six minutes nationwide because someone decided to dig without taking necessary precautions. And that can lead to service disruptions, serious injuries, and costly repairs.

No matter where you plan to dig in your yard, take five minutes to dial 811 first. This phone number will connect you to your local One Call Center. Tell the operator what kind of work you want to do and where you want to do it. A few days later, the utility companies will stop by and mark any underground pipes, lines, and cables in that area. The call and information are free.

In addition, make sure you know the locations of wiring and pipes for any landscape lighting, fountains, or water features in your yard.

Soil: nourish your plants from the ground up

Unleash more power from your fertilizer. Soil that's too alkaline or acidic can prevent your plants from absorbing the fertilizer you give them. That's like pouring fertilizer money down the drain. Fortunately, soil testing is easy and inexpensive. Just dig up a few samples and ask your local cooperative extension agent how to get them tested. The test results will reveal whether your soil is acidic or alkaline, which nutrients it needs, and how to fertilize or amend it so your plants and lawn flourish.

But remember, your soil test results are only as good as the samples you take, so be careful to do it right. Don't mix samples from the vegetable garden with samples from the flower bed, shrubbery bed, or lawn. After all, the kind of soil that grows a perfect lawn can differ greatly from the ideal soil for veggies. Pick which areas you want tested and take one group of soil samples for each. You'll be surprised how easy it is.

For example, go to your veggie garden, dig up several 5-inch-deep plugs of soil, and mix them together. Remove anything in the soil sample that isn't soil. Drop the sample into the container recommended by the testing lab and label accordingly. Follow the same process for the lawn or any other area you want tested. When you're done, you'll have perfect soil samples that may lead to the most dazzling yard and garden you've ever had.

Pantry tests give clues about pH level. "Soil testing lets you know what the plant needs and where the pH range needs to be for that plant to grow. If it's not in the optimum range for that specific plant, that plant will not take up the nutrients in the soil or the nutrients you've applied," says Kim Toal, Fayette County Extension agent with the University of Georgia Extension service.

Most plants in the garden would love to grow in a soil that is just a bit acidic, with a pH between 6.0 and 6.5. Grab items from the pantry and do a rough pH test.

Collect a soil sample and divide it in half. Add a few drops of cider vinegar to one sample. If it fizzes, the soil is alkaline. Wet the other sample, then add a pinch of baking soda. If this sample fizzes, the soil may be on the acidic side. That gives you a basic idea, but check with your county cooperative extension agency for a more accurate test.

Discover your soil type. Here's an easy way to find out what type of soil you have. In a glass jar, mix a generous handful of dirt with two-thirds of a quart of sterile water and a teaspoon of dishwashing soap. Shake it up and let it settle. Heavy sand will drift to the bottom quickly.

Leave your jar undisturbed overnight so medium-grade silt and the lightest clay can settle more slowly. You should see clear lines dividing the soil types. Dirt that is about 40 percent sand, 40 percent silt, and 20 percent clay is ideal, and it's called loam.

Try a simple drainage test. You don't need to send a soil sample off to the lab to figure out how much irrigation your garden needs. All you need is a shovel. Wait for the soil to dry out, then dig a hole about 1 foot deep and 1 foot across. Pour a bucket of water into the hole, and check the results.

- Good drainage. Water fills the hole then drains out completely within a few minutes.

- Sandy soil. Water seeps into the soil almost as fast as you can pour it into the hole. You'll need to water often to keep plants from drying out.

- Poor drainage. As you pour water into the hole, it quickly fills up. To keep plant roots from sitting in a swamp, consider amending the soil with compost or sphagnum peat moss. You may also try a raised bed system using an easy-draining soil.

Develop a sense of humus. Loam, humus, chocolate cake — whatever you call it, dark, rich, crumbly earth is the Holy Grail of every gardener. If your soil is yellow-gray and sandy, water will run through it too quickly, and your plants will die for lack of water and food.

Don't dig it up and add better soil. Instead, lay down a thick carpet of dried leaves, wood chips, or garden clippings. Mix the mulch with the top 4 to 6 inches of soil. The organic matter will trap moisture and break down to feed your plants and build humus.

Be patient with wet earth. If you till or work your garden beds before they have a chance to dry out, you'll compact the soil, leaving air and water no place to go. As if that's not enough, when the soil does dry out, you'll end up with big chunks of dirt as hard as bricks. Take your time and wait until spring is well underway before digging.

To quickly test your soil, make a ball out of dirt and throw it in the air. If it sticks together until it hits the ground, put your shovel away and wait for drier days.

Create top-notch topsoil. All loads of dirt labeled "topsoil" are not created equal. Dirt sold as topsoil typically comes from the top 2 inches of the ground, but it may not be good quality soil for your garden. It may be low in organic matter or high in weed seeds, depending on where it came from.

When buying topsoil in bulk, ask about the source and whether it's been tested for nutrient levels, acidity, and contamination by herbicides or other chemicals. Then plan to mix in some compost with your new topsoil before you plant in it.

Get perfect topsoil the lazy way. Turn rock-hard soil into soft, rich earth in one season — without exhausting yourself. There's no need to till when you let time do the work of breaking up the soil. Follow this no-dig plan for garden prep, and you'll also avoid pulling weeds later on.

- Put down a layer of newspapers about 10 sheets deep in the area where you want the garden. Use regular newspaper — not the glossy colorful sections. Don't bother digging, removing sod, or pulling weeds first.

- Water the newspapers well, then cover with a thick layer of compost and soil. Some gardeners like to add another layer of newspapers and organic material, watering it all well.

- Leave the layers for weeks or months, and weeds will rot while hard dirt softens up. By planting time you will find a thick layer of rich topsoil that plants will love.

Plant legumes to loosen compact ground

Don't waste your precious gardening time trying to break up hard soil. Sprinkle lupine, bean, or alfalfa seeds in your beds and let them do the work for you. These deep-rooted crops grow quickly in poor, hard soil, and their strong root systems crumble compacted earth and add nitrogen and air to it. Pull up these hard workers by the roots before they seed, and your soil should be ready for planting.

Make friends with an earthworm. Earthworms can till and aerate a whole plot of soil and fertilize it with their castings. They multiply readily and are an important ecosystem to develop. Regular gray earthworms are great in the garden since they burrow through the soil, leaving rich castings in their air-filled tunnels.

But for the compost pile, encourage red worms. These wigglers are easily identified by the red and brown stripes that adorn their body. Encourage these little guys by providing lots of garden waste, like grass clippings, straw, and leaves, and they will produce compost that is pure gold.

Seaweed turns your garden green. Organic gardeners know the value of chemical-free fertilizers, including "green manure." Seaweed is a great natural choice to mix into the soil or use as a mulch, and you don't even have to buy it. Collect it fresh on the beach, then rinse it off before you use it to remove excess salt.

Seaweed, or kelp, provides some of the main three minerals plants need — nitrogen, phosphorus, and potassium — along with other trace elements like magnesium and zinc. You can also add it to your compost pile, or chop it up and put it in the planting hole before you put in new plants. Along with adding nutrients to the soil, seaweed also helps ward off slugs. Be sure to follow local rules on gathering seaweed.

Keep in moisture with dryer lint

You need to empty the lint from your clothes dryer anyway, so put it to good use. Rather than throw it away, till it into the ground around your vegetables or flowers. It will help your soil retain moisture. It also makes a great addition to soil in hanging baskets, which are especially prone to drying out. Lint in the soil, or as a basket liner, will help keep hanging plants moist for longer while still allowing drainage. And if your lint is from a natural fiber, like cotton — no synthetics — it's also suitable for your compost pile.

Plant a cover crop. A cover crop, like oats or rye grass, can keep your soil in tiptop condition until you are ready to plant again. The cheapest source for seeds is birdseed or deer plot mix. Sprinkle the seeds thickly in a recently plowed or cleared plot, and let them grow for a few weeks. Just before the flowers mature, plow them under or cut them down. The rotting greens will quickly enrich your soil with nutrients and prepare it for the crop that follows.

Keep the chaff, throw out the seeds. Straw, especially straw that's been ruined by rain, is very cheap and easy to find in rural areas. Horses might turn their nose up at it, but it's perfect to till into the earth in the early fall. Straw breaks down readily and will enrich your soil. Make sure the straw is free of weed seeds, then lay it at least 6 inches thick around your plants. Lightly dig it in and let nature run its course. It will soon crumble into rich earth.

Don't pot with everyday dirt. It's tempting to save money by filling pots with dirt from your garden, rather than store-bought potting mix. But unless your yard consists of sandy, loamy soil, don't do it. The best soil for containers is not your "garden variety." Backyard dirt usually doesn't drain as well as potting mix, and that can starve plant roots of oxygen. And it's often loaded with weed seeds, unless you sterilize it first.

Ready to start a new bed? Dig it out by the light of the moon. Weed seeds only need a few seconds of sunlight to germinate. Even if they are immediately buried, they will find a way to the surface. Till by the moon and your weeds will never have a chance to grow.

Explore peat moss substitutes. Peat moss is endangered in some places, and it's very slow-growing. If you're creating a seed-starting mix, you'll probably need to include some. Otherwise, try these to get similar soil benefits. Many of them are free.

- sulfur or pine needles to lower soil pH

- compost, shredded leaves, or green manures to help soil hold water

- coconut fiber or aged pine bark to add bulk to potting mix without adding much weight

- vermiculite, packing peanuts, or shredded newspaper to store summer bulbs in the winter

Compost your way to black gold

A quick guide to making compost. Compost has been called "black gold" by gardeners. But you don't find it in mines. You help create it in your own backyard. Here's how.

Alternate layers of "brown" and "green" matter. Examples of brown, or carbon-rich, matter include leaves, straw, sawdust, and hay. Grass clippings, manure, weeds, coffee grounds, and fruit and vegetable peels count as green, or nitrogen-rich, matter. Aim for a balance of browns and greens, and let nature do the rest.

For best results, your pile should be at least 3x3x3. That way, it will get hot enough to speed up the decomposing process.

Water the pile occasionally to keep it moist, like a wrung-out sponge. Also turn the pile with a pitchfork once in a while so air circulates through it. When your compost is ready to use, it should be dark, crumbly, and sweet-smelling.

Turn your garbage cans into gold mines. If you're handy with a drill, you can convert one or two plastic garbage cans into compost bins. Drill rows of holes every 5 inches around the can, and add a few on the bottom for drainage. Fill with a 2-inch layer of sawdust or straw, then start adding yard waste and kitchen scraps.

You may get less compost in a can than with a large pile, but it's harder for pests to reach and easier to turn. Just fasten the can's lid on securely, and roll the garbage can on its side. What's more, your black gold should be ready in just two to four months.

Dig this easy method. Who needs a big, messy compost pile? Just dig a 1-foot trench and line it with kitchen scraps, dead weeds, and other plant material. Fill it in with topsoil, and plant vegetables in the trench row next year. The buried material will rot into compost and benefit the plants' roots. Worms will also flock to the buried treasure and leave behind valuable worm castings that improve the soil.

Build 2 for prime results. A compost pile is great, but you really need two — one heap of material that's been aging and rotting down for a while, and the other that you can constantly add to. That's because organic material — leaves, grass, wood chips, kitchen scraps — have to be broken down by bacteria before being put on your garden. If you put it directly on the garden soil, you risk drawing nitrogen from the soil and away from your plants. Your plants could end up starving for nitrogen for the next year. A two-pile system lets you add to one pile while you use compost from the finished heap.

Stick a pitchfork in your compost pile, and leave it there. That way, you don't have to fetch one every time you bring out kitchen scraps. It will always be there — all you'll have to do is turn the pile after you add to it.

Perfect compost in a hole. Prepare the ground for your rosebush by composting in the hole where you plan to plant it next year. Layer the main ingredients in 4-inch bands of brown, dried organic matter; soil; green grass clippings or weeds; soil; manure; and a final layer of soil. In between, sprinkle a couple of light dustings of fertilizer, limestone, or compost activator.

Cook up your own compost for free. You don't have to kick into full pioneer mode just to build better garden soil. Composting is surprisingly easy. Start by saving your leaves, straw, and grass clippings, plus plant-based kitchen scraps like fruit and vegetable peelings, bread, tea bags, and coffee grounds. Pile all this yard and kitchen waste into a heap roughly 6 feet wide and 3 feet high. In three to six months you should have beautifully rich compost your plants will love.

For a slightly more structured look, use leftover hardware cloth, concrete blocks, or wood pallets to form an enclosure for your yard waste. Because this pile is freestanding, you can turn it over occasionally with a pitchfork or shovel to help the compost develop faster. Just be aware that this easy access may also make it more attractive to animals and insects.

5 solutions for composting gone wrong. Here are five common composting problems and what you can do about them.

- Animals. Break up kitchen scraps into smaller pieces before adding them to the pile if critters are attracted to your compost. Mix the scraps with soil to disguise their smells. Always avoid meats, fats, and oils — even salad dressing on leftover greens. They're the most likely culprits to bring hungry animals running.

- Ants. These tiny insects are a sign that your compost is decomposing slowly, probably because it's too dry. Compost should be as moist as a damp sponge. Cover it if it's losing moisture, or take the cover off when it rains. In a drier climate, water your compost pile. Mixing well with a pitchfork or other tool distributes the moisture and adds air. This turns up the heat of decomposition and makes it uncomfortable for ants, earwigs, and other bugs.

- Cold and slimy. Three things are usually to blame — too much moisture, not enough air, and too little nitrogen-rich material. To boost nitrogen, add coffee grounds or grass clippings and mix well.

- Odors. If your pile smells like ammonia, it needs carbon. Charcoal, paper napkins and towels, dryer lint, and leaves are rich in carbon. To remedy a trash odor, turn your compost with your pitchfork and break up the large pieces. You can avoid this in the future by chopping items into smaller pieces and mixing them into your pile.

- Too wet. Add brown matter to the mix. Good choices include straw, newspaper, dry grass, and leaves.

Be prepared. Store dry leaves in a barrel, garbage can, or garbage bag and keep them next to your compost pile. When you add kitchen scraps to your pile, cover them with a layer of leaves. You'll keep away flies and other pests.

Turn trash into compost treasure. Pretty flowers, lush foliage, tasty vegetables. These are the things gardens are made of. But getting your garden to grow doesn't have to cost you a bundle. Household items you already have can go on the compost pile. Use this list to help.

- sawdust
- uncolored human hair
- sod and soil
- toadstools
- shredded corncobs
- shredded leaves
- crushed eggshells
- grass clippings
- pet hair
- hay and straw
- fruit and veggie peels
- citrus fruits
- tea leaves and coffee grounds

Careful sorting is key. Not everything from your kitchen can go into the compost pile. A reputation for being smelly and attracting wild animals comes from piles filled with the wrong items. The worst offenders include meat, bones, and other animal byproducts that decay and smell bad. Fence in the pile if raccoons or mice are still attracted. Also keep these other items out of the compost pile.

> Toss your meat and dairy leftovers in your trash can, but save your peels and your leftover fruits and vegetables. Drop these in your blender, add water, and blend until smooth. Use this to water your plants and you'll be feeding them, too.

- Roots of hardy weeds, like bindweed and couch grass. Burn these so they don't multiply in the compost heap.

- Man-made fabrics and carpeting since synthetic textiles won't break down. But you can include natural fibers like cotton and linen.

- Rose canes and prunings from other woody plants, which don't break down quickly.

- Eucalyptus and walnut leaves. These may harm other plants.

- Leaves from a potato crop, which are likely contaminated with potato blight spores.

Bag yourself some free compost. The best things in life are free, and that may include compost for your garden. Contact your city or county department for waste, sanitation, or recycling to find out if they have a program for free compost. The free compost may be available year-round or on a certain day each year. Ask what requirements you must meet to get your compost, including what containers to bring, whether you must participate in related programs, and whether you must bring proof that you are a local resident.

Mythbuster: sunflower seeds are A-OK for composting

You may have been told not to put sunflower seeds or their hulls into the compost pile. The fear is that sunflower seeds contain allelopathic — plant-killing — substances that can harm whatever plants you put the compost on. Don't worry. It's true that sunflowers contain these natural chemicals, but they will be broken down and harmless after the composting process.

4 smart tips for better, faster compost. Even if you've never composted before, you can have rich, organic fertilizer in no time.

- Place your compost pile in a well-drained, sunny area to encourage the heating process.

- Keep a side supply of dry grass, brown leaves, straw, and shredded newspaper or cardboard ready to layer with kitchen scraps.

- Avoid hay because it often contains weed seeds.

- Chop up and mix all ingredients well at the start, to speed up the composting process.

Casting call for worms. Everyone could use a little help. Even Santa Claus has his elves. Recruit your own army of little helpers by starting a worm bin.

Worms turn your food scraps into rich castings that make perfect compost for your garden and houseplants. It's easy to harvest the power of these helpful critters.

First, you need a bin. Any box with a lid will do. Drill holes in the bottom for drainage and air. Raise the box off the ground, and put a plastic sheet underneath it to catch leaks. Fill the box with bedding or damp, shredded paper.

Now you're ready for your worms. Make sure to get red worms, or red wigglers. You can find them at some garden supply stores or order them from catalogs or the internet.

Once you have your worms, feed them kitchen scraps, like fruit and vegetable peelings, coffee grounds, eggshells — pretty much anything besides meat and dairy products — and just let them do their thing.

Don't overdo. Some people say you can never have too much compost. That's not quite true. As with anything else, too much of a good thing is not good. If you overdo the organic matter in your garden, soil can become spongy, and plants can suffer from pests and disease. Stick with a 4-inch layer of compost.

> For a simple outdoor worm bin, stack three old tires. Fill with the usual bedding, food scraps — and, of course, worms.

Sniff out finished product. The decomposition process in your compost bin can take weeks or months. Check out these clues to help you know when your "black gold" is ready.

- Put a bit of the compost in a bucket, and take its temperature. If the temperature changes noticeably over about four days, it may still be heating up and processing. Give it more time.

- Take a sample and seal it in a plastic bag. Wait a couple of days, then open the bag and take a sniff. If you smell ammonia or another unpleasant odor, it's not ready. Finished compost will give off a pleasant, earthy smell.

3 ways to speed up your compost. Some like it hot. Bacteria, for instance. To speed up the compost process, help the pile heat up, and allow those helpful little critters to work faster. These easy tricks can encourage a hot compost pile.

- Add manure. The pile needs both green and brown matter, but damp organic matter will cause it to heat up and speed up.

- Chop up yard waste. Put dry leaves into a barrel, insert a string trimmer, and turn on your giant blender. Shredding leaves increases their surface area, giving the process a big head start. Besides that, it cuts down their volume.

- Keep it moist. A dry pile won't heat up, so you may need to spray it down.

Get the straight scoop on recycling yard and kitchen waste into compost at *mastercomposter.com*. You'll learn how to build a bin, what materials to include, how to involve worms, where to use your finished compost, and much more.

Allow time before planting. Add compost to your soil about three weeks before planting. That gives it time to blend with the soil. An even better idea is to mix the compost into the soil several inches deep. Plants will have an easier time establishing roots in the compost-and-soil mixture rather than in a top layer of pure compost.

Fertilizer: feed your plants for free

Think small to make a big difference. It's healthier to eat several small meals throughout the day rather than one big meal. Take the same approach to fertilizing your plants. In general, feed them lightly and often rather than heavily only once in a while. That way, you know the fertilizer will be used by your plants. Excess fertilizer just runs off into waterways and becomes pollution.

Super spreader strategies. Using a fertilizer spreader isn't exactly rocket science. But there are some tricks to keep in mind. First, designate a strip at each end of your lawn to give you some room to turn the spreader on and off as you turn around. Then go back and forth between the end strips, making sure to slightly overlap each row you make. That way, you won't miss any spots.

Gear up for safety. Applying fertilizer can be dangerous. But with the right gear, you should have no fear. Make sure you wear a long-sleeved shirt, pants, boots, and goggles. You might even want to slip on a dust mask. Avoid fertilizing on a windy day, and

Tired of spreading fertilizer the hard way? Give yourself a coffee break. Make a handy spreader for granular fertilizer by punching holes in the bottom of a large coffee can. A hand-held strainer will also do the trick.

keep children and pets off your lawn for 24 hours after applying fertilizer.

The ideal time to apply fertilizer. Pay attention to your local
weather forecast. It could save your lawn — and save you
money. Fertilizer can scorch your lawn if it's not watered in
right away. Apply fertilizer to your lawn just before it's supposed to rain. That way, you won't waste water.

An easy way to save. Can you give your plants all the nutrients they really need without spending a fortune on fertilizer
this year? Absolutely.

Buy generic. Read the labels on fertilizer packages very carefully. Compare the ingredients as well as the NPK (nitrogen,
phosphorous, and potassium) numbers. The NPK numbers
are usually separated by dashes, as in 20-15-5.

Does the cheap, generic
fertilizer contain the same
ingredients as the fancy one
labeled "Rose Food"? Are the
NPK numbers the same on
both packages? If so, give the
generic fertilizer a try, and see
if it performs as well as the
specialty one — for less.

> What's the best kind of
> fertilizer spreader? That
> depends on your needs. If
> you have a small lawn and
> precision is more impor-
> tant than speed, choose a
> drop spreader. For larger
> lawns where speed is key,
> use a rotary spreader.

Mighty manure. A good material for composting in your garden is farm animal manure. Check your local area for farms
that might give you free manure if you're willing to haul it
away. Manure is high in nitrogen, one of the three most
important nutrients for anything you grow. Horse manure is

highest in nitrogen, followed by chicken and then pig manure. Chicken manure will cause a gradual buildup of salt in your compost or soil, so don't use it for too long in one place.

Give your plants a taste of kitchen scraps. Don't throw it away! That's not garbage — it's plant fertilizer. Here are some kitchen scrap throwaways that your plants will love to eat.

- Toss eggshells and banana peels into your potted plants instead of the trash can. Banana peels give your plants a boost of potassium and phosphorus, while crushed eggshells provide extra calcium.

- Save the water from boiling potatoes or spaghetti, let it cool, and use it to water your plants occasionally. Plants adore this "starchy" water.

- What do you do with leftover chicken bones? They smell bad in the garbage, you can't put them down the disposal, and they attract unwanted varmints to your compost heap. Instead, try drying them in the microwave oven. Then put them in a strong paper bag and crush them with a hammer. Sprinkle them around the base of your garden plants. They'll thrive on the extra nutrients.

> Local farms and horse stables can be good sources of free manure, but so can rabbit rescues. Visit the House Rabbit Society website at *rabbit.org* to find a shelter near you. Offer to volunteer, and you'll get floppy-eared cuddles along with free manure.

Free coffee grounds for your garden

Some Starbucks stores offer several pounds of spent coffee grounds to gardeners for free. Call your local shop to see if they participate in this Grounds for Your Garden program. If they don't, call around to other coffee or donut shops. You may get free grounds from one of them.

Sprinkle these coffee grounds around evergreens, roses, azaleas, camellias, and rhododendrons. Use them in your worm bin or compost bin. A coffee-grounds mulch can even help outdoor containers that stay too waterlogged. But mulch lightly or your plant won't get water at all. Coffee can also cause caffeine poisoning in dogs, so avoid using it if dogs frequently pass through your yard.

Rotate fertilizers for top-blooming roses. You can buy fertilizers labeled for use on rosebushes, but you'll need to change what you use over the course of a season. Pay attention to the numbers. Roses need a different blend of the three main nutrients — nitrogen, phosphorus, and potassium, or N-P-K — at different times of the year.

Early in the season, when roses want to put out leafy growth after they've been pruned, give them lots of nitrogen. That means selecting a fertilizer with roughly equal amounts of N-P-K, like one that says 7-7-7 or 10-10-10 on the label. But later in the summer, when it's time to put out lots of flowers, give your rosebushes a boost of phosphorus to encourage flower growth. Pick one with a high middle number, say 9-27-15.

Rev up your roses with a secret ingredient. Brew up your own "liquid gold" for your roses. Here's how. Shop for alfalfa pellets or alfalfa meal. You'll need at least one-third cup of alfalfa for each rosebush, so be sure to buy enough. Pour the alfalfa into a container and add one gallon of water for each bush you'll feed. Let this alfalfa tea brew several days before using it to water your roses. Repeat this process once every three or four months. If you don't have time for tea, push a handful of alfalfa pellets into the soil around your rosebushes instead. Roses will devour it and reward you with luscious blooms.

Feed flowers with fruit. Roses love banana peels, so cut some up and mix them in the soil at planting time. They rot quickly, releasing minerals that roses need — calcium, sulfur, magnesium, and phosphates.

You can also make a banana peel tonic for use after the plants are established. Just soak chopped pieces in a closed jar of water for two weeks. Pour the remaining mush under the rosebush. If that's too much trouble, chop the peels and scratch them into the soil below the plant.

Rock solid way to boost your roots. Blending rock dust into your garden soil is a great way to provide a mineral boost for roses, veggies, trees, and grass. You can get it from your garden center or a nearby quarry. Minerals in rock dust, including calcium, iron, and phosphorus, improve soil's ability to hold water, plus they provide important nutrients plants need.

But for this kind of inorganic mineral source to do much good at spring planting time, you need to add it in the fall. If you don't have that much time to wait, use a plant- or animal-based amendment like compost tea or seaweed.

Free fertilizer from an unlikely place. You won't believe what you can put in your garden soil that works just like organic fertilizer. Come springtime, you may have a good supply of ashes from your wood-burning stove or fireplace. Wood ashes are rich in nutrients plants love, and you can scatter them directly in your garden as fertilizer.

For lawns, approximately 12 pounds will feed 1,000 square feet. For flower and vegetable gardens, use around 10 pounds for 500 square feet. A half pound will do the trick for individual shrubs or rose bushes.

Ashes increase the pH level of soil — a good reason to test your soil before you try this. Don't use ashes if your level is 7 or above. Scatter them carefully and keep away from acid-loving plants, such as blueberries and azaleas. Only use ashes from burnt wood, like hardwood trees, not pressure-treated, painted, or stained wood. And never use ashes from burned trash or cardboard.

> Some plants just love eggs. Indulge them. Crush some calcium-rich eggshells into the water you plan on giving your ferns or blooming perennials. Let the solution stand for a couple days, shake well, then water as usual and watch your garden grow.

Pickle your posies for fabulous flowers. Don't dump out the juice left in the jar after you eat the last of the pickles. Mix it with water, and pour it around your flowering gardenia and azalea bushes. These acid-loving plants will appreciate a slightly lower pH from the vinegar in pickle juice. But keep the solution weak to avoid doing any damage to your prize bloomers.

Go low-budget for great results. Epsom salts contain magnesium and sulfur — two nutrients plants need. Mix one tablespoon of Epsom salts in a gallon of water, and treat your plants to a healthy feast. It's a great homemade fertilizer for roses, vegetables, and houseplants.

Revive plants with vinegar. Apple cider vinegar is chock-full of trace minerals your houseplants need. Mix a tablespoon of apple cider vinegar with a gallon of water to create a mighty tonic. A monthly dose will also do wonders for azaleas and radishes.

Fertilize with a 10-cent kitchen wonder. Don't pay for expensive fertilizer when you can grab that bottle of ammonia from under the kitchen sink. Household ammonia contains nitrogen, a major ingredient in commercial fertilizers. Some gardeners suggest using around one-quarter cup of ammonia with some liquid hand soap in a 20-gallon hose-end sprayer. That might work, but you need to check three things first.

- Calibration of your sprayer. Be sure it's set to deliver a diluted mixture of ammonia and water so you don't burn your plants.

- Tap water pH. If it's higher than 7.0 — on the alkaline end of the scale — your plants may be harmed by toxic aqueous ammonia from the solution. But if your water has a pH lower than 7.0 — acidic — then ammonium ions will be released to plants. They'll consider that a treat.

- Soil pH. If it's alkaline, skip using ammonia to avoid the risk of toxic aqueous ammonia.

Call on a hairy helper. Even better than manure, human hair is a rich source of nitrogen for your garden plants. If you have a friend in a barber shop or hair salon, see if she will collect hair trimmings for you. Spread them on loose garden dirt and work them well into the soil. This will also help keep deer from foraging in your garden.

Beware homemade bone meal recipes

Search the internet long enough and you will find several recipes for making your own bone meal from the bones saved from cooking. The recipes may sound easy and tempting, but the bone meal they produce may not be effective — or safe.

"Cooperative extension does not recommend that homeowners make their own bone meal," says extension agent Stephanie Ray Butcher. "The process required to make a safe product is quite labor intensive, and it is difficult for homeowners to acquire the quantity of material needed to gain any benefit from it in their soils."

Plan ahead for great spring growth. Your garden may look empty and tired in the fall, but that's not the time to stay inside and rest. Add some lime to the soil after the growth season, and you'll get a bonanza of blooms in the spring.

Lime takes about three months to alter your soil. It's an alkaline ingredient, a natural "soil sweetener" for ground that's too acidic. Lime blends more easily with dry soil, so wait for a dry spell, then mix it into the top 10 inches of your soil.

Pantry cure for lime-dry skin. Even dedicated gardeners who don't mind the thought of dirt under their fingernails hate what garden chemicals can do to skin. Lime, in particular, is a harshly alkaline powder that can leave skin dry and leathery. After you handle lime, treat your hands to a rinse with vinegar, an acidic solution that can neutralize the lime. You'll get back your soft, supple skin in no time.

Don't mix these two ingredients. Lime and manure are a bad combination, so never add them to your soil at the same time. Together they produce ammonia, which can destroy your plant.

Mulch: defense against weeds and weather

Timing is everything. Deciding when to mulch can be tricky — too early and you smother tender shoots, too late and you have a full-blown weed problem. As a rule of thumb, mulch early in the spring around well-established plants, like shrubs and trees, and later around perennials and seedlings. Early mulching may slow plant growth a little because the ground takes longer to warm up. Mulch vegetable and annual gardens after they are well-established. This will keep the plant roots cool during the summer and prevent water from evaporating.

Wait for freeze in fall. In summer, mulch helps keep water in and weeds out, but in winter, it serves a different purpose. Mulch helps keep the soil temperature warmer, preventing damage to plant roots. But wait until after the ground is frozen, or nearly so, to apply the mulch. Otherwise, the ground might stay too warm and encourage tender, new growth at the wrong time of the year.

Spy on sprouts under wraps. If you spread a thick layer of mulch in the fall, peek under your carpet regularly in the spring to check for emerging plants. A thick layer of mulch will smother not only weeds, but bulbs and perennials making their return appearance. If you see bulb tips pushing through, remove the mulch so they can grow. Do the same around your perennials. If you staked your plants before you cleaned your garden bed last summer, it will be easy to find your hidden sprouts.

Calculate your ground cover. Once you choose your mulch, it's easy to figure out how much you need. Measure your garden in feet and multiply the width by the length. Now multiply that number by the thickness of mulch you need (in inches). Count on 2 to 3 inches for heavier, finer mulches, like wood chips and gravel, but at least 4 to 6 inches of lighter fluff, like pine needles, straw, and paper. Divide this number by 324 to find out how many cubic yards of mulch to order.

Clean the curb for a fall harvest. Mulch is easy to come by in the fall. Make your neighbors an offer they can't refuse — do curbside pickup of their discarded leaf bags or piles. You can also contact your local waste management company. They often collect limbs and leaves and shred them, offering the free mulch to the community. Just be aware that recycled mulch may have weed seeds or garbage in it.

Enrich your soil for free. Why spend money on mulch when you can get it at no cost? Here are the best free mulches you'll find and a few you should avoid.

- Grass clippings. Be sure they're free of weeds, herbicides, or weedkillers. Then dry them and use as cover, about an inch thick. They'll suppress weed growth and add nutrients as they decompose.

- Autumn leaves. Rake the leaves into rows, about 6 inches deep. Set your lawn mower on the highest setting, and run over the rows repeatedly, to thoroughly chop up the leaves. Use this fine mulch around acid-loving shrubs, flowers, or vegetables to add organic matter to the soil.

- Straw, hay, and wood chips are sometimes available for free, too. But be sure before you use them that they don't contain weed seeds. If so, they're a bargain you'd be better off without.

Uncover great deals on mulch. You will be surprised at how many ways you can get the mulch you need for cheap or even free.

- Use leftovers. Contact local arborists or tree trimmers who frequent your area and ask if they will dump their leftover wood chips at your house.

- Benefit from your tax dollars. Check with your local government's parks or public works department or your local cooperative extension agent to see if your local government offers wood chips or other types of mulch for free.

- Let sleeping dogs lie. Leave pine needles and leaves where they are if they fall into beds or islands. Otherwise, collect them and redistribute them to the beds and patches where they can do the most good. Grass clippings can also be good mulch as long as they are

Peanut shells make excellent mulch, and you can get them for free from many restaurants. Just remember to warn guests before you take them out into your garden. If they are allergic to peanuts, even the dust of this mulch can provoke an allergy attack.

free of herbicides, are allowed to dry before use, and are spread thinly.

- Always be ready. Keep an old shower curtain, tarp, painter's drop cloth, or old bed sheet in your trunk for collecting mulch. You never know when you might stumble across a freebie.

- Reuse the newspaper. Mulch with several sheets of newspaper or with shredded newspaper in your vegetable garden. Just be sure to put organic mulch on top of the newspaper so it will not blow away.

- Buy bargain bags. Check your local garden centers or home improvement centers for a pile of deeply discounted, torn bags of mulch. Check to see how much mulch has been lost before you buy.

Christmas is over, but you can still give your acid-loving plants a present. After you take down your Christmas tree, put it through a shredder. Then spread the mulch around your plants. It will provide cover and help to enrich the soil.

Keep plants warm with straw or hay. It's important to mulch tender plants in the winter to keep the freezing and thawing ground from spewing up their roots. The best mulches are light and fluffy, using air itself to insulate and warm. Try laying a thick carpet of evergreen boughs, straw, or hay around plants that prefer warmer weather.

Let "living mulch" choke out weeds. Farmers sometimes plant what's called a cover crop to avoid leaving bare ground between rows of the main crop — typically a clover, alfalfa, or rye grass. This type of ground cover prevents erosion, crowds out weeds, gives nutrients back to the soil, and keeps soil nitrogen in balance. You can get the same benefits in your vegetable garden as long as you pick a living mulch plant that doesn't compete. Here's how to make it work.

- Be sure your garden is free of weeds before you begin.

- Plant the main crop, and let it become established for about five weeks.

- Sow the seeds of your living mulch carefully between the rows of the main crop.

- Plan to plow the living mulch under at the end of the season to boost the soil's nutrient content.

Prepare bed with a good soaking. Mulch is great for keeping weeds at bay in your garden. But be sure to water the ground before you lay it down, or you could be doing your plants more harm than good. Once the mulch is in place, rainwater will have a harder time getting through to the soil. That's why it's best to start with damp ground — for both organic and inorganic types of mulch. Be sure to water again once the mulch is down to keep small pieces from blowing away.

Spread a light, even layer of mulch by using a flying disc like a Frisbee. Just pick up a handful of mulching material on an upside-down disc, then flip your wrist to toss it evenly. No need to pour mulch from a heavy bag.

Prevent pests and mildew around trees. Don't heap mulch around tree trunks, creating a volcano appearance. Instead, pull the mulch back from the trunk about 3 inches, leaving a donut of breathing room around the tree. Mulch piled up around trees and shrubs keeps the plants from getting acclimated to winter temperatures, plus it retains moisture that can cause mildew damage and attract pests.

Mix it up for fluffier leaf mulch. Big, flat leaves like maple leaves don't always make the best mulch. They tend to mat down into a solid mass, creating a barrier that keeps air from reaching the soil. Mix in oak or beech with maple leaves to create an airy mulch that allows for ventilation.

> When you need a new mower, choose a mulching mower and let it drop the grass clippings onto your lawn. Experts say this can save you up to 30 percent on lawn fertilizer.

Mow leaves in a circle. Take the bag off your lawn mower, and use the mower to chop up fallen leaves to make mulch. Walk in a circular pattern from the outside to the inside of the circle, directing the cuttings toward the center. When you get to the center, you'll have a tidy pile of shredded leaves.

No need to fear termites. You might think organic mulches would be a magnet for termites, but it's not true. Some woods used as mulch actually produce natural chemicals that repel termites and other pests. Any termite with a choice would prefer munching on a cardboard box to nibbling your wood chips.

But place only a thin 2-inch layer of mulch near the foundation of your house. That will allow soil to dry out in that area and prevent a bridge that termites can cross without touching your treated soil.

> ## Get creative with rocks
>
> Crushed granite, smooth river rocks, gravel, and even glass beads make a permanent mulch that will look great around trees and shrubs in your yard. Just keep these three cautions in mind.
>
> - Don't plan to plant anything else in those beds. These mulches are almost impossible to remove.
>
> - Don't use crushed limestone or marble chips, unless you want to increase the pH of your soil. These rocks will neutralize the soil's acidity, resulting in alkaline soil.
>
> - Shiny, light-colored stone mulch can brighten up your garden beds but will also reflect sunlight and can raise the temperature around your plants.

Repel pests for free. Save your money. Instead of buying expensive cedar mulch at the garden center, ask local friends and family for pruned branches from their eucalyptus, cedar, juniper, and arborvitae. Put these branches through a chipper shredder, and you'll have your own pest-repelling mulch. Just remember, only local plants will do.

Watch out for stinky mulch. Before you buy or spread hardwood mulch, take a quick sniff and check its temperature with your hand. If the mulch smells like ammonia, vinegar, or rotten eggs or is hot to the touch, it has been stored improperly. This causes the mulch to produce byproducts that can harm your plants within 24 hours, and may eventually kill them.

Put old carpet to work in your garden. Use carpet to help make a weed-resistant garden pathway. Lay down carpet first and then cover it with mulch or stone. The carpet prevents weeds from poking through while keeping stones or mulch from sinking into the ground. But that's not the only way you can use carpet in your garden and yard. Consider these ideas, too.

- To convert a grassy area into a flower bed, vegetable garden, or landscaping island, lay carpet down over the grass. The lack of light kills the grass and weeds after a few weeks.

- Lay carpet in already-prepared beds to help control weeds there, too. When you need to plant, simply cut an X into the carpet and turn in the flaps.

- To help prevent tomato blight this year, just lay wide strips of old carpet around your tomato plants when you plant them. The carpet should prevent soil diseased by blight from splashing on the plant when you water.

For any of these uses, make sure you choose carpet with an open-weave back instead of a rubber back. The open-weave backing allows water and fertilizer to soak through. And remember, any carpet you use in your garden or yard should be carpet-side up, the same way you lay it in your home.

Turn secondhand stuff into garden goodies

6 surprising places shrewd gardeners go for bargains. The next time the garden center runs out of a sale item, don't give up hope. Go where no one else thinks to shop, and you'll get the freebies and deep discounts everyone else is missing.

- Browse your local dollar store for seeds, gloves, small tools, and other basic supplies.

- Shop flea markets and yard sales for plants and garden supplies. Also, try the bargain bins at home improvement stores. Just be sure to check the health or quality of the product carefully before you buy.

- Check out recycling retailers like the Habitat for Humanity ReStore. You'll often find great deals on gardening tools, plants, and more.

- Check your local farmers market for perennials. Not only will you find plants proven to survive in your climate, but you may get lower prices than at the plant nursery.

- Keep your eyes peeled for construction sites where the trees and shrubs haven't been cleared yet. Ask if the plants will be removed. If so, ask if you can dig up a few to take home with you. You can also try to negotiate for some free rocks or bricks off their scrap heap.

- Ever noticed how some businesses regularly change out the flowers in their landscaping displays? If you see gorgeous autumn chrysanthemums at one of these firms, call and ask if they're just going to throw the poor things out in a few weeks. If the answer is yes, ask if you can have the plants for free, instead.

Ingenious ways to pay less — or nothing — for gardening supplies. Make your yard and garden look like a million bucks for a fraction of the cost. Here's how to get plants, supplies, and more for cheap or free.

- Swap instead of shop. Save extra seeds to swap on online gardening forums, seed exchanges, or websites such as *craigslist.org*.

- Buy used garden tools, pots, and other supplies. Shop yard sales, estate sales, thrift stores, flea markets, newspaper ads, Craigslist, or even *freecycle.org*.

- Split the cost. Go in with your neighbors on a flat of seedlings or mass of bulbs.

- Check what people are giving away for free on websites like Craigslist and Freecycle.

- Compare local, in-store prices with online deals on seeds and bulbs.

- At end-of-season sales, haggle with the salesperson for a lower price.

4 offbeat paths to seasonal savings. You could spend loads of money on planters, plants, and garden supplies, but you'll probably like these bargains and freebies better.

- Ask your county extension agent how late you can plant spring bulbs so they still bloom this coming spring. If the right time is after the New Year, buy during spring bulb closeout sales when you could get up to 75 percent off.

- Don't buy fresh annuals every year. If you live in the southern half of the country and your annuals don't reseed, dig them up, pot them, and keep them in your garage until replanting time. Get advice on overwintering annuals from your local county extension agent.

- Stock up on garden supplies at end-of-season sales. Don't buy anything that's not on sale. You can always try again when the season resumes next year.

- Find out which trees and plants can be put in the ground near the end of the growing season and which ones you could success-fully overwinter inside. Those are the trees and plants to buy at end-of-season discounts.

Do your yard in a patch-work job. Buy scraps — odd-sized roll ends — of sod at your local sod farm. It will take some time to patch these together to cover the ground you need, but you'll save money. If you like working puzzles, this will be fun.

Save $65 with DIY backyard bubbler

Formal English gardens often include an elegant fountain — beautiful and soothing. Can you bring this little piece of luxury to your own backyard without breaking the bank? Sure you can.

While purchasing a small pot fountain could set you back as much as $100, if you have an eye for repurposing and recycling, you can make your own for around $35.

Pick up a fountain pump at your local home improvement store, then hunt around for an old glazed ceramic urn, cast concrete pot, or other type of waterproof container. You'll need a plastic liner or bucket and a few miscellaneous supplies listed with the pump directions. Check with friends, local restaurants or supermarkets, newspaper ads, and *freecycle.org* for some of these items. In no time at all you'll have your own charming water feature for a steal.

Take the thrifty route to a garden path. You can make an inexpensive garden path from locally available products. Depending on where you live, this may include buckwheat hulls, mushroom compost, pine straw, cherry pits, or delicious-smelling cocoa shells. Check your local garden center. If you don't find what you're looking for, ask the garden center staff or a landscaping service where to go. You may also be able to get path materials for cheap or free from a local business or processor. For example, if buckwheat is grown in your area, a local processor may welcome the chance to get rid of some buckwheat hulls.

But if you're unfamiliar with the material, ask whether it's safe to use in all gardens. For example, The American Society for the Prevention of Cruelty to Animals reports that cocoa shells are toxic to dogs and recommends that pet owners avoid using them.

Discover hidden gardening goodies you didn't know you had. Free gardening stuff is everywhere if you think outside the box. Here are just a few leftovers and extras that can be reused to enrich your garden.

- Call a local granite yard and ask if you can have the cutouts left from creating holes for sinks. Then use these flat pieces as stepping stones or to smother weeds.

- Clean that plastic clamshell container your spinach came in for a seed-starting mini-greenhouse.

- Your old patio umbrella frame can become a trellis.

- A layer of packing peanuts can line the bottom of large flowerpots to improve drainage and keep them lightweight.

- A broken pot can still be filled with succulents, herbs, moss, and ferns pouring out of the crack in a whimsical garden display.

- A chipped or cracked coffee mug can be a free planter for your windowsill.

- An old fireplace screen can become a trellis. So can those lighted wire frame Christmas reindeer when their lights stop working.

- The sandbox your kids don't want anymore can be turned into a raised bed.

Make stepping stones for your yard or garden

Who would have thought — attractive, inexpensive stepping stones from plastic food containers, like margarine tubs. Select the same type of container for uniformity, or different sizes and shapes for variety.

Coat the inside of the container with petroleum jelly, mix up a bag of concrete (follow directions on bag), and put about 2 inches of the mixture in each plastic container. Stir gently to get rid of any air bubbles, and smooth the top.

After about an hour, you can add decorative touches like trinkets, pebbles, writing, or leaf imprints. Let sit for a couple of days before removing your stepping stones from the containers.

6 ways to reuse plastic nursery pots. You hate to throw out those plastic nursery pots, but they're beginning to pile up. Put them back to work with these tips.

- Use plastic cell packs to organize small garden items, or use them to start plants from seed next spring.

- Turn a pot upside down and use it to protect a small plant from early autumn or late spring frosts.

- Donate nursery pots to a plant sale, a school garden, or another charity; offer them to a plant nursery; give them to a grower at your local farmers market; or offer them on *freecycle.org*.

- Line a large one with a plastic grocery bag and use as a temporary garden wastebasket for wrappers, paper towels, and other disposable items you'll later throw in the trash.

- Store small garden tools in them.

- Paint the outsides of the pots with paint made for plastic. Some paints can make your plastic pot look like it is made of stone or copper.

Make an imitation stone planter. Use 14-inch or larger plastic nursery pots as molds for hypertufa planters — pots that look like concrete or old stone but weigh much less.

To make the hypertufa mixture, you'll need perlite, peat moss, and Portland cement from your local home improvement store. Spread a dropcloth or plastic sheeting over a shady work area, and put on gloves and a dust mask. Then follow these steps.

- Mix three parts perlite, three parts peat moss, and two parts Portland cement in a wheelbarrow or plastic tub.

Add enough water to give your mixture the consistency of
cottage cheese.

- Spray your plastic nursery pot with nonstick cooking
  spray. Let dry a little and line the inside of your pot with
  handfuls of the mixture. Aim for smooth walls at least
  3/4 inch thick on the sides and about 1 1/2 inches thick
  at the bottom.

- Create a drainage hole by pressing
  a wooden dowel through the existing drainage hole at the bottom of
  the pot.

- Cover with plastic and let cure for
  several days — then separate the
  mold from the pot.

- Put the pot back under plastic for
  10 days, remove the plastic, and
  let dry for two more weeks. Your
  pot is now ready for planting.

8 sensational, easy-to-make plant markers. Plant markers
not only help you identify your plants, they can be great-
looking features for your garden. Best of all, they don't have
to be expensive or hard to make.

- Broken flowerpots. Don't throw away broken clay pots —
  reuse the pieces by writing on the rim of the pot and
  sticking the broken edge into the ground. They look so
  good you might even break a few pots just for fun.

- Stones or bricks. Brush off smooth stones you find in your garden, or old bricks that are lying around. Paint a bit of fancy lettering on a smooth area, and make them uniquely your own.

- Small pot on a stick. Turn a mini terra-cotta flowerpot upside down, and write the plant name on it with a permanent marker. Place it on top of a stake.

- Seed packet. It's practical and clever to keep the plant's information close by. Put the seed packet on top of a stake, then cover it with a clear jar to keep moisture away.

- Nursery label. This is really useful if you have more than one variety of tomato. Cut a little slit at the top of a stake and slip the nursery label in. Place them at eye level for easy identification.

- Wine bottle. Permanent colored marker on a wine bottle stuck upside down in the ground makes a distinctive identifier.

- Milk jug. Cut the plastic sides into strips, label each one with permanent magic marker, and push into the appropriate spot in the ground.

- Golf club. Have old golf clubs you don't use? Instead of letting them gather dust in a basement or garage, put a label made from waterproof tape on the face of the club. Cut off the grip, and stick the shaft in the ground. They can double as plant stakes, too.

Get creative with planters. Looking for inexpensive but creative garden planters? Try these creative substitutes.

Watering cans, discarded toilets, an old bathtub with a working drain, rusty strainers, toy trucks and wagons, driftwood, a used wheelbarrow, tea kettles, even an inverted umbrella can make original and whimsical planters for your garden.

What about spraying an old pair of shoes with outdoor paint? And if you add a coat of paint and plant a few flowers or vines inside an old barbecue grill, you've instantly turned an eyesore into an attractive planter for your patio.

The next time you're out and about, look around with a fresh eye. You might find some junk just waiting to be turned into plant treasures.

2 outdoor uses for milk jugs. It's a breeze to make nifty garden helpers from an empty one-gallon or half-gallon milk jug.

- Soil scoop. Cut off the bottom inch from a half-gallon milk jug. Lay the jug on its side with the handle facing up and grab a magic marker. Notice that the handle is on a corner between two sides. On each of these sides, draw a diagonal line that starts near the bottom end of the milk jug and ends an inch or two below the handle. Cut along these diagonal lines and you'll have a scoop that's good for soil and many other things in your garden.

- Portable harvest holder or portable trash can. Cut a hole out of the top corner opposite the handle in a one-gallon milk jug. Use it as a portable holder when you pick berries, cherry tomatoes, or nuts. Cut another jug the same way to create a portable trash can when you are weeding. Cut a wider, deeper hole and you can use the jug as a portable storage bin for small items.

Transform ladders into an arbor. Pull your old wooden ladders or stepladders out of storage, and put them to work beautifying your garden. You need three ladders or two stepladders to follow these instructions.

- Remove the backs if you use stepladders.

- Cut the ladders to equal size if they are not the same height.

- Attach posts to the legs of each ladder with screws.

- Position the two ladders so a stepladder back or third ladder can span the space between them.

- Sink each post deep in the ground so it's firmly seated.

- To complete the arbor, fasten the ladder back or third ladder across the tops of the standing ladders with screws or twine.

- Grow grapevines or annual flowering vines up and over your new arbor.

Turn old junk into a new trellis. Pick up an old metal headboard from a yard sale. To prepare it for use, remove the rust or let it be part of the headboard's charm. You can even prime and paint the headboard. To anchor your new trellis:

- Choose metal stakes or posts at least 2 feet high, but not taller than the headboard's outer posts. You can paint these stakes to match the headboard, but let them dry completely before using them.

- Pound a stake a foot deep into the ground where you want each headboard leg to sit.

- Sink the headboard legs into the ground in front of the posts.

- Attach the headboard to the posts with wire or a few zip ties near the top of each stake and several more a few inches above the ground.

Turn castoffs into garden accents. An old freestanding bathtub is a fine container for a water garden — especially if you can find one cheap at a yard sale or flea market. For a rustic touch, turn a watering trough or whiskey barrel into a water garden container just by adding a liner. What's more, if you give up water gardening or decide you want a pond, any of these containers can be recycled into planters.

Join a community garden and save. If you have no space at home for a garden, join a local community garden. This can be a cheap way to get space to grow vegetables, fruits, herbs, flowers — whatever you want. At some community gardens you can rent your own small plot, maybe 8x10 feet, for less than $100 each growing season. The cost may also include water and expert gardening advice.

In an established garden, you may get a bed with good-quality soil that's already built and prepared, so you won't need to replace native dirt. Some community gardens even provide soil testing. Check the website of the American Community Gardening Association, *communitygarden.org*, to find a community garden near you. With more than 18,000 community gardens across the United States and Canada, there's likely one nearby.

> Don't buy garden tools or equipment if you only need them a few times each year. Instead, borrow or trade tools with other gardeners. For larger, rarely used items, renting may be cheaper than buying.

4 ways to snag free plants for your garden. There's no need to make a big investment in plants if you're just getting started in gardening. Here are some sources to consider when looking for something to grow. Be flexible, and see what's offered.

- Landscaping crews. They often toss perfectly good plants when they change displays or redesign someone's yard. Ask nicely, and you may be able to adopt some.

- Garden club. Consider joining a local or online gardening club, which may host plant swaps among members. Or ask a neighbor about a trade.

> Don't spend money on more greenery when you can divide your perennial plants and move some to new ground. Doing this helps plants that tend to form crowded clumps stay healthy. It works well with hostas and daylilies. Do your dividing in the spring.

- Membership. If you want trees, consider joining the national Arbor Day Foundation for just $10. You'll get 10 trees in return, along with access to advice and a support network for your tree-growing adventures.

- Volunteers. Be on the lookout for volunteers — plants that come up unexpectedly — and make the most of these happy accidents.

Get landscaping plants on the house. Ask garden centers for plants they are throwing out, recommend bargain-hunting experts. You may have better luck at small, locally owned places, since many big box stores have strict policies against giving plants away. But by taking their "trash" off their hands, you save them dumping fees — many dumps charge by the pound.

Rules for foraging free plants. Native plants, or the varieties that grow wild in your area, have a good chance of surviving a move to your yard. But follow these rules for foraging when you gather free-growing plants.

- Ask before you take plants or seeds from private property, even if it's clear the plants are being removed for construction.

- Don't take an entire group of wild plants. Leave a few so they can grow back.

- Never take a rare or endangered species.

- If you're gathering wildflower seeds, spread a few where you found them so they can continue growing.

- Finally, be sure you have the knowledge to transplant successfully. If you don't know how to deal with a certain variety, you may kill it rather than save it.

Dig up plant savings. You can buy from the same plant nurseries as your neighbors but pay significantly lower prices than they do. What's the secret? Buy and plant in autumn.

This tactic can be successful no matter where you live. Experts say many plants, particularly perennials and trees, thrive after an autumn planting. This happens because the still-warm soil temperatures encourage better root growth than the cooler soil temperatures of spring. So contact your county extension agent to find out exactly when to do fall planting in your area.

Many garden centers and garden departments also have clearance sales during autumn to reduce inventory for the winter or make room for holiday products. Just remember that some of these clearance plants may be potbound or have other problems, so be sure to check the plant over carefully before buying or planting. Your new purchase may need a little tender loving care in order to thrive.

Make sure your bargain is actually a bargain. Next time you're shopping for plants, just say "no" to plants that look like they need a little too much TLC. These deals may not be worth the trouble or expense if the plant shows certain signs of ill health.

- Dead leaves. These can signal disease, neglect, or both.

- Spots or odd growths on leaves. If the plant is carrying a disease, it might spread to your entire garden.

- Roots that have grown into a solid mass, filling the pot. The plant may not grow well even when planted in the ground.

- Weeds growing in the pot. They're a sure sign of neglect.

- Large gaps between leaves. Another sign of neglect.

> Buy six-packs of the plants you want rather than a single larger plant. You'll pay less and — depending on how green your thumbs are — end up with six times the greenery. If you're really patient, start plants from seeds and grow a whole crop for pennies.

- Soil with a hard, crusty surface. This plant has been in the pot for a long time.

Signs a dormant plant is a good deal. You can save up to 50 percent buying shrubs and trees in the winter, then either planting them immediately if the ground is not frozen or saving them in a cold frame until spring. But check to be sure your bargain is dormant rather than dead.

- Scratch the bark of a woody plant to be sure you see green underneath the outer bark.

- Pull the plant out of the pot and look for roots that are healthy and firm — not black, moldy, or crumbling.

- Check the leaves and stems of evergreens to see if they're healthy and supple rather than brittle and brown.

Wait until spring to fertilize a dormant plant to avoid waking it up too soon.

Spend less for quality trees and shrubs. Get the best deal possible if you're buying from the plant nursery. Bypass that tree in the 10-gallon container and buy the smallest size available instead. Not only will you get a dramatic discount, but your tiny tree will probably be the same size as the 10-gallon version in just a few years.

That may sound unlikely but consider this. Because a 10-gallon tree is container-bound for several years, it can't grow as rapidly as a younger tree planted where roots can spread out. So buy small when shopping for trees, shrubs, and perennials. Your new plant may become just as big and impressive as its older brothers in a few years, but you'll save big today.

Plan ahead for your weekend projects, and shop for plants at the garden center on Thursdays and Fridays. You'll find a better selection after weekday restocking and avoid having to settle for picked-over plants.

Look for hidden treasures when buying plants. Peek under the leaves for extra baby plants in the soil next to the main stem when buying a potted plant at your garden center. You can separate these hidden treasures when you transplant, allowing the seedlings more room to grow. Best of all, you just bought two or three plants for the price of one.

Stock up on free seeds. Stop paying for common vegetable, herb, and fruit seeds. You can easily get them for free.

- Join a seed swap. Local gardening clubs sometimes hold seasonal seed-swapping events, sharing surplus seeds and growing tips. Or start your own through your church or community center. If you have access to a computer, join an online swap group and mail seeds to one another.

- Save your own. For tomatoes, simply scoop out seeds and gently rinse away the jelly-like goo surrounding them. Spread them in a single layer on a paper towel to dry for several days.

Get instructions for finding free seeds from the International Seed Saving Institute's website at *seedsave.org*.

Become swap savvy. Follow these basic rules at a plant or seed swap so other gardeners will be happy to share with you again next time.

- Alert the swap organizer that you are planning to come so she can make space.

- Find out if the swap has basic rules for participation. Some groups assign monetary values to different types of plants or seeds to encourage fair trades.

- Prepare plants by potting them and labeling with genus and species names.

- Feel free to bring seeds, bulbs, and tubers to trade, but be sure they're in plastic bags with labels.

- Avoid taking plant cuttings to offer, since they can be difficult to transport.

- Bring your own reusable bags or boxes to carry items home.

- Don't remove plants from another gardener's table without asking if he would like to make a trade.

Fresh produce at half the price

One in three households grows at least some of their own vegetables, fruits, berries, and herbs. Half do it specifically to save money.

They're on to something. Most gardens are small — less than 100 square feet, or 5 feet by 20 feet. Despite this modest size, home-growers still come out on top. They invest an average of $53 a year in their vegetable gardens. Yet a 100-square-foot garden can yield 50 pounds of produce worth $100 at in-season store prices.

It's like paying half price for produce. Plus, you know where it comes from and what pesticides have or haven't been used. Give gardening a try, and see how much you save.

Reap big savings from your garden. In his book *The $64 Tomato*, author William Alexander tells how aiming for the perfect garden led to an average cost of $64 per tomato. But experts claim you can save money by growing your own herbs, vegetables, and fruits.

The trick is to plan carefully so your garden doesn't cost more than the delicious food it produces. Start with these tips.

- Choose produce that's expensive at the supermarket. Determine which vegetables, fruits, herbs, and spices give you the most sticker shock, and make a list.

- Grow stuff you like to eat. If you never use it, you can't save money. Remove items you dislike from your list.

- Pick items you can store a long time or preserve. Narrow the list further by emphasizing items that have a long storage life or can be preserved by canning, drying, or freezing. Preserving prevents waste when your plants produce more than you can eat, and allows you to use your extra produce out of season.

- Consider options with a great track record. In many parts of the country, tomatoes, sweet peppers, cucumbers, green beans, or leaf lettuce can provide good savings, but herbs may be your top bet for saving money. For example, herbs like basil and parsley are economical and easy to grow, but the same herbs bought fresh at the supermarket are pricey.

- Avoid garden dropouts. Investigate your garden candidates to make sure they can survive long enough to help supply your kitchen. Ask your gardening friends, family, and neighbors what kinds of produce and herbs grow well in your area — and which varieties are best.

Gather free information to create your perfect garden.
To find more information and investigate specific plants, use these resources:

- Surf to *extension.org* to find links to your local extension office's website.

- Visit your local library or the internet.

Look for answers to questions like these:

- What soil, drainage, and other conditions does the plant require?

- How hard is the plant to grow, and what are your chances of success?

- Does your yard get enough sunlight for the produce you want to grow?

- How can you protect the plants from pets, wildlife, insects, and disease?

- How big will the plants get, and how many can you fit in your available space?

Start small. To keep costs down, limit yourself to just a few items the first year, especially if you are a beginning gardener.

Handy tricks and tips for the toolshed

Help garden tools last longer. Simple ingredients you may already have lying around your house will help you sanitize and store your tools properly, so they stay in tiptop shape for many years.

First of all, be ruthless when it comes to dirt and germs. Clean and disinfect all gardening tools — including shovels and pruners — after each use. Make sure you get all the dirt and plant debris off when you clean. Surprisingly, many experts recommend you take it a step further and disinfect pruning tools after each cut you make or after each plant you prune.

Disinfect with a mixture of one part bleach to nine parts water, but remember that bleach can be corrosive. You can use rubbing alcohol instead of bleach, but it's more expensive.

If you use bleach, coat the metal with a thin layer of oil before storing, so the tool won't rust.

Make cleaning your tools child's play. A good way to keep your gardening tools clean and well-oiled is to prepare a sand-box. Not for your kids, but in your toolshed. Mix 40 pounds of sand with one quart of motor oil and keep it in an open box. After using tools, rub through the gritty, oily mixture a few times to clean them off and lube them up for storage.

Your tools can last a lifetime. You can use household items you already have to make your garden tools work better and last longer. Try these simple tricks, and you'll spend less on replacements.

- Spades and shovels. Big or small, the treatment is simple. Use a wire brush to take rust off the blade. Sandpaper makes it even smoother, and running a file quickly along the edge will keep it sharp and easy to use. Rub in a little cooking oil to prevent rust and make digging easier. Keep a bucket of sand in your shed or garage, and stick your tools in it at the end of the day. It helps keep them dry, and you'll know just where to find them the next day. For wooden handles, sand down any splinters and rub linseed oil on the whole handle to stop it from cracking and splitting as it ages — especially before you hang it up for the winter.

- Clippers. Put a little car wax on the hinge for a better cut. The paste that keeps your car shiny helps the clipper blades avoid a jam and glide more smoothly. You can also spray the blades with cooking oil — it keeps them lubricated and cutting freely. If some pine pitch or spruce sap sticks to the blades while trimming, put a little olive oil on a rag and rub. The blades will be smooth and clean again. Another wipe or two will take the sticky stuff off your hands, as well.

- Wheelbarrow. Make it roll with ease — keep the tire at the right pressure with your bicycle pump.

Keep gardening tools sharp with these simple tips. You want your tools to perform effectively and safely. That's why you want to keep blades sharp on your pruners and loppers. And sharpening the blades on your hoes, shovels, and trowels keeps them in tiptop shape. Here's how to do it.

- Wipe down blades with WD-40 or another lubricant.

- File edges with a whetstone or 10-inch flat mill file.

- Follow the bevel of the blade and apply light pressure as you move the file or whetstone away from you.

- Smooth out any nicks or burrs.

Great garden tools on the cheap. Don't spend a fortune on tools for your garden. Secondhand tools are often made of better-quality steel than some newer ones, plus they're a great deal. Check out these sources.

- Flea markets and yard sales.

- Pawn shops, thrift stores, and consignment stores. Look for a Goodwill store or Habitat for Humanity ReStore in your area.

- Estate sales in rural areas.

- Internet exchange sites, such as *craigslist.org* and *freecycle.org*.

- Your gardening-expert neighbor, who may be willing to lend you a tool — along with good advice.

When purchasing garden tools, don't buy the cheapest tool or the most expensive. Stick with the tools in the middle. The cheapest tools tend to break easily and the most expensive tools are usually geared towards the experts.

Take advantage of tool lending libraries

There's always another tool that would come in handy in your garden, but costs add up. If gardening is your hobby, save your money for plants and seeds, and borrow tools you won't use very often from a local tool lending library.

Some nonprofit tool lending libraries, like the North Portland Tool Library, lend tools for free to local residents. Others, referred to as "tool banks," charge a small fee and may lend only to charities and other groups. Ask local gardeners or do an internet search to see if there's a tool lending library near you.

So when it's time to trim your rhododendrons, you could spend around $46 to buy a new pruning lopper, which will sit in your garage for a year, getting dull and gathering dust. Or you could borrow a lopper from a tool lending library and bank that $46 instead.

Take the strain out of carrying tools. Let your garden tools do the work for you — not the other way around. This clever idea will help make heavy tasks light. Attach a plastic window box to your wheelbarrow for a permanent tool holder — just a couple of screws will do. Drill through the window box into the handles of the wheelbarrow, or use the drainage holes if they

line up right. Pop in the screws, and off you go. Keep small tools, your water bottle, even your cellphone, close by and easy to get to.

Find a few 5-gallon buckets. They are the gardener's equivalent of baby food jars for storing stuff. Clean them out and use them for fertilizer, grass seed, birdseed, potting soil, and anything else you want to keep dry and safe from bugs and rodents. And it's also a good idea to put inside the bucket that part of the original sack that has handling and application instructions.

Original contents of these great containers include paint, joint compound, and swimming pool chemicals. If you don't know anyone who uses these things, you can also buy brand new buckets at any home improvement store.

Don't forget lids to keep the contents airtight. Lids also let you stack your buckets to save floor space — just be sure to label the outside.

This tool will make gardening buckets of fun. Use a 5-gallon bucket to carry your small gardening tools. As a bonus, you can flip it over and sit on it as you weed, plant, or just take a breather. Add an S-hook to the bucket handle, and hook it on to your wheelbarrow, and you won't even have to carry the bucket.

Simple, low-cost dry sink for your shed. There's no need to put expensive plumbing in your shed. Instead, make a dry sink. Use it for holding and rinsing flower cuttings, or controlling soil spill when you're potting.

First, find something to use for the sink. It could be a big bucket, like those for drywall joint compound, or a plastic dish pan. It could even be an actual sink you find at a yard sale or thrift shop. If so, make sure you also have a bucket to put under the drain. Make an outline of your container on a wooden potting bench, then cut a hole that's just big enough for the container to slide into and rest snugly.

Make it even more useful with a portable water source for rinsing your hands. Get an empty laundry detergent bottle with a push-button dispenser, rinse it out thoroughly, and add water — instant convenience. You could also use a plastic beverage dispenser — the kind with a spigot, or an old water dispenser designed to sit on a shelf in your refrigerator.

3 ways to stop a leaky hose. Garden hoses are constantly sprouting little leaks, but instead of tossing them out, try one of these quick fixes.

- Plug it up temporarily with some chewed gum.

- Make a short-term repair by pressing the point of a toothpick into the hole. Water will cause the toothpick to swell, plugging the hole. Break off the rest of the toothpick and wrap the area with duct tape.

- Cauterize it. Simply heat up the tip of an ice pick with a flame, then gently melt a tiny bit of the rubber around the hole until it melts back into a seal.

New life for a leaky hose. If your old hose has been punctured, turn it into a soaker hose. Simply poke more holes down the length of the hose with a nail. Then cap the end and lay it in your lawn or garden.

Stow away garden hoses on your patio. Get garden hoses out of your garage and closer to where they're needed by coiling them up inside those large planter pots you have sitting on your patio. They'll be neat, tidy, and out of the way. Plus you won't have to haul them back and forth. When cold weather approaches, make sure you drain them as you coil them, if you plan to leave them outside through the winter.

Guard the blade on sharp saws. Recycle a leaky, old water hose and get a free blade guard for your saws at the same time. Cut a piece of hose the same length as your saw blade. Slit the hose down the middle on one side, and slide it over the saw teeth. This trick works on axes and other sharp blades, too.

An old tire inner tube can serve the same purpose on a miter or circular saw. Just slit it open and slide over the round blade.

Keep hoses kink-free. Save a sturdy metal coffee can and put it to good use in your garage. Drill a few holes in the bottom and bolt or screw it to the garage wall. Wrap your garden hose around it in winter, or hang bulky outdoor extension cords over it to keep them tangle-free and off the floor. Store the hose nozzle or other small parts inside the can so you can find them easily later.

Choose a rubber or rubber-vinyl garden hose, and it will last longer, advises Trey Rogers, lawn expert and author of the book, *Lawn Geek*. Rogers also suggests buying the highest ply hose you can.

2 ways to tame your garden hose. No need to buy something expensive — these free solutions will tame the tangle and keep your hose handy.

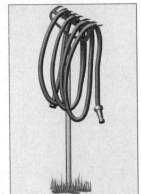

- Rake. Replaced your garden rake lately? Give the old one a clever update that's both useful and ornamental. Secure the handle firmly in the ground — no wobbling — then use the head of the rake for hanging a hose. Loop the hose loosely, and the spaces between the tines of the rake will keep it neatly in place.

- Wheel rim. Got an old car tire sitting around? Take off the metal rim, and attach it securely to your house or a fence. Your hose will curl up nicely around the rim and will unroll easily without tangling. Paint the rim to match your house, and it will blend right in.

What to do before you pick up a rake. The U.S. Consumer Product Safety Commission reported that about 28,000 people needed medical treatment in just one year for injuries related to using nonpowered garden tools. Follow these raking rules to avoid becoming a statistic.

- Stretch the muscles of your arms and legs before you begin — just like you do for any other exercise.

- Don protective gear, including gloves, closed-toe shoes or boots, long pants, and sun protection.

- Use the right rake for the job. A light, fan-shaped rake is great for gathering up leaves, while a flat-headed, metal rake might work better for smoothing a surface.

> Hang a sturdy rake on your garage wall, and its fingers will make great hooks for your smaller pieces of gardening equipment.

- Pick a rake that fits you, avoiding one that's too heavy or too large to handle comfortably.

- Change positions as you work, alternating which hand and foot are in the front.

- Never set a rake down with the teeth pointing up.

Lightweight reel mowers are packed with advantages. Your old gas-powered mower finally conked out, and you'd like a less-expensive mower that requires less maintenance. Maybe it's time to take a new look at the reel push mower.

"I think a lot of people are under the misconception that they're really hard to use," says Lars Hundley, owner of Clean Air Gardening, a supplier of environmentally friendly lawn and garden products. He explains that modern reel mowers are far less heavy and much easier to push than older push mowers. Some even weigh as little as 17 pounds. Consider these other advantages.

- You won't have trouble starting a push mower, and you won't need to haul it to the repair shop for maintenance. "With a push mower, you push and it mows," says

Hundley. "It's pretty mechanically simple, and there's really not that much that can go wrong with it."

- The reel mower is better for your lungs and sinuses because it creates no smoke and pollution. Gas-powered mowers are heavy polluters. "Even though they're only burning a little bit of gasoline, they're putting out more pollution than an automobile for every hour you push one," Hundley explains.

- You can carry your cellphone when you're mowing and hear it ring.

- Of course, reel mowers aren't perfect. Their blades still need sharpening every few years, and they don't mow well in yards full of rocks, sticks, or tall weeds. And if your yard is quite large, you might really need a self-propelled power mower. But otherwise, you may find that you prefer the new reel push mowers. Not only do they have all the advantages Hundley describes, but their cleaner cutting style is also better for your grass.

Say sayonara to sticky grass clippings. You can forget about cleaning your mower. Spray WD-40 on its underside so grass clippings can't stick there anymore. Then, when you're hot and tired after mowing, you won't need to pry clippings off your mower deck. Instead, you can check that deck, smile at how clean it is, and go inside for a cold, refreshing drink.

Keep your mower blades sharp to save your lawn. Mowing should help keep your lawn looking sharp, but a dull blade can weaken turf, says Dr. Aaron Patton, assistant professor and extension turfgrass specialist for the University of

Arkansas Division of Agriculture. "Sharply cut leaf blades increase turf health by improving recovery, decreasing water loss, and increasing photosynthesis," he says, adding that lawns mown with a dull blade heal more slowly, have greater water loss, and simply don't look as nice.

Diagnosing a dull mower blade is simple. If the grass blade has a single, clean cut across the top, the mower is in good shape. However, if the edge is ragged or there are signs of previous, incomplete strikes on the grass blade, there's a good chance the mower blades need sharpening.

"Sharpen mower blades at least twice a year or more often for larger lawns," Patton recommends.

Cool your engine before storing your mower. You're understandably excited to be done mowing your yard. But take some time to let your hot riding mower cool down before driving it into your garage and shutting the door. Otherwise, you'll risk an explosion or fire.

New uses for old rubber gloves. The best thing about buying new rubber gloves is recycling your old ones.

- Get organized. Make large rubber bands by cutting the wrist and palm of the glove into strips. Use these strips to bind items together in your tool shed. Or wrap the rubber bands loosely around your string trimmer cord or other cords to keep them coiled up.

- Hang more tools. If the hanging hole in your tool is too small, thread one end of your "rubber band" through the hole. Now one end of the rubber band is behind the hanging hole, while the other end is in front. Use one finger to hold the front end open so you can thread the back end through that loop. Pull it tight so one end surrounds the handle of your tool while the other provides a "hanger" large enough to slip around a hook.

- Make a tool grip. Snip off the glove's fingers at the base and trim the tips. Slip the fingers over the handles of your garden tools.

- End slips and slides. Cut out the palm of the glove. When you bring cut flowers in from your garden, place the palm under your flower vase to provide a nonskid mat.

- Add a garden jar opener. If the lid for your fertilizer or pest control product is too tight, don't run for the jar opener in the kitchen. Instead, keep an old rubber glove with your outdoor supplies to use only in the garden.

Easy care for gardening gloves. Gardening gloves can get sopping wet if you work during the morning dew or right after it rains. Here's a great way to dry them. Remove the bottoms from two small, plastic pots and slip a glove over each one. Set the pots on an old baking rack or dish rack to help them dry.

To store your gloves, clean out a tall, plastic canister or jar with a screw-on or snap-on lid. Good choices include large peanut butter jars from warehouse clubs or a tennis ball canister. Put your gloves in the jar, put the lid on tight, and store your gloves in your garden shed without fear that bugs will burrow inside them.

Get a better hold on tool handles. Arthritis can put a crimp in your fix-it plans, making pruners, trowels, and other yard tools hard to hold tightly. Get a better grip by wrapping the handles in insulation.

Cut a piece of foam pipe insulation to the right size, and duct tape it around the handle. Or wrap a length of self-adhesive foam weatherstripping around and around the handle, sticky side down.

Spread bug killer more effectively. Buy an old flour sifter at a yard sale — one you won't use for food. Paint the handle a bright color and store it with your garden tools to minimize the chance you'll use it in your kitchen. When you need to spread small amounts of an insect-killing powder, use the sifter. It can help spread the powder evenly so you're less likely to miss a spot or use too much in one place.

Easy store, easy pour. Here's a nifty way to make small, sturdy, plastic bags filled with seeds or fertilizer easier to handle. Before recycling a plastic bottle, cut off the top, including the collar and screw top. Pick a bottle with an opening that's the right size — the bigger the bag, the bigger the bottle. Unscrew the cap and feed the top of the plastic bag through it. Fold the edges of the bag over the bottle top and screw the cap back on. It's now air-tight and secure. Want a handle, too? Use a plastic milk or juice bottle in the same way, but cut carefully to include the handle.

Never hunt for missing garden items again. Easily organize hand tools, plant labels, and other items you need for gardening. Get a hanging shoe organizer with clear plastic pockets. Drop your trowel and similarly sized items into the pockets. Then slip clear plastic cups, resealable baggies, or other small, transparent containers into the remaining pockets. Fill each one with twist ties, garden pegs, or other small items. You can even label the pockets so you can find everything at a glance.

Hammer out weeds. A plain, old hammer can be a useful tool for weeding your garden. Slam it into the soil, catching the weed between the claws, and pull it up, just like you would with a nail.

Make lugging your tools around child's play. If you're looking for an easy way to move tools and supplies around in your garden, buy a child's plastic sled. It can carry a great deal of weight. And since it's low to the ground, it's convenient for planting and other on-the-spot gardening chores.

Mail call — your tools don't ever have to be out of reach. Maybe your yard is too small for a tool shed. But you can still have your gardening hand tools close by. Just paint an old mailbox to fit your garden style and install it. Keep gloves, a trowel, pruning shears, and other small tools tucked neatly inside until you need them.

Reflect on this handy bug tool. Make a homemade bug finder by gluing a mirror to an old mop or broom handle. No more crouching, bending, or playing a frustrating game of hide-and-seek with pests. Just stroll through your garden, glancing at your makeshift mirror on a stick to spot bugs lurking on the underside of leaves.

Keep your boots spider-free. Stretch a pair of old socks, pantyhose, or tights over the tops of your gardening boots when you leave them in the shed overnight. That will keep spiders, scorpions, and other creepy-crawlies out of your galoshes.

Dig this homemade scooper. Make a cheap, yet sturdy, scooper out of an empty bleach bottle. Just rinse it out, and slice off the bottom diagonally. Then grip the handle and start digging.

Dabble in homemade dibbles. Instead of spending money for a dibble — and bending over to use it — try making your own. Sharpen one end of an old broomstick handle or just use a walking stick with a brass tip. That way, you can simply walk through your garden and poke holes for your seeds.

> Before you decide to throw away that rusty trowel or other gardening tool, try soaking it overnight in cider vinegar. Wipe away the residue with a cloth, and you may find it's as good as new.

Make your tools measure up. Turn your hoes, rakes, and shovels into handy rulers. Just paint or notch marks for inches and feet on the wooden handles of your tools. That way, you'll always have a measuring device when you need one.

Take the comfort of your computer outdoors. Gardening can be tough on your knees, so here's a tip that's bound to click. Kneel on old computer mouse pads to cushion your joints. As a bonus, you'll also keep your pants clean.

Add rust protection to your toolbox. Tired of the same sad story of the gardener and the rusty tools? Then check out this absorbing tale. Put a charcoal briquette or a piece of children's sidewalk chalk — the thick, colorful kind — in your toolbox during the winter to absorb moisture. This time, your story will have a happy ending.

Keep tall tools in line and out of the way. Tall tools were once tricky to store, but not anymore. Set cup hooks into two exposed wall studs in your garage. Stretch a bungee cord across the space between the beams, and hook each end onto a cup hook. Now you can stand rakes, hoes, brooms, and other long-handled items between studs.

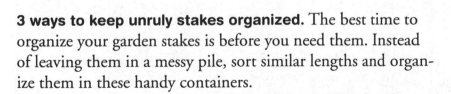

Not all workshops feature exposed studs. If yours doesn't, then improvise. Turn an old bar stool upside down and place it in the corner. Stand tall tools in it, handles down, for super-simple storage.

3 ways to keep unruly stakes organized. The best time to organize your garden stakes is before you need them. Instead of leaving them in a messy pile, sort similar lengths and organize them in these handy containers.

- Plastic crates. Take two plastic crates that have lots of openings in the sides and base, and stack them upside down on top of each other. Put stakes upright through the holes, and they won't go anywhere until you need them.

- PVC pipes. Use them as a sleeve for your stakes, and lean them in a corner out of the way.

- Chimney pipes. Discarded chimney flues are sturdy and stand upright on the ground — perfect for keeping your stakes ready for use.

Keep that worn-out golf bag. You bought a newer, nicer golf bag, but you can't bear to throw out the old one. Move it from the sports equipment pile over to the lawn and garden section of your garage and hang it securely on the wall. Now you have a place to store your rakes, hoes, and other long-handled items.

Prepare power tools for storage

Your outdoor power tools that use gasoline — a snow-blower in the winter and a chainsaw and lawn mower in the summer — need a little TLC before you put them away in the offseason. Experts say to drain the gasoline from the fuel tank to be sure the engine starts up again when you need it. Use an old turkey baster to remove all the gas you can, then run the engine until it stalls. You can even put the drained gas into your car. Check your tool's owner's manual, which you can probably find on the internet, to see about these other maintenance steps.

- Change spark plugs and oil, and inflate tires.
- Lubricate fittings and other parts.
- Inspect for worn belts, frayed cables, and loose bolts.
- Look for wear on skid plates and other parts.
- Sharpen blades.

Tricky ways to keep your twine in line. Never misplace your roll of twine again. Try one of these clever ideas to keep it handy and tangle-free.

- Flowerpot. Put your roll of twine into a spare clay or plastic pot and run the end through the drainage hole. Place it upside down, pull, and cut. Make it portable by adding a cover — tape a bit of cardboard over the top, and away you go.

- Baby wipes container. Whether it's a plastic box or flip-top cylinder, just remove the lid, add twine, replace the lid, and run the twine back through the opening in the lid.

- Plastic pitcher. Reuse an old pitcher with a lid to keep your twine organized. If the lid has a flip-top, run the twine through the hole. Otherwise, pull it through the spout.

> You hate throwing anything out. So don't toss your split tool handles. Rescue them by prying open the split and applying wood glue or epoxy. Clamp the area until it dries, then sand the handle so it's smooth. Just like new.

Turn a heavy sprayer into a wheeled delight. To you, "heavy metal" isn't a music choice, but that 5-gallon pressure sprayer you have to lug around the garden. End the misery. Take a couple of bungee-style cords and strap your heavy sprayer to a wheeled luggage cart or a dolly. Then let the good times — and your sprayer — roll.

Stop losing your tools in the grass. Golfers finally got smart and started playing with brightly colored balls. Now they can search for a fluorescent orange ball in a field of long grass, rather than having to pick out a tiny white blip. The same idea can work with your garden tools — to make them more noticeable when you leave them lying outside.

- Mark a spot or stripe on the handle of your shovel or hoe with fluorescent spray paint.

- Tie a length of shiny holiday ribbon on the handle. Use curling ribbon so it really stands out.

- Attach a brightly colored luggage tag to the handle.

Water without wasting a drop

11 ways to save money on outdoor watering. The average household uses as much water outdoors as indoors, so you can make a big dent in your water bill by limiting the water used in your yard. Start with these tricks and tips.

- A lawn measuring just 32 feet by 32 feet can require more than 600 gallons to water it 1 inch. Cut your lawn in half, and your bill will shrink accordingly. This spring, expand your garden beds by spreading mulch over the lawn and simply planting through it. Set garden paths between the beds and leave only a patch of grass. Native plants need far less water than a lawn, and once established, they can be left to fend for themselves during a dry spell.

- Water your lawn once a week, instead of daily. Place an open tuna can nearby, and give the grass a good, slow soaking. When an inch of water has collected in the tuna can, turn off the water.

- Mulch trees, shrubs, and beds so they'll lose less moisture to evaporation and won't require as much watering.

- Use drip irrigation around trees and shrubs.

- Fertilize your lawn less, and use slow-release fertilizers.

- Attach a pistol-style sprayer to your hose so the water won't run continuously.

- Collect water from your gutters with a rain barrel, and use it to water your flowers and grass.

- Adjust your mowing height to 2 inches, and leave clippings on the grass instead of bagging them. Your grass will retain more moisture and need less water.

- Sweep your patio and driveway with a broom instead of hosing them down to clean them.

- If you wash your car at home, don't turn on the hose until you are ready to rinse.

- Avoid planting grass on steep inclines that are hard to water.

Sneaky way to lower your water bill. One of the best ways to conserve water is to keep plants in groups depending on their individual water needs. Place all the moisture hogs together and water frequently. Plants that need "well-drained soil" and "full sun" will probably appreciate a dry spot. With different watering schedules, you can provide the ideal environment for each plant to flourish — and save water doing it.

Recycled water gives your plants a boost. Time to stop letting water go down the drain without thinking about the cost. From now on, save water and use it to nourish your plants.

- Cooking. How often do you simply pour away the water used to cook vegetables or boil eggs? Instead, let it cool and give this nutrient-rich water renewed purpose by taking it out to your garden or giving it to your houseplants.

- Pet water. Pouring out your pets' bowls to give them clean water? Keep a container handy and pour the old water in there instead of down the drain.

- Shower or bath. Put a container in your sink or shower to catch excess water that would otherwise wash away. You may not get it all, but every little bit helps — and a few suds won't harm your plants. The same is true after a bath. Any water you can reuse rather than sending down the drain is a saving on water costs and a benefit for the environment.

> If you collected and used every drop of rain off a normal-sized roof, you could potentially recycle almost 32,000 gallons of free water — a savings of almost $50 off your water bill every year. Rain barrels can cost up to $400 each, so look for local programs that give them away or make your own.

- Milk cartons. Before you recycle your empty milk cartons, fill them halfway with water and swish it around. The liquid makes a nutritious drink for alkaline-loving plants — African violets, particularly, love this homemade milkshake.

Make your own rain barrel. Buy a large, plastic trash can with a fitted lid. Elevate it on a stack of bricks so it reaches the downspout. Cut a hole in the lid the same size as your downspout and fit the two together. Drill a hole near the base of the trash can, high enough to fit a bucket underneath. Thread a water spigot through the hole from the outside and attach it with a gasket. Now, when rain fills your barrel, you can attach a hose to the spigot and water your plants.

Turn functional into fantastic. Dress up a drab rain barrel by turning it into a planter.

- Wrap coarse netting or chicken wire around the barrel, securing it in the back with twist ties.

- Plant clematis or morning glories at the base, and let them grow up through the netting. Soon your flowering vines will hide the barrel.

- Keep the vines in check so they don't block the downspout.

Salvage water from wading pool. When the kids finish playing in the wading pool, use a garden hose to drain it onto your thirsty plants. Just put one end of the hose in the bottom of the pool and suck air from the other end until the water starts to flow. To avoid swallowing dirty water, make a fist around the end of the hose and suck with your lips against your hand. You will be able to feel the water pressure and move your mouth before the water gets to it.

Best ways to garden during a drought. A water shortage can doom plants, but not if you follow these guidelines for survival.

- Water whole areas, not single plants. The dry soil near a plant will suck moisture away from its roots.

- Add another 2 inches of mulch around plants to help conserve water.

- Don't bother watering the worst-off plants. They may tug at your heartstrings, but they will never fully recover. Save water for plants with the best shot at survival.

- Put off fertilizing. Added nutrients spur growth, which makes plants even thirstier.

- Cut back flowering annuals. They may rebloom if the rains return.

- Make perennials, trees, and shrubs a priority over short-lived annuals or vegetables. Their loss would leave a bigger hole in your landscape — and your wallet.

Keep your grass green with less water. Chances are over half your water bill is for outdoor watering. But there's a good possibility you can water less and still keep a green lawn. Instead of watering sidewalks and driveways, or just spraying water into the air so it can evaporate, you need a simple way to give your lawn the water it needs, without the big expense of wasted water.

Depending on your climate, soil, and variety of plants in your yard, you may opt for an automatic sprinkler system, or you may find that the right hoses, timers, sprinklers, and drip systems will do the job just as well.

No matter what your system, wait until the top 6 inches of soil are dry before you water your lawn. Then water long enough to soak the soil below the root zone. Shallow watering encourages shallow root growth, which leads to drought damage and even more watering. It also lets weeds get started.

Vegetables and flowers need water all the time, but deeper-rooted shrubs and trees don't need to be watered as often.

3 unmistakable signs your lawn needs water

Don't wait until your lawn turns brown. Try these tricks to know when to water before it's too late.

- Look at your lawn through polarized sunglass lenses in direct sunlight. If it looks blue-gray instead of green, it's time to get busy with the garden hose.

- Walk through your lawn, then turn and look back. If there are footprints left from where you stepped, your grass needs a drink to give it more bounce.

- Push a 6-inch screwdriver into the ground. It should go in easily and all the way, if the lawn has enough water.

It's better to water deeply and less often. Frequent, shallow watering can cause shallow roots, thatch accumulation, and compacted soil.

Most lawns need 1 to 2 inches of water a week, and it's good to give it a half inch to an inch twice to make the total.

Moisten where it matters. Every drop counts in a drought, so make sure you're watering the neediest plants first. At the top of your list should be hanging pots and porch containers, which need water every day. Expensive, rare, or mature trees and shrubs are next, with vegetables that are forming fruit and perennial beds right behind them. Low on the list should be annuals that are easily replaced and lawns that can tough it out.

Look to your indicator plants for advice. You don't need to check on every single plant in your garden to see if it's time to water. By watching certain plants, you can tell the perfect time to get out your watering can. In your vegetable garden, keep an eye on how your squash or melon plants look. When their big leaves start to droop, it's probably a sign to water everything. And if you plant impatiens or coleus in the root zones of a tree, look to these little indicator plants to know when the tree is getting thirsty. You'll notice their wilting leaves long before the tree shows signs it needs water.

> Your soil will tell you how often you need to water. Sandy soil absorbs water easily, but lets it go just as fast. Water it often but in small amounts. Clay soil takes longer to soak up water, but holds on to it. Water it less frequently, but more deeply.

Timing — the key to a solid soak. Use the right watering tool at the right time to make sure all the water gets to your plants. If you water with a sprinkler, do it in the morning. Up to 40 percent of the water can be lost to evaporation if you run the sprinkler during the warmer, sunny afternoon hours. On top of that, morning watering allows leaves to dry before evening when damp leaves are more likely to "catch" fungal diseases. But if you water with a soaker hose or drip system, do it at night so the water has more time to sink into the soil.

Scale back your work when watering a hanging plant. It's not easy to see when your hanging plant needs water. Don't climb a ladder to check the soil —
use an old fish scale for a simple and reliable visual check from the ground. Hang the scale on a hook, then hang the basket on the scale. Before you water, make a note of the starting weight shown on the scale — and then again after you water. Your plant will weigh more. When the weight goes back down, the plant is ready for more water.

In hot weather, when hanging baskets dry out faster, use a sneaky, slow-release solution. Put a few ice cubes on the soil and let them melt. It's easier than using a watering can. Also, the soil has more time to absorb the precious moisture, and you won't have excess water running out of the basket.

Make a handy rain gauge. After it rains, you may wonder if your garden got enough water or if you need to turn on the sprinkler. To solve the mystery, place empty coffee cans here and there in your garden. When the rain stops, just measure the depth of the water in the cans. If you have at least an inch, there's no need for additional watering.

Clever way to check soil moisture. It's usually time to water when half the moisture the soil can hold has dried out. Here's a way to check soil moisture without getting your hands dirty. Insert wooden dipsticks at several places in your garden, and leave them there for an hour or more. Then pull each one out and check to see if the bottom is damp. If not, it's probably time to water. Use wooden paint stir sticks, craft sticks, or other light-colored wooden sticks to do the testing.

How to water a slope successfully. Watering downhill is an uphill battle. That's because water usually rushes down the slope before it has time to seep into the earth. You could buy soaker hoses, but here's a cheaper alternative. Water for a few minutes — or until you see runoff — and then stop so moisture can sink in. Return a little later for a few more minutes of watering and then stop again. Repeat this process until you're satisfied you've watered enough.

Some plants advertise their resilience. Hairy, gray, and silver foliage are a sure sign a plant is drought tolerant. The color is actually a reflection of the sunlight off millions of minuscule hairs that trap moisture evaporating from the leaves and return it to the plant.

Build a moat to hold water. Trees need a lot of water while they get established. To keep water near their roots, build a moat around the base of your tree. The larger the root base, the larger the moat. Turn a hose on low and set it in the basin for a thorough soak. As the tree grows, make sure the moat does, too. Otherwise, the roots will stay in the wet spot, and the tree could get top-heavy and topple.

Design a watering system like a pro. Choose the most water-efficient irrigation method for your outdoor space. Sprinklers are only effective on lawns. Drip systems are great for trees and shrubs that need infrequent deep watering. Soaker hoses are easy to install and ideal for plants that need water delivered directly to their roots, like vegetables and perennials. A hose or bucket is the method of choice for container gardens.

Choose the right equipment for your yard. Sometimes a professionally designed underground sprinkler system is the most efficient way to go — if you can justify the front-end expense. But if your growing season is short, your climate wet, or your yard less complex, you can go shopping for other equipment that is less expensive, but just as effective. Here are a few things to keep in mind.

- You can use timers to turn on the water early in the morning to avoid evaporation in the hot midday sun. Set them to start and stop the flow so water will soak in instead of puddling up and running off.

- When you buy a hose, remember that a larger diameter hose delivers more water.

- Look for sprinkler heads that will let you aim the stream where you want it to go. It's better to have a large-droplet spray because mists evaporate quickly.

- With soaker hoses and drip systems in your gardens and flower beds, you will use less water and do more good. You can also put timers on them. It's always a good idea to install a back-flow preventer to keep dirty water from backing up and polluting your tap water.

Make tomato stakes that water roots. You could install both tomato stakes and root-watering pipes, but you'll like this clever two-for-one trick much better. For every tomato plant you plan to grow, cut a 5-foot length of 2-inch PVC pipe. Make a mark about 10 inches away from one end of each pipe. Next, use a posthole digger to make holes near each spot where you plan to place a tomato plant. Dump the displaced dirt on a plastic bag near each hole.

Drop the first pipe into one of the holes. Push it down into the soil as far as you can. Place a 2-inch thick piece of board over the top of the pipe. Hammer the board directly above the

PVC pipe to push the pipe further into the soil until the mark on the PVC pipe is even with the ground. Roughly 4 feet of PVC pipe should remain above the dirt. Fill in the space emptied out by the post hole digger and dump any leftover dirt back down the pipe. Repeat this process for all the other poles. When you're done, you'll be ready to plant tomatoes. Just make sure each tomato plant is only a few inches from a pipe.

When you're ready to water, turn the hose on extra low and put the nozzle end in the pipe. Allow the pipe to fill and move on to the next pipe. Check back on the first pipe a few minutes later. If the water drains quickly, you may need to refill the pipe a few times. As the tomatoes grow, tie them to your PVC stakes. Wrap your tie around the stake first, knot it in place, and then tie the remaining lengths to the tomato plant.

Retain moisture with double potting. Unglazed terra cotta makes an ideal container for plants since it breathes. But it also loses water through evaporation. Instead of watering every day, set your medium-size potted plant in a large, decorative plastic or ceramic planter. Fill the space between the two pots with sphagnum moss and pour water into this outer pot. The clay will absorb enough water to keep the soil damp, but it won't lose any to the outdoors.

Water your plants while you're away. You can vacation without worry when you train your plants to water themselves. Set up a self-watering system using a plastic soda bottle.

- Heat a thick needle or tiny nail over a candle, and poke a small hole in the bottle's plastic lid.

- Fill the bottle with water and screw on the cap.

- Turn the bottle upside down and check the water flow. It should stay in the bottle for a minute, then slowly begin to drip out the hole. If no water comes out, loosen the cap slightly to release the vacuum.

- Place the bottle upside down into the top of the soil near the plant you want to water. Depending on the size of the bottle, you can be sure your plant is getting a slow stream of water for up to several weeks.

You can also use a clean, plastic milk jug. Poke a small hole in the side of the jug, near the bottom. Hold a finger over the hole as you fill the jug with water. Position the hole near the stem of your plant. Tighten or loosen the cap to adjust the flow.

Make a hose highway. If your garden hose must run right over a flower bed to get where it needs to go, give it an alternate route with a few wire coat hangers. Cut the hooks off the hangers and bend them into the shape of an M. Stick these in the ground, making a raised path across your flowers, then guide your hose into the middle bend of each M. Voilà — a garden monorail.

Buy the right size hose. The diameter of your hose makes a big difference in the time it takes to water. To drench a 1,000-square-foot garden to a depth equal to 1 inch of rain at an average water pressure of 50 pounds per square inch will take one hour and three minutes with a half-inch diameter hose. Upgrade to a five-eighths inch diameter hose and you only have to leave it on for 37 minutes. Fastest of all, a three-quarter inch diameter hose will water the same yard in just 24 minutes.

Catch fog droplets. In the dry, coastal areas of Chile and Peru, the natives harvest water from fog with a series of nets. Where misty mornings are the norm, you can try this, too.

Tightly stretch a fine nylon net between two poles on a slope facing the wind. Use a brightly colored net so birds will see it and not get caught. Plant low-growing plants or lay an old piece of gutter under the net. Condensation will collect on the screen and run off into the gutter where it can be diverted to your flower bed or a holding tank.

Take the challenges out of watering. It's as certain as death and taxes — watering your garden. Yet this important task can be a challenge if you have trouble walking or lack the strength of your younger days. Consider which of these tools can make the job easier on you.

- An extra faucet installed near your vegetable garden means you don't have to lug a long hose across your yard.

- Drip irrigation systems or soaker hoses can let you do the job by flipping a switch.

- Lever faucets are easier to turn off and on than those with round handles.

- Hose-end shutoff valves keep you from wasting water while you move to a new part of the yard.

- A long-handled watering wand lets you put water where you want it without bending.

How far will your hose go? Don't plant a garden only to discover your hose won't reach the distant corners. Check the length you'll need with this tricky tip.

Tie a string to your spigot and unwind it as you walk to the farthest spot you want to water. Cut the string at this endpoint. Next, fold your string in half, then in half again. Measure this piece and multiply the length by the number of folds. Add 10 feet to that measurement and you have the ideal length of hose to cover all your watering needs.

Shortcuts to success with seeds

Planting can be dirt cheap. Who says you can't grow money? A study by Burpee Seed Company found just $50 invested in seeds and fertilizer can produce $1,250 worth of groceries each year. Think about this. At the supermarket, a single pound of spinach will set you back $3.83. But for less than a dollar, you could buy seeds and grow up to 6 pounds of spinach. Check out these expert tips to learn how gardening from seed helps you cash in on crops.

"These days, it's expensive to go out and buy your own transplants," says consumer horticulturist Robert Westerfield. The little plants you find at the store then transfer to your garden are easy to work with, but Westerfield warns, "You're paying sometimes a couple of dollars for a plant that you could have produced on your own for a few pennies."

Start seeds right and watch your savings bloom. "In general, most of the cucurbits — squash, cucumbers, melons, gourds, and pumpkins — are easy to grow by direct seeding," says Westerfield. "You take the seeds at the proper time of year, plant them in the garden, and blooms are going to sprout and develop into a bearing plant."

However, solanaceous crops, like tomatoes, peppers, and eggplants, grow best if you start seeds indoors about six weeks prior to the planting season, then transfer the sprouts to the garden. "Don't try to direct seed them," he explains, "because they are very susceptible to temperature changes as well as some soil diseases — things that cause them to fizzle before they ever get to size."

Go to seed for free. The easiest way to get free seeds is to save some from a previous harvest. For best results, you want true-to-type seeds, or ones that will produce new plants exactly like their "parent." That means you should avoid gathering seeds from any hybrid plants you may have in your garden.

You can also snag seeds for next to nothing by participating in seed exchanges. Some are free and some require a membership fee. Contact local gardening clubs or organizations, or search online to find programs available in your area.

More than books at the library

Who knew you could find seeds in a library? Visit *seedlibraries.net,* and you'll find plenty of places where you can borrow seeds to grow your own flowers and vegetables.

Just imagine the different types of seeds you'll find while traveling. It's a cheap and easy way to try something new in your garden.

If the plants grow well, let a few go to seed, and bring or send the seeds back to the library. You'll be continuing the cycle and helping other gardeners.

Free seeds for the swapping. Give your garden some variety without buying seeds or plants when you join a seed swap. These informal gatherings, usually held in the spring, let gardeners trade surplus seeds and growing tips.

Tips for seed-catalog shopping. The most avid gardeners shop from mail-order or web-based suppliers. Convenience, unique merchandise, top quality, and reasonable prices are the biggest reasons people use these companies, but early ordering incentives, specials, and coupons can yield savings of up to 50 percent on flowers, bulbs, and seeds.

When shopping this way, only buy quality seeds. Many times cheaper seeds have low germination rates or purity. When that's the case, fewer seeds will develop into plants or the plants will not exactly match the variety description.

You can save money by buying packets with fewer seeds. After all, there's no point in buying 100 seeds when you're only planting two 25-plant rows.

And limit the number of companies you use and orders you send in. Every order costs a few extra dollars for shipping and handling, and if you only order a few packets of seeds, it may cost more to send them than to pay for the seeds.

An inexpensive photo album or old CD wallet can be the ideal place to keep your seed packets. Slip the packets in the pockets and you're set. For extra convenience, you can use sticky notes to make index tabs for each "page" or to tack notes on an individual pocket.

Dig up ideal keepers that cost nothing. An empty, plastic pill bottle from your last prescription is an ideal place to store seeds. Unlike seed envelopes, the bottles keep your seeds visible and in one place if the container tips over. They'll also keep your seeds dry and protected. So when you're done using a pill bottle, just clean it out, let it dry, and drop your seeds in. You can even label the bottle. If you don't have enough pill bottles, ask friends and family members to pass along their empty bottles when they no longer need them.

No-fuss way to keep seeds dry. Keep your seeds from molding in storage with a little household drying agent. Take a couple of tablespoons of powdered milk and place on a paper napkin. Fold and roll up the napkin into a small packet, sealing the ends with tape. Place your homemade desiccant pack into the container with your seeds and seal. After six months, put in a fresh pack of powdered milk so it will continue to absorb moisture.

Don't use hybrid seeds in the garden. "Hybrids are crosses from one plant to another to get a certain color fruit or certain growth habit or disease resistance," says Melinda Myers, nationally known horticulture expert and host of TV and radio's "Melinda's Garden Moment." "When you save and grow from those seeds," she says, "you're not going to get exactly the same as the parent plant."

The key to following seed instructions is using the last frost date in your area as your transplant goal. So if the tomato instructions say to sow the seeds six weeks before transplant, that means start the seeds indoors six weeks before the last frost.

Let your finger be your guide. Your index finger can tell you how deep to sow a seed. Just stick it into the soil as far down as your entire fingernail for radishes, lettuce, and Spanish onions. Bury up to your first knuckle for the planting depth for cabbage, carrots, beets, cucumbers, and squash. Sow bush and pole beans and corn as deep as your second knuckle.

Plant early during drought. Get seeds in the ground as soon as possible during a drought. Potatoes, onions, garlic, lettuce, peas, and spinach can be sown as soon as you can work the soil. These plants will bloom earlier, miss the high temperatures of summer, and need less water. It's also a good idea to use short-season varieties for your crops. They'll be in the ground fewer days, so they'll need less water.

Plant without back pain. Don't let back trouble stop you from planting seeds in your garden. You can sow without bending. Cut a length of PVC pipe between 3 and 4 feet long. Make sure it reaches higher than your waist when you rest one end on the ground. Place the pipe where you want a seed planted and drop the seed through the pipe. Use the end of the pipe to push soil over the seed.

A large paintbrush will come in handy when planting a garden row. You can brush just the right amount of soil over the seeds.

Sow tiny seeds easily. Those itty-bitty petunia seeds are tough to see, let alone sow. To make sowing easier, thoroughly clean an old saltshaker, let dry, and find a measuring spoon small enough to fit through the mouth of the shaker.

Use the spoon to help deposit equal amounts of seed and sand in the shaker. When you are done, screw the lid on the shaker, and sow your seeds.

Space seeds in your garden. There's a quick way to get the right space between seedlings in your garden rows. Just use a plastic drink bottle with the same diameter as the distance the seed packet says to space them. Beginning at the end of the row, press the bottle into the soil firmly enough to leave an impression. Place one or two seeds in the center of that circle. Make the next circle by placing the bottom edge of the bottle beside the first circle. Continue this process to the end of the row. Your plants will come up neatly spaced without all that tedious measuring with a ruler or string.

Make your own ready-to-plant seed tapes. Instead of buying expensive seed tapes, make your own using toilet paper. First, roll out a length of toilet paper. Line your favorite seeds down the center and fold lengthwise into thirds. Dampen the paper slightly so that it sticks together. Let it dry. When you're ready to plant, lay the tapes in your garden rows and cover with moist soil.

> Dampen a length of string and dip it into your container of seeds — the seeds will stick along the string. Then stretch the string out in your garden and cover with dirt. You'll end up with a straight row of plants.

Shield your investment. To prevent pests from digging up or eating that row of seeds you just planted, lay down some gutter guard mesh over the row. This is the strip of mesh used to keep leaves out of your roof gutters. Hold down each end of your mesh seed protector with rocks or bricks.

Trade achy back for a planting stick. For a quick and easy way to dig holes at exactly the right depth for each vegetable seed, simply wrap a rubber band around the handle of your hoe. Turn it upside down and adjust the rubber band so it marks the exact depth for corn or bean seeds. Now simply go down the row and push the stick into the ground to the correct depth. You can easily switch to a different seed — just adjust the height of the rubber band and start a new row.

Pick the right light for strong growth

Most seeds don't need light to germinate, but keep them moist so they don't dry out and die before they become seedlings. Then that's the time to make sure they have plenty of light. If seedlings don't get enough light they grow leggy — with weak, spindly stems — while reaching out trying to find light.

Seed starting for tightwads. You can make most seed-starting kits cheap or free. Here's how to create a seed-starting station that provides warmth, light, humidity, and the best odds of success.

- Don't waste your money on plastic pots. Instead, poke holes in the bottom of cleaned out avocado skins or eggshells. Now you have free "pots" for your seeds.

- Seeds thrive on humidity, so place your "pots" inside clamshell plastic containers. Once closed, these containers keep humidity inside. You get these containers any time you order take-out food. Just save them and rinse them out.

- The inside of your refrigerator may be very cold, but the top is nice and warm. Set up your seed starters there.

- Seeds demand light, so place fluorescent lamps above them.

Save young plants from an early death. Young spring plants are in danger of getting eaten by birds. To keep your vegetable seedlings safe from beady eyes, cover them with plastic mesh baskets, the kind strawberries and mushrooms come in. By the time the plant pushes up against the roof of its cage, it won't be tender or interesting to the birds anymore.

Start seedlings for less. Get an early start on your spring garden and save money, too, by using egg cartons as starter trays for your seedlings. Just fill the cups with soil, plant your seeds, and keep them in a sunny window. If you use cardboard cartons, you can separate the cups and plant them directly in the soil when the

A set of plastic picnic silverware can be useful for those delicate gardening chores. Spoons in particular are good for putting just the right amount of soil or fertilizer in the right spot during potting or seeding jobs.

threat of frost has passed. If you use Styrofoam cartons, remove the seedlings from the cups before you transplant them.

Nurse your baby plants in a bottle. Create a mini greenhouse from a plastic 2-liter soft drink bottle to give your garden plants an early start. Cut a 3-inch-wide flap in one side of the bottle, beginning at the neck and stopping several inches from the bottom. Punch some drainage holes in the opposite side. With the bottle resting on its side, lift the flap and put in a few inches of potting soil. Plant and water your seeds, and place the bottle in a sunny window with the flap closed. Moisture held inside will help the seeds sprout, but you can open the flap to adjust the humidity as needed. If established plants grow too large before it's time to transplant them, you can cut the flap away to give them more room.

> Seeds and soil don't mix. Use milled sphagnum moss to start seeds instead. Add vermiculite to help the moss hold water and provide seeds with magnesium and potassium. And to lighten the mix, toss in perlite.

Give seedlings a head start. Aluminum foil and a shoebox are handy helpers when you start plants indoors from seeds. Line the box with the foil, shiny side out, extending an inch or two above the sides. Punch drainage holes through both foil and shoebox bottom. Add potting soil up to a few inches from the top of the box and plant the seeds. Put it in a sunny window and wait. The foil will reflect heat to the seedlings as they grow. Your plants should be big and healthy when it's time to transplant them to your garden.

Get a jump on spring. To start your garden before the last frost, save these throwaway items to recycle into covers that will protect your plants.

- Cut off the top part of a half-gallon waxed milk carton, leaving about 6 to 8 inches from the bottom. Turn it upside down and cut three sides of the bottom square to make a flap. Press the sides of the carton a few inches into the loose soil, and plant the seedling in the center. Open the flap to let in air and sunshine, but close it at night if there is danger of frost. After the plant grows tall and the danger of cold damage has passed, leave the open carton in place as a shield against some bugs.

Cut the bottoms out of coffee cans and put them over newly planted seedlings in the spring garden. At night put the plastic lids on for protection. Take them off during sunny days. Remove the cans when the threat of frost damage has passed.

• Grab a plastic milk jug or soda bottle. Cut off the bottom and place it over your plant. Leave the top off for air and water.

Make your own cold frame. A cold frame can help you harden off seedlings in the spring or grow cool weather crops in autumn or winter. It uses sunlight to keep plants warmer than the outside air, so choose a spot facing south where your cold frame can get direct sunlight for at least half the day. All you need is an old window and materials for a base, like scrap lumber, bricks, or cinder blocks.

Once it's built, your cold frame will resemble a box with the front end sunk into the ground so its roof slopes downward. The slope helps rain drain off and allows more sunlight into the frame. Design the size of your cold frame to match the size of the window you use as a roof.

To start, mark off where the south wall and north wall of your cold frame will rest and measure the distance between these marks in feet. Your cold frame must slope toward the south, so

dig a sloped bed with the
deepest edge at the south
end of your frame.

Remember the distance in
feet between the north and
south wall? That number is
also how many inches deep
your trench should be. In
other words, if the distance between the north and south walls
is 6 feet, make the trench 6 inches deep. Dig toward the north
wall so you end up with a sloped bed that starts at ground
level at the north end and slopes down to the depth of the
trench at the south end — a 1-inch drop per foot of distance.

Create a frame from your choice of materials that rests just
inside the edges of your sloped bed. If the frame is wood, you
may need to assemble it before placing it in the bed. Bricks or
cinder blocks can simply be layered along the bed's edges.

Make this frame between 1 and 2 feet deep. If you use cinder
blocks, stuff the holes with newspaper or dirt. Place your
window on top to complete your cold frame.

Beat damping-off. A simple ingredient from your kitchen
pantry can stop this fungal bully from picking on your yard
and garden. First, drink some chamomile tea and drop the
used tea bag into 3 3/4 cups of water. After the tea bag has
soaked awhile, remove it, and pour the water over your
seedlings. For severe cases, use a fresh tea bag straight from the
box. Fungi hate it when you do that.

Hardening off doesn't need to be hard. The traditional method of hardening off seedlings to make the transition from indoors to outdoors involves a week or two of daily moves — outdoors during the day to get used to the sun and wind, then back inside at night.

Skip the hassle of all that moving by placing your seedlings in a transitional place, like a covered porch or along the east side of your house protected from the wind and sun. Assuming the weather is mild, you can leave them here for the days and nights of hardening off, then move them straight to your garden.

Give your precious garden babies a jump-start on growth. Mix a teaspoon of baby shampoo into a quart of water and use it to water trays of newly planted seedlings. The mild soap prevents a tough crust from forming on the soil surface.

Transplant seedlings damage-free. The first pair of leaves most plants put out are "false leaves," part of the plant's embryo. Don't transplant your tiny seedlings when you see those. Wait until the plant produces the first true leaves, usually the second set of leaves. Handle the seedlings by these leaves rather than by the stems, which are easily damaged. The plant can grow new leaves, but it can't spare its delicate stem.

Prepare tender seedlings for a careful transplant. Some vegetables don't transplant as well as others. Squash and cucumbers, for example, have long roots that are easily damaged in the process. You can, however, improve their chances of success. Start them in the kind of plastic basket you buy fresh strawberries or blueberries in at the grocery store. Just line the container with newspaper, add the soil, and plant four or five seeds. Grow them in a sunny spot until time to take them to the garden. Snip off the tops of a couple of seedlings to give the others more room to grow. Cut the bottom out of the basket and plant it, container and all into the ground. The roots can continue to grow without ever being disturbed.

Make a miniature greenhouse. You can start your seedlings in the garden earlier with the proper protection. Cut the hooks off of wire coat hangers. Straighten the wires, then bend them into U-shapes. Press them into the soil over the rows, spaced about 12 inches apart. Drape clear plastic over them and anchor with rocks or bricks. Leave the ends open so air can circulate. On sunny days remove the plastic. You can quickly replace it when temperatures drop. When frost is no longer a threat, pull it all up and store it until next year.

Annuals: amp it up with color

Add pizzazz to your landscape. Annuals provide a lot of color in the garden. They show off their beauty best when planted in groups of the same kind, rather than interspersed with other colors and varieties. Some of the best bloomers that require the least amount of care are nasturtium, coleus, marigold, dusty miller, impatiens, periwinkle, zinnia, spider flower, sweet alyssum, and yellow cosmos.

Flowering herbs do double duty. Your flower garden turns into a functional kitchen garden when you mix in lovely culinary herbs like rosemary, chives, lavender, and German chamomile. Flowering herbs fit so well among the other blooms, you may forget to pick them when it's time.

Just be careful with flowering annuals like basil, dill, cilantro, and chervil. Once these herbs start making flowers, leaf production slows down or stops. Harvest them often to enjoy their fragrant leaves and delay flowering.

Tomato fertilizer isn't just for tomatoes. Use this high-potassium liquid fertilizer to help your annuals flower. Too many leaves and not enough flowers could be a sign that you're overfertilizing. Lay off the high-nitrogen fertilizers and manure, and use tomato fertilizer instead.

Give budget wildflowers best chance for success. Seed packets claim you can create a lush field of flowers with a quick scattering. Wildflower seeds can save money over buying pricey annual flowers. But sow them right so you get more than unsightly weeds.

- First, be sure your wildflower mix is right for your region and your use, such as a dry area.

- Next, prepare your seeds by soaking them in water overnight to speed up germination.

- Clear weeds or grass from small patches of ground, loosen up the soil, and press seeds into it. Use twice the amount of seed the package recommends.

- Finally, water your seeds just like you would other young flowers.

Your field of wildflowers will be less spectacular next year because some of the annuals won't come back, but you can repeat the steps if you like the results.

Save big with self-seeding flowers. Imagine getting five years' worth of annuals at 80 percent off and only having to plant them once. Self-seeding annuals can do this for you because these low-cost "annuals" come back year after year. Examples of popular self-sowing annuals include Mexican aster (*Cosmos*), pot marigold (*Calendula officinalis*), spider flower (*Cleome spinosa*), and snapdragon (*Antirrhinum*). Discover what your garden center may not tell you about starting and caring for these cost-savers.

- You may already have some self-sowers in your yard. In early spring, check for "volunteer" seedlings from flowers that you did not sow or plant. They may come from flowers you already have or from your neighbor's garden — and they cost nothing.

- If you must buy self-sowing annuals, look for hardy annuals. Your best bets are native plants or plants from places with similar climate and soil.

- Make sure your self-sowing area stays undisturbed. Plant your annuals where water will not wash the seeds away, and water gently enough to keep from washing the seeds away yourself. Mark the area so you will not accidentally clean it up, mow it down, or prepare it for different plants.

- When you "deadhead" to remove dead flowers, be sure to leave a few untouched so you can harvest those seeds later. The more seeds you want, the less deadheading you should do.

- You have three ways to get more flowers from self-sowers. You can let the seeds fall near the original plant for a clump of flowers. You can transplant any volunteer seedlings to wherever you want them once they develop three sets of leaves. Or you can collect the seeds that often hide behind fading flowers. Wait until these seeds have dried to harvest them. Then collect them in an envelope and keep in the refrigerator until time to plant.

- Contact your county extension agent for more advice on the selection, care, and overwintering of self-seeding annuals in your area.

Get perennial color from annuals. Save money by keeping this year's annuals for next year's garden. Dig up your healthiest begonias or geraniums in the fall, put them in pots, and store them in a garage or cool basement. Water them monthly, then plant them in the yard come springtime.

You can also try keeping geraniums by shaking the dirt from their roots and hanging them upside down in the basement. Another option is to keep them in their original nursery pot and insert them into another pot that has been planted in the ground. At the first threat of frost, simply remove the original pot and bring the plant indoors.

Bigger and "bloomier" isn't always better. When you are shopping for annuals, tall plants or those in full bloom may attract your attention first. But in the long run, you'll have healthier plants if you make bushy, dark greenery your highest priority.

Encourage marigolds to return in the spring. Don't clean up your garden too quickly when flowers stop blooming in late summer. In mild areas, some annuals will reseed themselves. Marigolds, pansies, and zinnias, for example, will give you a new season of blooms the following spring. But you have to let seed heads develop, dry, and drop their seeds to the ground so they can come up again.

For wildflower patches, when the plants turn brown, mow them to a height of about 5 inches. This will scatter the seeds and provide some mulch, too.

And be on the lookout for the new seedlings when spring rolls around. Don't mow them or pull them up thinking they are unwanted weeds.

Annuals add variety to perennial beds. Who says you can't mix annual and perennial flowers? A blend of various types of plants brings some zing to flower beds.

- Mix unusual potted annuals in your perennial bed, changing them with the seasons. Move the pots around to meet changing water or lighting needs of each flower.

- Plant annuals in the ground among the perennials. A variety of plants mixed together — called polyculture — helps all the plants thrive because they don't compete for identical nutrients. Plus, they're less likely to share the same diseases. So your zinnias may enjoy greater health if you plant them next to your hostas.

- Use annual flowers that won't spread or grow above 10 inches to fill in the spaces between newly planted shrubs or ground cover. These compact plants can camouflage bare spots while the permanent residents reach maturity.

Want to know when to plant annuals? A good way to tell when to put out your bedding plants is to watch the flower beds in parks, shopping centers, and other public places. Professional landscapers know the best time to get things growing. Transplanting needs to happen as early as possible to get the most blooming time, but if there's still a risk of frost, you could be in trouble. Annuals need warm soil to grow well. Cold weather will slow them down and put them behind later-planted flowers.

Impatient for your impatiens to grow? Try stimulating them with a daily dose of cold tea. Potted plants benefit from the many minerals in this everyday beverage.

Beat spring rush with fall seed planting. Spread out the gardening chores by putting your annual seeds in the ground in the fall — the same time as you plant bulbs. Aim to sow seeds just before the rainy season in a warm climate, or right after the first killing frost in a colder area. You'll enjoy a colorful surprise in the spring when it's sprouting time. Annual poppies, pansies, and larkspur are good candidates for fall sowing.

Let annuals soak up the sun. Sunshine is important for growing annual flowers. Their entire lifespan is less than a year, so they need to soak up lots of energy in a short time to make their beautiful blooms. Plot the sun's passage before choosing the flower bed for your annuals. They need six to eight hours of midday sun every day. Early morning and late afternoon sun is not as intense and doesn't do as much good. Keep in mind the changes that the seasonal movement of the sun, cloud cover, and progress of leaves on the trees will bring.

> Give tiny seeds a chance at life. Follow the package directions when you plant flowers that come from tiny seeds. California poppies, columbine, shasta daisies, and similar flowers need light to begin germination. If you bury the seeds too deep, they won't make it out of the ground.

Give impatiens their own sun shade. Provide temporary shade for sun-fearing flowers like amethyst, Persian violets, and shade-loving impatiens with an old umbrella. You can "plant" it in your garden where you need it or make an umbrella-shaded pot for a sunny deck.

- Find a large, heavy container to use as a pot, and dig out a big umbrella — possibly an old golf umbrella or canvas market umbrella.

- Keep the umbrella upright in the pot by wedging bricks around it or placing it inside a short length of PVC pipe.

- Add a layer of sand to the pot, then potting soil.

- Place your plants so that the tallest grow near the umbrella at the center of the pot. You may want to do the planting with the container in its final location since it will be heavy.

Prompt petunias to bloom twice. Freshen up your flowering plants and encourage a second bloom with a midsummer makeover. Many annuals, even the more forgiving varieties like petunias, can become leggy and tired by the middle of the growing season. Give them a good pruning, and top-dress the soil with about one-half inch of vermicompost — compost helped along by worms. Then water thoroughly to help nutrients reach the roots. Sit back and wait for a new show of flowers from your refreshed bloomers.

Strike the right balance in timing your transplanting. Move flowers too early in the spring, and a surprise freeze could put a chill on your efforts. But wait too late, and your annuals won't have enough time in the warm soil to do their best blooming.

Plant vintage treasures among the blooms. Get that cottage garden feel without spending a dime on a new gazing ball or pricey iron sculpture. The key is to select interesting vintage items and place them in your garden so the plants appear to be growing around them. Try an old metal sign planted among your impatiens, or petunias growing up through a cracked crock. Even a broken spice cabinet looks great when zinnias are sprouting from the drawers.

Mr. Smarty Plants to the rescue. Get gardening help from the experts at the Lady Bird Johnson Wildflower Center in Texas. "Ask Mr. Smarty Plants" is a free online service provided by the staff and volunteers, offering advice on all things related to native plants. You can even get help with plant identification if you send a digital picture of your mystery plant. Navigate to *wildflower.org/expert* to find answers to all your gardening questions.

Here's an easy watering cue. Figure out which flower bed dries out first and which holds the most water. Then use these as your cues to know when to water all your plants. There's no need to check every bed or flower once you decide which area works as the canary in your coal mine.

Bulbs: seasonal secrets to blooming beauty

Become a bulb expert. The next time you shop for spring or summer bulbs, remember these tips from Wayne Juers, horticulturist and plant doctor for Pike Family Nurseries headquartered in Norcross, Georgia.

- "Make sure the retailer has them displayed in a somewhat of a cool, dry place," says Juers, "because if they've been exposed to sun or moisture, they will start to rot."

- Look for bulbs that are firm, never mushy.

- Larger bulbs may cost more, but consider the benefits. "You're going to get more plants out of the bigger bulbs," Juers says. "But sometimes for value, the little bulbs are fine. Just buy more of them, and you might get a better deal."

- For spring bulbs, Juers offers two extra pieces of advice. "Make sure there's lots of paper-like skin on the outside," he says. And, instead of buying bagged bulbs, look for single bulbs packed in Styrofoam or shredded straw. "You get a better quality bulb when you can hand select," he explains.

Be careful after buying bulbs, too. Plant them at the right time and the right depth. "People make a lot of mistakes because the bulbs become available much too early to plant," says Juers. Plant spring bulbs by September and October if you live in the colder areas like the Northeast, but wait until November or December if you live farther south. Cold-area gardeners should plant summer-flowering bulbs in late May or June, while Southern growers can plant their bulbs in April.

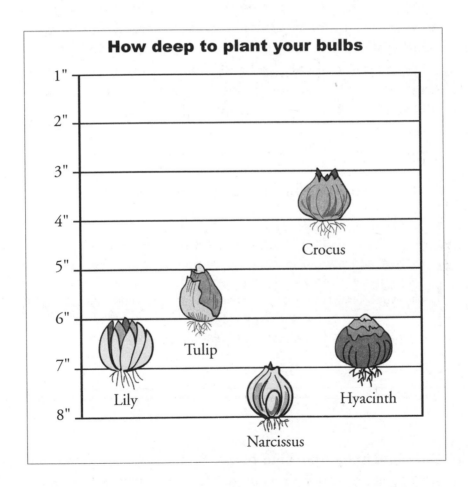

How deep to plant your bulbs

Take planting cue from nurseries. Spring-flowering bulbs, summer-flowering bulbs — different varieties of bulbs grow and bloom at different times of the year. How do you know when to plant them? Companies that sell bulbs take out the guesswork. They typically offer bulbs for sale near the time of year they should be planted. So if you see tulip bulbs offered for sale and that's the flower you want, buy them now and plant them soon.

Knock out disease with 1 simple step. Crop rotation, or moving the location of plants from year to year, keeps bulbs healthy. When you plant bulbs in a new area, you keep last year's soil-borne diseases and pesky insects from returning this season. So replant summer bulbs like gladiolus and begonias that you lifted last fall in a new place this spring.

Speed-plant bulbs for less digging

Skip the tedious chore of planting bulbs one by one. You can get all your tulips or daffodils in the ground in less than an hour with this quick method. It's as simple as digging a few large communal holes and tossing in your bulbs. Then just turn them pointed end up and cover with dirt. Figure four large bulbs per square foot you dig. That means you can plant about 100 bulbs in a 5 x 5-foot bed.

Get more bang from your bulbs. Bulbs, especially daffodils, are a good investment in your garden. Buy a few and in time they'll fill your landscape. Daffodils are known as "the poets' flower." They are easy to grow, and they tolerate any kind of soil except boggy land. They multiply quickly, yet take years before they need to be divided. An added benefit — rodents find them unappealing and leave them alone.

Daffodils, tulips, and other bulbs like to be buried deeply, but that doesn't mean you have to dig a deep hole. Instead, only dig down about 3 inches. Bury the bulbs and cover them with soil. Then take mulch, compost, or more soil and mound it on top for another 3 inches of "depth."

Then again, don't try overly hard to be thrifty. You might try to double your money by looking for daffodil bulbs with two "noses." It's true you'll get two flower stems, but these bulbs are more likely to go "blind" — stop producing flowers. Stick with a single-nose bulb for more flowers in the long term.

Bulbs bloom without bone meal. The old advice was to put bone meal in the bottom of the hole when you plant bulbs. But now the experts say it's not necessary to fertilize bulbs the first year. And you won't have dogs and rodents, attracted by the smell of bone meal, digging up your bulbs.

Turn your trash into garden treasures. "There is no shortage of items you can repurpose in the garden," says Colleen Vanderlinden, freelance writer and author of *Edible Gardening for the Midwest*. "Some of my favorites are items that would normally end up in the landfill or in my recycling bin."

The mesh bags that oranges or onions come in are a good example. "Put freshly dug tender bulbs in them, hang the bag in your shed or basement, and let your bulbs dry out a bit before storing them," suggests Vanderlinden. She also recommends putting one bag inside another. "Fill with potting soil, and sift over newly planted seeds," she says. And at the end of the season? "Ball them up and use them as a great scrubber for cleaning out flowerpots." But that's not all.

"Use old, worn serving spoons as garden tools. They work especially well in planting up container gardens, when typical trowels are often too large for such a small space," advises Vanderlinden.

"Another item I use in the garden is small, single-serving plastic yogurt containers," she adds. "I use them to start vegetable seeds indoors by washing them thoroughly, drilling or poking several holes in the bottom for drainage, filling with soil, and planting seeds. Tomatoes, peppers, and eggplants all do wonderfully grown this way, because they develop large root systems in a short amount of time. You can also use yogurt containers as measuring scoops when mixing up homemade potting soil. For example, if your recipe calls for eight parts peat to one part perlite, you'll know to add eight containers full of peat and one full of perlite, and your mixture will be perfect every time."

> The secret to healthier bulbs? Make sure the bulb packaging says "for naturalizing" if you want to leave your tulip bulbs in the ground year after year. To guarantee the bulbs reappear every spring, dose the bed with a low-nitrogen fertilizer in the fall.

Plant bulbs and seeds without a backache. Instead of kneeling and crouching to create holes for bulbs and seeds, make it more like a walk in the park. A broken shovel with a D-handle makes a great new tool — a dibble. Sharpen the broken end to a point and use it to make holes as you walk the row you want to plant. Likewise, an old walking stick or cane with a metal tip can serve the same purpose. Or use the handle from an old rake or broom.

In addition to sharpening one end, use a yardstick to mark inch and foot measurements on it for a complete bulb hole tool. When you want to space your bulbs and seeds uniformly, you've got your measuring stick right there with you. And when you need to plant at a particular depth, measure the right length from the end of your stick, then get a rubber band and wrap it around at that mark — you'll reach the perfect level every time.

Choose rodent-resistant bulbs

You can prevent mice, gophers, and squirrels from digging up or eating your bulbs, particularly if you are ready to switch to new flowers or you are planting bulbs for the first time. Just plant the kind they don't like. Bulbs that are poisonous or intensely disliked by these four-legged pests include daffodils, narcissus, camassia, fritillaria, alliums, bulb irises, snowdrops, ivy-leafed cyclamen, chionodoxa, magic lily, Spanish bluebells, and Siberian squill.

Simple secret ends squirrel damage. Don't want to tempt hungry squirrels? If you plant bulbs they like, you can protect your blooms by cleaning up the bulb's papery skins after planting and laying a window screen on the ground over the bulbs. Weight the edges down with rocks or boards and remember to remove the screens before your flowers emerge from the ground.

Saving bulbs from outdoor critters. Backyard critters may love your bulbs, but one trip to the kitchen could fix that. Sprinkle cayenne pepper or Tabasco sauce on the soil around the bulbs and neither raccoons nor squirrels will stick around. You can also try black pepper. Just remember, you'll need to "reheat" the area with a fresh round of pepper or Tabasco after each rainfall.

Soapy solution to garden thievery. Get out your kitchen grater, take a bar of pungent soap, and sprinkle soap shavings on the soil after you plant bulbs. Stearic acid from the soap works to deter squirrels and other critters from digging down to eat your bulbs. The soap shavings should last several weeks. When you can't see them anymore, repeat the process.

Two flowering bulbs, daffodils and narcissi, are poisonous. Don't store them in an area, like the cellar or refrigerator, where they might be mistaken for onions. It's best to keep these in a completely separate gardening area.

Trick bulbs into blossoming. Spring-flowering bulbs, like tulips, hyacinths, and crocuses, need to lie dormant for a period of cold weather before they can grow and bloom. That's how these bulbs know to sprout and bloom during spring rather than in the middle of winter. It's a natural process called vernalization, and it's no problem if you live in a cold climate like Minnesota or

Maine. But if you live in a mild climate like Florida or Texas, you can get brilliant blooms with this refrigerator secret.

- Pre-chill bulbs in the fridge at around 40 to 45 degrees Fahrenheit to make them think it's wintertime. Your crisper drawer may be perfect for this.

- Start about eight to 15 weeks before planting, depending on the variety of bulbs.

> If you don't have an indoor space to store bulbs over the winter, keep them outside on a porch or under the house in an inexpensive Styrofoam cooler. Just pack them in peat moss and leave the cover open slightly so air can circulate.

- Be sure to keep apples and other fruit away from the bulbs. Ethylene gas from ripening fruit will kill your flowers.

Your bulbs will "believe" they had a rough autumn and will be itching to bloom.

Give bulbs breath of fresh air. Store bulbs over the winter in a sack that gives ventilation. If you use airtight containers or plastic bags, your bulbs might come out damp and moldy. You can use mesh bags made for storing bulbs or substitute a paper bag. Old pantyhose also work great, since they let your bulbs breathe freely. Hang the bags in a cool, dry place like the basement.

Perennials: many happy returns

Perennial power: save time and money with fabulous blooms. That showy flat of annuals is cheap and oh-so eye-popping — just what you want for instant color and curb appeal with pow. But a gardener in it for the long haul will save more money — and get as beautiful a display — with perennials.

Say you have two areas you need to fill with flowers. In the spot near the porch, you plant 12 impatiens, at a cost of around $10. You fill the other bare patch with five purple coneflowers and pay almost $30. The annuals are so much cheaper, it sounds like a no-brainer, doesn't it? But don't be fooled.

"Annual plants are a way to add seasonal color to your landscape," says Kim Toal, Fayette County Cooperative Extension Agent with the University of Georgia Extension Service. "But perennial plants add continuous color year after year." Even though each annual costs less than a perennial, Toal is quick to point out, "These plants will need to be replaced every year."

After seven seasons, you've spent about $70 to put in impatiens every year. But you'd pay nothing beyond your original investment for the purple coneflowers. "If you look at a cost comparison of an annual versus a perennial," Toal says, "a perennial is much cheaper due to the fact you're going to be seeing that same plant year after year."

Planting perennials also means you've spent a lot less time and energy every year clearing out the spent plants, digging, and replanting. What's more, each perennial you buy can be a source of additional plants, since some reseed and others can be divided into more plants. Choose perennials wisely, and they can give you years of beauty without requiring much care or cost.

Plant flowers that care for themselves. Make your garden self-sufficient by picking virtually indestructible flowering plants. Best bets are plants that are suited to your climate and the conditions of your yard. Look for plants that don't need lots of pruning, staking, or dividing, and have some resistance to disease and pests. The ability to tolerate variations in temperature and humidity, as well as expected life spans of five years or more, also make them great choices. And be patient while your new plants are getting established. Before you head to the nursery, be sure to check out this list of the top 10 low-maintenance, garden-ready flowers.

- morning glories
- moonbeam coreopsis
- impatiens
- daylilies
- black-eyed Susans
- irises
- lavender
- marigolds
- peonies
- columbine

Clever way to find the best plants for your yard

You'll have more success if you plant perennials that are best for where you live. You can find out for sure which ones will do well in your yard by paying attention to the plants in your area — not by visiting a website.

Look around town to see what plants are thriving in old graveyards, around neglected farm yards, or near old houses. Droughts, storms, and all manner of bad conditions — these flowers have seen it all. They have survived for years with little or no care, so they should stay healthy in your yard, too.

Simple way to keep your columbines pure. Plant only a single variety of columbine flowers in your yard if you want to keep their color the same every year. Planting more than one type — even at opposite ends of your yard — allows birds and bees to cross-pollinate them, and the colors won't stay true.

Save even more in the offseason. Planting perennials in autumn can save you money three ways.

- Many nurseries run late-season specials on great perennials. Be sure to plant them six weeks before the first frost. Skip mums, asters, and other late bloomers, though, because they won't get established before winter.

- You're less likely to have pest and disease problems during cooler months so you won't need to buy remedies.

- You won't need fertilizer, since you don't want to encourage new growth during autumn.

Buy once, harvest every year. Every backyard gardener bears the same burden — year after year, you have to start all over again. Wouldn't it be nice if your vegetables came back each season like your perennial flowers? Well, the word perennial doesn't just refer to pretty blooms. You can grow vegetables, fruits, and herbs that make a comeback every year. Gardening expert Melinda Myers shares the best part of growing perennials. "Once established," she says, "you've got decades of harvest without investing in more plants, just weeding and maintenance." That means less time and money you have to put into your garden and more tasty treats you get to harvest.

Boost the blooms in your rose bed. In May and June, give your roses a little extra push to keep blooming. Sprinkle one teaspoon of Epsom salts per foot of height beneath each shrub.

Grow $40 of this crowd favorite every year — asparagus. "If you grow them properly and cultivate good beds, asparagus plants can last 20 to 30 years," says consumer horticulturist Robert Westerfield. Still, he's quick to remind that, in most cases, asparagus plants take two years to start producing. "The first year, you let all the energy go back into the plant, and it's from the second year on that you can begin the harvest."

This is a real money-saver, since fresh asparagus might cost $3.21 a pound at the supermarket. Buy 25 plants for $16.95 and, once they start producing, you could get more than 12 pounds, or about $40 worth of asparagus every year. Over the lifetime of your plants, that adds up to at least $1,100 you get to trim off your grocery bill.

Encourage your plants to keep on blooming

When blossoms die, it gives the plant the idea its job of producing flowers is done. So it stops blooming and puts its energy into producing seeds instead. You can trick it into thinking its job isn't finished by deadheading — or pinching off the dead blossoms before seeds form. If there are still buds on the stems, just remove the dead flower head. If there are no more buds, cut the stems back to the base.

If deadheading doesn't appeal to you, try planting flowers such as impatiens, begonias, ageratum, alyssum, and lobelia. As "automatic deadheaders," they do the work for you by dropping their dead blossoms without any help.

Enjoy a giving garden. Plant pleasing perennials for a garden that keeps on giving. Like all produce, your success with perennials will depend on where you live. Check out these popular plants that will return every season for years to come, and see if you can grow them in your gardening zone.

- Veggies: Jerusalem artichokes, scarlet runner beans, radicchio, rhubarb

- Herbs: shallots, garlic chives, bronze fennel, German thyme, sorrel, spearmint

- Fruits: blackberries, blueberries, strawberries, raspberries

- Fruit trees: apples, peaches, plums, pears

Double your perennials for free. Dividing your perennials not only gives you more at no cost, it also helps you contain overgrown plants and revitalize tired ones. Most perennials need to be divided once every three to five years.

For best results, divide your spring and summer bloomers in autumn at least four weeks before the ground freezes. Divide autumn bloomers in the spring as soon as you spot new growth.

Before you divide a plant, water it thoroughly, prune the stems and leaves to around 6 inches high, and prepare the planting space.

To divide the original plant, lift its root ball out of the ground. Insert a sharp shovel, flat-edged spade, or spading fork in the soil at least 4 inches away from the plant. Press down until the end of your tool has penetrated below the root level and pull your digger back out of the ground. Use this technique to make a circle around the plant. Slip your shovel under the plant and lift the root ball out.

Some plants can be pulled apart with your hands or cut apart with a knife. If your perennial is too big or thick for that, insert two pitchforks in the root ball so they are back to back in the center of the plant. Position them so both handles are vertical. Pull the handles of the pitchforks apart to separate the plant, but be careful to avoid breaking the handles. After dividing, plant your "new" perennials right away.

When not to divide perennials. It's best to divide perennials like coneflowers and black-eyed Susans in spring or early fall. But you'll do more harm than good if you try to divide them at these dangerous times.

- when the weather is very hot

- after a long drought

- in late fall, close to the first freeze

Spray away diseases. Try this homemade spray to protect roses from fungal diseases like powdery mildew and black spot. Mix two or three tablespoons of baking soda with a gallon of water and a few drops of dishwashing liquid. Spray your bushes once or twice a week. It's a safe, effective alternative to chemicals and poisons.

Extend gardening season for pennies. Imagine making a season-extender that won't blow away or break the bank — no matter how many you use. All you need are 2-liter bottles and duct tape. Place one bottle as your center marker and form a circle of bottles around it. Wrap duct tape around the outside of the circle to bind all the outer bottles together. Then remove the center bottle, and you have a new cloche.

For best results, position the cloche around the plant in the morning and fill each bottle with water and a pinch of salt to help hold the heat. The sun will heat the water during the day. That will keep your plant warmer during chilly nights because water retains heat better than air does. For extra protection from frost, throw a sheet of clear plastic or a transparent old shower curtain over the cloche.

Give unwanted bamboo the boot. Bamboo blowing in a gentle breeze makes a pretty addition to your garden. But it can get out of hand quickly if you leave the new shoots unchecked. Fortunately, if you act while the shoots are still tender, you can easily break them off at ground level with your foot.

Protect plants from an overnight frost or freezing temperatures with kitchen garbage bags or old pillowcases. Once you tuck a pillowcase over a plant, it will be as toasty "in the sack" as you are.

Fruit: easy picks for tasty treats

How pick healthy strawberry plants. The first step to luscious strawberries is a healthy plant that can take whatever challenges your local weather and soil can dish out. So look for strawberry varieties that grow well in your area. Your local extension service or a good nearby plant nursery can help. To make sure you get plants that aren't struggling with hidden diseases, buy only plants that are certified virus-free.

Discourage birds with tough berries. As soon as you see green strawberries on your plants, paint small rocks red and place them where birds might be looking for a snack. When the birds try to bite the "fruit," they'll quickly realize these berries aren't good enough to eat. By the time your strawberry crop ripens, they'll be gone, and you'll keep all those berries for yourself.

> Keep strawberry plants high and dry. If better drainage might help your strawberry plants, try growing them on raised rows 6 or 8 inches high. For best results, keep rows about 25 inches wide and space the plants 18 inches apart.

Try a trick from the strawberry pros. Join the strawberry farmers who beat weeds and get better strawberries by treating their plants as annuals. Starting in summer or early fall, put the plants in the ground and give them a plastic mulch. Water regularly for the best results. After harvest, remove all the strawberry plants to make way for next year's planting.

Enjoy summer's harvest all year long. When spring or summer berries are in season — whether growing in your garden or plentiful in the supermarket — freeze some to enjoy in winter. Put them in the freezer on a cookie sheet. When they are frozen, transfer them to freezer containers. They won't stick together, so you can use just the amount you need without defrosting extras.

Cinder blocks make great homes for strawberry plants. Fill the holes with a mix of half compost and half potting soil, and place a plant in each. Water frequently and pinch off the runners. Give the plants a dose of liquid fertilizer twice a month.

Simple way to beat the bare years. Do your fruit trees bear bushels of fruit one year and almost none the next? When fruit-bearing is sparse in alternate years, it's called biennial bearing or alternate bearing. You may be able to break the cycle if you thin even more fruit than usual from the trees during a heavy-bearing year.

Outsmart worms with apple "footies." Try these nontoxic, no-spray tactics to help stop worms, coddling moths, and apple maggots right in their tracks — but be prepared to start early. When your apples are nearly the size of a penny, shield them with one of these.

- Slip a small paper lunch bag over each apple, and staple it shut across the top. Leave no gaps for bugs to sneak through.

- Gather a pile of stretchy little nylon footies, the kind some people use when trying on shoes. Slide a footie around and over each apple, and tie it around the top of the stem to enclose the apple.

These clever tactics may not be practical to try on tall apple trees, but they should work well on espaliers, semi-dwarf, and dwarf trees.

> For the tastiest apples and pears, don't water your fruit trees too much. The excess water can also make soft fruits, like figs, split open as they ripen.

Grow sweeter grapes. Plant your vines where they'll get the most sunshine, and you'll be rewarded with sweet grapes. A south-facing wall or slope is ideal. And if you grow them in rows running north to south, your plants will receive the most sunlight and will be more protected from wind damage, as well.

Turbocharge your vines for better grapes. You can train your grapevines to produce bigger harvests of higher-quality grapes. Use this strategy for American varieties on a two-wire trellis.

- During your first growing season, tie one shoot to the top wire. In late winter of the second year before buds appear, tie one cane to the left half of the lower wire and another to the right half. Using the same pattern, tie one cane to each half of the upper wire for a total of four canes on the trellis. Remove all other canes.

- Your vine also grows green shoots. Select the four healthiest shoots that are near the trunk, and cut them back to four buds. These "renewal spurs" will become next year's canes. Remove all other shoots.

- During late winter of the third year and all future years, remove old canes that have fruited, cut new canes back to 40 buds, and tie them to the wires like you did the second year. Cut four new shoots back to four buds, and remove all other shoots.

Grow a tree from supermarket lemons. Collect seeds from three supermarket-bought lemons, and rinse them in warm water. Soak overnight, let dry, and choose three small containers with drainage holes. Fill each container with sterile potting mix, plant each seed one-half inch deep in its own container, and set the container in a dish. Water and cover the container with a clear plastic bag. Place it where temperatures stay around 70 degrees and continue to water regularly.

When plants appear, uncover the containers, and move them to a sunny spot. You must wait at least five years to find out whether your lemon tree will produce lemons, but it should make a lovely houseplant in the meantime.

Go natural for better-sprouting seeds. If your lemon seeds haven't sprouted after eight weeks, try again with fresh lemons from a natural foods market or farmers market. According to the Rare Pit and Plant Council, many supermarket fruits are treated with tiny amounts of radiation. This radiation should not harm you, but it may prevent supermarket lemon seeds from sprouting.

Harvest melons from a small space

You can grow watermelons, cantaloupes, and pumpkins on a tiny patch of land with this ingenious method. Train each vine on a large, sturdy trellis, and nestle each fruit in a sling made of pantyhose, an onion bag, cheesecloth, netting, or an old T-shirt. Use pantyhose slings for smaller varieties, but choose the stronger options for bigger fruits.

Slip the melon or pumpkin into its sling when the fruit is small, tie off both ends to envelop the fruit, and tie those ends to the trellis. Be sure to hang your sling high enough to keep the melon or pumpkin off the ground, even after the fruit becomes full-grown.

Get gardening advice for free from a master. You can get free advice via telephone or email from a local master gardener. These volunteers have undergone many hours of training, so they're experts about local planting. To find a master gardener near you, go to the American Horticultural Society website at *ahsgardening.org*. Navigate to the Gardening Resources tab, then click on the Master Gardeners link.

Veggies: grow all you can eat

Shop your backyard for high-priced produce. "I've seen bell peppers at the grocery store selling anywhere from $1 to $1.50 a piece," says Robert Westerfield, Horticulture Extension Coordinator for the University of Georgia. "But a pepper plant, even if you buy the transplant, costs about $2. By the time it's said and done — with nutrition, fertilization, and water — you've got about $8 in that plant." However he's quick to point out you won't get just one pepper from your plant, but as many as 50. "It's going to put out peppers as long as the plant's happy," he says. That's up to $75 worth of peppers from your $8 plant — quite an impressive payback.

"Just about any herb you can think of will be expensive to buy in stores, but relatively economical to grow at home," adds horticulture educator Jennifer Nelson. Of course, not all homegrown foods save you loads of money. Vegetables like potatoes, cabbage, and onions are already pretty cheap at the supermarket. But you can sprout great savings by growing pricey produce like tomatoes, squash, leafy greens, peppers, green beans, and berries.

Enjoy richer flavors and more nutrient power. Heirloom varieties of vegetables have been around for decades, but they aren't grown by commercial farmers. Yet research suggests heirloom varieties are tastier and far more nutritious than the same vegetables from your supermarket.

A study of 43 garden crops found that today's crops have significantly less vitamin C, calcium, iron, vitamin B2, phosphorus, and protein than the produce people ate in 1950. Experts suspect that breeding vegetables for the high yields sought by commercial growers results in less-nutritious vegetables. Grow heirloom vegetables, and you may enjoy both farm-fresh flavor and a richer treasure-trove of nutrients.

Grow tastier tomatoes and beat blossom end rot

If you constantly battle blossom end rot, you could grow your tomatoes in extra large tomato cages. Caged plants resist blossom end rot better than staked tomatoes. But there's a better solution. For the sweetest, juiciest tomatoes ever, add powdered milk to their water. It nourishes your tomatoes with calcium, so they're far more tantalizing and delicious. That extra calcium can also defeat blossom end rot before it starts.

Stop tomatoes from cracking. Use these two easy tricks to keep prized tomatoes from spoiling.

- Be very consistent with watering. Cracking is more likely when the plant receives wildly varying amounts of water over time. Water regularly, and don't let the soil dry out too much or stay too soggy.

- Grow crack-resistant varieties.

Grow prize tomatoes in limited space. Make an easy-to-build tomato pole.

Measure out a 6 x 3-foot rectangle in a flat, sunny space. Mark the four corners and the midpoint of each long side. At each marking, loosen soil and pound a 2" x 2" 8-foot-long wood post about a foot into the ground.

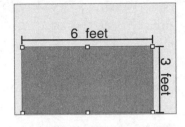

Angle each pair of posts so they cross 1 foot below their tops. Tie each pair firmly together with thick, sturdy twine to make three triangle shapes.

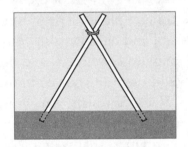

Connect the triangles with horizontal 2" x 2" 6-foot-long wood posts. Place three along each slanted side of the triangles at equal intervals. Tie in place with twine. Rest the last 6-foot-long wood post on top in the V-shaped slots of the triangles.

Prevent pests and diseases in container crops. It's the biggest mistake people make when planting container gardens. And they do it year after year — plant in the same diseased, nutritionally depleted soil.

Tomato plants, for example, get in a bad way. You can rotate these garden-based crops to help them escape pests and diseases lurking in a particular patch of soil. But pests and diseases can overwinter in your tomatoes' potting soil, too. That means you are just inviting fresh rounds of pests or disease if you plant next year's tomatoes in old soil. What's more, the soil's nutrients have already been depleted, and that could make your new tomato plants more vulnerable to blossom end rot and other problems.

Instead of rotating the tomatoes away from the soil, move the soil away from the new tomato plants. Throw out the soil and old plants in your tomato containers, and don't add them to your compost pile. When you plant next year, use new potting soil, and choose containers that weren't used to grow tomatoes this year.

If you're a smoker and a gardener, milk can protect your tomato plants. Before handling tomato plants, rub your hands with milk. It retards the growth of tobacco mosaic virus, which could be transferred from your hands to the plant.

Harvest more vegetables with colored mulches. You can pick up to 30 percent more tomatoes from the same plants if you place red plastic mulch around them, but other vegetables also benefit from colored plastic mulches.

- Green. May produce more squash and melons where summers are cool. Dark green is particularly effective with melons.

- Dark blue. May lead to nearly one-third more cucumbers.

- Silver. May pump up your pepper plant production and help fight thrips.

You can find these plastic mulches in gardening centers or online. For best results, place soaker hoses beneath the mulch except where drainage is poor, install the mulch during the warmest part of the day, bury the edges, and cut holes for planting. Remember that all plastic mulches warm the soil, so avoid using them with plants that cannot handle the heat.

Shed light on fruiting vegetables. Peppers and tomatoes need radiant heat to produce large, full-flavored crops. You can ripen tomatoes faster with aluminum foil. Simply cover the ground under the plant with strips of foil, or drape a nearby fence with a wall of silver to keep developing fruit nice and toasty. Foil mulch will also squelch weeds and keep viruses away from your plants.

Winning ways to ripen tomatoes. What's black and white and red all over? Tomatoes wrapped in newspapers. All joking aside, this trick really works. Find out how your daily paper can make your tomatoes better.

Once you hear the news about a hard freeze coming, reach for your newspaper. Pick your green tomatoes, wrap them individually in newspaper, and store them at room temperature to ripen.

If wrapping them individually seems like too much bother, you can put the unripe tomatoes on a shelf and cover them with sheets of newspaper. The idea is to trap ethylene gas to speed up ripening. Make sure to check your tomatoes often. Remove the ripe ones as well as any that have begun to rot.

Here are some more helpful hints for ripening and storing tasty tomatoes.

- To really ripen a tomato in a hurry, put an unripe tomato in a brown paper bag with an apple or banana. These fruits give off ethylene gas to hasten ripening.

- Tomatoes that have turned pink, but not yet red, can be picked and left in a warm place out of direct sunlight to ripen.

- Once ripe, tomatoes should be stored at room temperature — not in the refrigerator. To make them last even longer, place them stem-end down on your counter. This blocks air from entering and moisture from leaving your tomato.

Pick spinach off a vine. Spinach shoots up in early spring, but by summer, the delicious green has gone to seed. To enjoy fresh greens from your garden all summer long, grow Malabar spinach. Not a true spinach, this vine is originally from India. It loves the sun and tastes surprisingly like its namesake. To harvest it, pinch off the tender leaves, and let the older, tougher ones nourish the plant.

Many gardeners find that some plants grow too slowly to start from seeds. Tomatoes and peppers take six weeks or longer to reach the transplant stage. You'll probably do better buying those as transplants, especially if you live where the growing season is short.

Rescue your spinach seeds from harm. You may have heard that you should soak spinach seeds in vinegar

overnight before planting them, but this may be taking a useful garden trick one step too far.

"The purpose of pre-soaking seeds is to soften the seed coat in
an effort to improve germination," explains extension agent
Stephanie Ray Butcher. She adds that large seeds, such as the
ones from corn, snap beans, or cucumbers, can be soaked in
water overnight so they will be ready to plant the next day. But
spinach is different.

"While spinach seeds can be pre-soaked in water without
harming the seed, it germinates easily without the pre-soak,
and avoiding this unnecessary step saves time and energy."
What's more, soaking spinach seeds in a vinegar solution could
harm the seeds, Butcher says.

Sow a gourmet salad

Spring salad, or mesclun as the French know it, is a
refreshing and colorful mix of lettuce, endive, chervil, and
arugula leaves. You can easily grow these trendy greens.

Just mix together the various seeds and sprinkle them
on a prepared bed. Sow only enough seeds to produce
greens to feed you for a week. Plant another batch the
following week for a continuous harvest. Once they are
a few inches tall, chop down the greens to within an
inch of the ground and fertilize the bed. Your greens will
be ready to pick again in a month.

Grow cholesterol-busting super sprouts. If you think broccoli is good for you, try broccoli sprouts — broccoli seeds that have been germinated and sprouted over three to five days.

People who ate about 3.5 ounces of broccoli sprouts daily for just one week had lower "bad" LDL cholesterol, while actually boosting "good" HDL cholesterol, found a small Japanese study.

You can find broccoli sprouts in some health food stores, but growing them is simple and fun.

Soak a handful of seeds overnight in room temperature water. Place a thin layer of potting soil in a shallow pan and moisten with a small amount of water. Sprinkle your seeds over the soil, then cover with another thin layer of soil. Cover with plastic wrap and poke a few holes in the plastic for air to circulate.

Keep away from direct sunlight in a warm, dry area. You should see sprouts in about two days. They're ready to eat in three to five days. Grab a bunch and toss in a salad, garnish a bowl of soup, or add to your favorite sandwich.

Wonder food for health and garden. Eating garlic can do wonders for your health. Some researchers say it can attack atherosclerosis, clobber cholesterol, bring down blood pressure, banish bacteria, and crush blood clots. Plus, when you grow it in your garden, it keeps aphids away.

In fall, when temperatures are cool, plant cloves 4 to 8 inches apart in fertile, slightly moist, well-drained soil. Harvest garlic before the temperature gets too warm. Usually that means May in the South and July in the North. Eight to 10 days

before harvest, stop watering
and let the soil dry thoroughly
before digging up the bulbs.

Save your tea bags after
you use them. When you
plant root crops, such as
carrots or onions, tear
open an individual-size
tea bag, and dump the
leaves in the planting
hole. This should keep
root maggots away.

3 reasons to grow kale. Kale
can pretty up your plate and
protect your vision. Plus it
grows well in cold weather.
To enjoy the best flavor of this
hardy, healthy treat, harvest it
after a frost. Pick leaves from
the center of each stalk. Don't bother with the bottom leaves
— they are too tough to eat. Leave the undeveloped tender
leaves at the top to grow next week's harvest.

Raise potatoes in a garbage bag. You don't need a big yard
to have a garden. Grow your own potatoes inside a 30-gallon
trash bag. Here's how.

- Prepare your seed potatoes at least one week before you
  begin planting.

- Cut several drainage holes in the bottom of the bag. Fill
  the bag half full with soil, and roll the sides down to near
  soil level. Place the bag where it can receive at least four
  hours of sunlight daily.

- Plant the seed potatoes 5 inches apart. Bury them 2
  inches deep with eyes pointing upward. Water after planting, and keep watering regularly.

- When the plants are about 7 inches tall, add enough extra
  soil so only a few leaves remain above soil level.

- Keep adding soil as the plants grow.

- When the leaves yellow and die back, stop watering and wait three weeks.

- Slit the bag to harvest your potatoes.

A word to the wise about rhubarb. Rhubarb leaves are toxic. They contain dangerous levels of compounds called oxalates. The stalks contain oxalate, too, but in safe amounts. Oxalates can contribute to kidney stone formation, so avoid eating rhubarb if you suffer from kidney disease or urinary problems. If you grow rhubarb, just trim the leaves as you harvest the stalks, then toss them in the compost. They won't hurt garden soil.

Stake your peas with Christmas trees. Make a trellis for your veggie garden in three easy steps:

- Prune a couple of trees down to their trunks (save the branches for winter mulch on your beds).

- "Plant" them upright near your peas or pole beans.

- Run a few lines of string between them.

Voilà! An environmentally friendly trellis.

Name that vegetable — plant a marker that sticks. A lot of plants look the same while they are small. To keep up with what you planted where, use a permanent marker to write the names on used popsicle sticks. Place them in the proper rows as you plant. They will last a full season. And at harvest time you can pull them up and toss them on the compost heap. They'll rot and become part of the soil for next year's garden.

Smart ways to increase your pickings. Reap more from your garden space, even if it's small. Here's how.

- Try succession planting. Your corn is harvested, and the plants are spent, so you pull up those old plants, recondition the soil, and plant peas to fill out the growing season. This is called succession planting. It works well for one-time producers like potatoes, corn, carrots, and greens, which you can follow with peas, other vegetables, or herbs.

> Grow fresh produce year-round in containers. Lettuce, radishes, and small-fruiting tomatoes and peppers do especially well indoors. So do parsley, chives, cilantro, and thyme. Place pots in a bright, sunny, south-facing window during winter. For fruiting vegetables, supplement weak winter light with a fluorescent fixture.

  To make sure your second crop can produce before the growing season ends, start seeds in containers at least one month before you expect to transplant them to your garden.

- Get more from tight spaces. Fit more plants in your space and get more from each plant by growing them on trellises, cages, stakes, or even a fence. Try this with peas, cucumbers, pole beans, tomatoes, squash, and melons. You can easily make a trellis by tying string between two end posts or repurposing old bed springs.

Also, choose plants that produce many fruits or vegetables, such as tomatoes, carrots, and green beans.

Garden without a yard. You can grow your own food even if you live in an apartment with no yard.

If your balcony or windows receive enough sunlight, try container gardening. You can grow salad greens, beans, peppers, cucumbers, cherry tomatoes, squash, radishes, beets, and chard in pots or other containers successfully.

If your light is too poor or container gardens are not permitted, check whether a community garden is available. A community garden provides the land for growing flowers or food. In some community gardens, you take home part of the harvest in exchange for tending the garden and helping to buy seeds and supplies.

To find a community garden near you, visit *communitygarden.org*.

Build up a bed for better harvest

You can plant earlier than your neighbor and enjoy a longer, more fruitful harvest simply by planting in raised beds. A raised bed drains and dries much quicker than the ground nearby. Because of its small size, you can custom build your soil, plant your vegetables closer together, and harvest a bigger crop.

The only problem is that improved drainage means your bed can dry out fast in the full heat of summer. So make sure you install a watering system and mulch these beds well, and you will reap the bounty soon after.

Grow more in less space. You can have all the garden vegetables you want in half the space. Follow these tips for a cheap and easy container garden.

- Consider container size. A container should generally be at least two-thirds as deep as the full-grown plant is tall, and at least as wide as the leaf spread.

- Pick the right plants. Stick with vegetables that take up little space, like carrots, radishes, and lettuce. Even better, plant crops that bear fruit over a long period of time, such as tomatoes and peppers.

- Don't go too small. Some gardening experts warn against dwarf or miniature varieties, saying they don't tend to produce as well as standard varieties.

- Look at lighting. The amount of sunlight you get may determine what you can plant. Root crops and leaf crops can usually tolerate partial shade. Fruiting vegetables need at least five hours, preferably eight to 10 hours, of full, direct sun each day.

- Ditch bad dirt. Don't fill plant pots with dirt from your yard. Sure, it's free, but most yard dirt is too heavy, coarse, and infertile for potted plant growth. It also tends to pack down in containers, choking the roots.

- Invest in potting soil. It's lightweight and free of insects, diseases, and weed seeds. Avoid soilless mixes such as peat-lite, however. They contain few nutrients and are so lightweight they may not give enough support to plant roots.

- Double up. Grow different vegetables together in one container to make the most of limited space. Plant lettuce, spinach, and herbs between tomatoes, peppers, and cabbage. Use tall, trellised plants like cucumbers to shade cool-weather greens underneath.

- Make adjustments. Don't let shade end your gardening dreams. Boost the light your vegetables receive by placing reflective materials around them. Lay out sheets of aluminum foil, or paint surrounding surfaces white.

- Fight wilting. Punishing heat can dry soil fast. If your plants wilt every day, consider grouping the containers together, so the foliage creates shade to cool the soil. Also, put pots on pallets or other structures to get them off a hot concrete patio.

A match made in gardening heaven. Get double duty from your limited garden space — plant tomatoes and potatoes together.

When your tomato seedlings have grown two sets of leaves, scoop out the center of an Irish potato for each seedling. Fill the holes with potting soil and transplant the tomatoes. Place them in containers with a couple of inches of soil. When the soil is warm enough, plant the potatoes containing the tomatoes in the garden.

The tomatoes will grow and produce fruits during the summer. In the fall you can harvest the potatoes.

Prevent plant problems with perfect partners. Companion plants can be surprisingly helpful in your garden, particularly when it comes to repelling pests. When planting your garden, arrange good companions together. On the other hand, some "enemy" companions may prevent nearby plants from thriving. Read more about plant friends and foes in this handy chart.

Plant this	Near this	But not near this	Here's why
marigolds	tomatoes		Marigolds reduce aphids on tomatoes.
French marigolds	tomatoes		French marigolds fend off nematodes.
cucumbers		potatoes	This combo results in poor plant health.
nasturtiums	squash		Nasturtiums help repel squash bugs.
mint	cabbage		Mint helps repel cabbage moths.
dill		carrots	Dill may slow carrot growth.
onions	lettuce		Onion scent helps keep slugs and snails away.
parsley	carrots		Parsley's fragrance can keep carrot flies from finding the carrots nearby.
tomatoes	asparagus		Tomatoes repel asparagus beetles.
summer savory	beans		Summer savory helps repel bean beetles.

Companions help each other out

The practice of growing certain plants together started long ago, before there were any ready-made chemical treatments for the garden. Native Americans planted corn, squash, and runner beans together. The squash leaves provided shade, tall corn acted as stakes for the beans to grow on, and the beans added nitrogen to the soil to benefit the other plants.

Stretch your growing season. Extend your growing season farther into autumn with this easy-to-make hot cap. Cut the bottom off a 2-liter plastic bottle, soak the label to remove it, and place it over the plant you want to protect. Push it down into the soil a little to keep the wind or animals from pushing it over. If the plant is too bushy for a 2-liter, try a bottomless plastic milk jug.

Unlike some hot caps, you don't need to remove these bottles from your plants every day. Instead, just remove their caps. This lets hot air vent up and out of the bottle so your plants don't overheat on warm, sunny days. Just be sure to put the caps back on at sunset to keep your plants toasty all night long.

Fit even more in your garden. Interplanting fast and slow growers is just one way to sneak more vegetables into your garden. Experiment with other kinds of interplanting, and you may discover you have even more planting space than you thought.

For example, you can combine shallow-rooted plants like radishes, broccoli, or spinach, with deeper-growers such as carrots, parsnips, winter squash, or tomatoes. Or interplant heavy feeders like cabbage, squash, cucumber, or celery with lighter feeders such as carrots or garlic. Better yet, interplant those heavy feeders with beans or peas, which enrich the soil by adding nitrogen to it.

Simple secret for early veggies. Plant borage in pots throughout your vegetable garden. You'll attract bees that can help bring you an earlier crop. If you're short on pots, don't plant borage straight into the ground. It can be as invasive as mint. Instead, check yard sales and flea markets for discounted pots in good condition.

Stop veggies from going on strike. Timing is everything when you harvest beans, squash, cucumbers, tomatoes, and okra. Don't leave even one overripe vegetable on the plant because that can trigger a chemical that discourages blossoming — and vegetable production. Check plants every other day during the growing season to make sure you harvest everything on time. This may mean you pick a few vegetables before you need them, so have a plan for what to do with extras.

Wider rows work better. Neat rows of lettuce, carrots, and radishes are the standard of many old-time gardens. But

An online survey found gardeners are more likely to eat vegetables than people who don't garden. But that's not all. The National Gardening Association suggests a 180-pound person burns 80 calories in just 15 minutes of raking or planting, 90 calories during 15 minutes of mowing or weeding, and 100 calories during 15 minutes of digging.

break with tradition and you may find your harvest increasing dramatically. Instead of one narrow, straight row, plant in an area as wide as your rake. Just mark it off with string, then sprinkle your seeds loosely. Greens that grow this close will keep down weeds, preserve water, produce more, and last longer as they stay cool and resist bolting.

A plastic laundry hamper can help keep your kitchen clean at harvest time. Use it to gather fresh vegetables from your garden. Then stop by the water hose and wash away the grit. Let it drain completely before taking it into the kitchen.

Secret to free food all year long. You pay a premium in stores for produce during its offseason. Freeze the extra from your garden for year-round food at a price that can't be beat.

Start by blanching. Nearly all vegetables must be blanched — scalded with boiling water or steam — before freezing. Blanching halts the work of enzymes in food, preserving flavor, color, texture, and vitamins. Begin by boiling one gallon of water per pound of vegetables. Lower a wire basket of vegetables into fast-boiling water, then cover with a lid. Start marking time as soon as the water returns to a boil.

Beets, pumpkin, winter squash, and sweet potatoes should be cooked rather than blanched before freezing. For the rest, follow the guidelines on the following page for water blanching.

Cool them quickly. Remove the veggies and plunge them into cold water, below 60 degrees. Let them cool for roughly the time they took to blanch. Change the water or add ice as needed to keep it cold. Drain them thoroughly before freezing.

Food	Blanching time (minutes)
Snap, green, or wax beans	3
Lima, butter, or pinto beans	2 to 4, depending on bean size
Broccoli	3
Carrots, whole, small	5
Cauliflower flowerets	3
Corn on the cob	7 to 11, depending on ear size
Eggplant	4
Collard greens	3
All other greens	2
Okra	3 to 4
Blackeye and other field peas	2
Green peas	1 1/2
Sweet peppers	halves 3; strips 2
Summer squash	3

Cheap way to preserve extra produce. Your freezer is full, but your vegetable garden keeps producing. Turn those extra vegetables into dried vegetables, and you can enjoy them weeks or months down the road. Drying may even help you take advantage of buy-in-bulk bargains on produce at your farmers market.

Best of all, produce takes up less space after it's dried, so you can store more in the same amount of space — and you can store most dried produce outside the freezer for several months.

An old screen door over two sawhorses makes a great surface to wash, drain, and dry vegetables from your garden. Place it in reach of the water hose, but in the shade where the sun won't scorch the produce.

You might think you need a dehydrator to dry produce, but your oven can do the job. Keep in mind oven-drying only works if you can set your oven so it maintains a constant temperature of 140 degrees with the oven door propped open a few inches. Use an oven thermometer to check. For drying racks, use shallow wood or plastic trays with slatted or perforated bottoms.

Although the drying process varies widely depending on what food you use, this is how you dry vegetables.

- Wash in cool water; cut into small, uniform chunks or slices; and blanch.

- Arrange the vegetables in a single layer on each drying tray while the oven preheats.

- Once the oven is ready, put the trays in and check the temperature and vegetables regularly until the vegetables are crisp.

- Cool the vegetables and pack them in clean, moisture-resistant containers, such as glass jars with tight-fitting lids. You can store them in a cool, dry place for months. To reconstitute your dried veggies, soak them in water.

You'll need additional details to successfully dry your own fruits and vegetables, so visit the National Center for Home Food Preservation at *uga.edu/nchfp* and click on Dry, or contact your local extension agent for more information.

Make extra dollars from leftover crops. You have too much zucchini or other garden produce to freeze, can, or dry for the offseason, so consider selling some using these clever ideas.

- Spread the word through friends and family that you have produce for sale.

- Put up a notice on community bulletin boards at your church, library, and other public outlets.

- Sell produce as part of your yard sale.

- Write a classified ad, and place it for free at *craigslist.org*. Include what you are selling, the price, a description, your availability, as well as the where, when, why, and how of the sale. For safety's sake, only accept cash, and make the exchange in a public place.

And remember, you can also make money from selling your extra seeds, herbs, or seedlings.

Homegrown herbs inside and out

Heart-healthy ways to perk up flavor. Use your lovely herb garden to season your food without using salt. You will discover a whole new world of flavors, while adding ingredients that may help protect you from heart attack and stroke. Start with this herb list for all kinds of food.

- Basil: fish, soups, stews, sauces, Italian or Spanish dishes

- Bay leaves: lean meats, stews, sauces, French or Caribbean recipes

- Chives: lean meats, soups, sauces, Chinese dishes

- Cilantro: Mexican or Chinese dishes

- Dill: fish, chicken, soups, German recipes

- Fennel: fish, Italian or German dishes

- Garlic: fish, lean meats, chicken, vegetables, soups, sauces, Italian or Greek dishes

- Marjoram: French and Caribbean dishes

- Oregano: soups; Italian, Greek or Mexican dishes

- Parsley: lean meats, vegetables, fish, soups, sauces, Italian or Caribbean dishes

- Rosemary: fish, chicken, sauces, French or Greek recipes

- Sage: lean meats, fish, stews, Mexican dishes

- Thyme: lean meats, soups, sauces, Caribbean recipes

Sit back and enjoy a cup of tea. You don't have to drink
the same old tea day after day. Start an herbal tea garden for
a fragrant array of fresh choices. Many tea gardens include
chamomile (*Matricaria recutita*), peppermint (*Mentha piperita*),
spearmint (*Mentha spicata*), pineapple mint (*Mentha suaveolens
variegata*), and lemon balm (*Melissa officinalis*). To make
herbal tea, add one cup of boiling water to a tablespoon of
fresh leaves or a teaspoon of dried leaves. Let steep for 10
minutes and strain.

Make herbs more scent-sational

Cut back herbs like basil and oregano at midsummer to
improve their fragrance and prevent them from bolting
to seed. Just be careful to remove no more than half
the leaves.

If you grow your herbs in containers, fertilize them, but
at a low application rate. Large amounts of fertilizer
weaken the fragrance and flavor of herbs, but consistently limiting fertilizer may help your herbs develop
stronger tastes and scents.

And be careful even after harvesting your herbs. Some
experts say that rinsing herbs too heavily may remove
the essential oils that give them their flavor and scent.
So rinse lightly, and pat dry with paper towels.

Pick the perfect time for picking. The early bird may catch the worm, but early morning is also the prime time for something much tastier — herbs. Gather your herbs early in the morning, after the dew dries but before the sun warms them too much. That's when the leaves have the most essential oils — and the most flavor. Here are more handy tips.

- Harvest herbs right before they bloom, when they have the highest concentration of oils.

- Use sharp shears or scissors. You want to cut stems cleanly to avoid damaging the plant.

- Remove insects and any damaged leaves from your harvested herbs.

- Keep the herbs out of strong light. A cool, dark place works best for drying and storage.

- Give herbs time to settle in. Don't harvest perennial herbs too heavily the first year.

- Get in the zone. If you live in a warmer zone, you can harvest up to two-thirds of your herbs' leaves at a time, once in the spring and again in the summer. But if you live in a cold zone, take only one-third each time and stop harvesting five to six weeks before the first fall frost.

- Tie a piece of cheesecloth or a nylon stocking around the seed heads to catch ripe seeds as they fall. Don't use plastic bags, which trap moisture that can lead to mold.

Give dried herbs an airtight alibi. Don't let the herbs from your herb garden go to waste. After washing and drying them, place them on a clean paper towel and microwave them for 30 to 40 seconds. Crumble the dried herbs and store them in an airtight container for up to three months. If you have leftover fresh ginger, the best way to store it is in your refrigerator, unwrapped.

Dried herbs lose their flavor over time. To revive old, tired herbs, push them through a mesh sieve or crush them between your fingers. This will release the herb's flavorful oils.

Freezing gives herb flavors a longer shelf life. Your garden herbs will keep their flavor even longer if you store them by freezing. Most people recommend drying herbs to store them, but fresh herbs stored by freezing taste better than dried herbs — for up to several months.

However, you must freeze them as quickly as possible after harvest, so pick them at their peak flavor, wash, shake, and let dry. Then immediately spread them on a cookie sheet or drop into freezer bags, and place in the freezer. After freezing, store your cookie-sheet herbs in freezer bags, and label those bags. Some herbs may keep better or become easier to use if you chop the herb, blend with water or oil, and pour the mixture into an ice cube tray to freeze.

Prevent foul flavors in freezer foods. Be careful how you package herbs when you freeze them. Store strongly flavored herbs like chives or rosemary in closed jars before you put them in the freezer — even if they are already in bags or frozen into ice cubes. If herbs like these are not in jars, their scents may seep into nearby foods, making those foods taste odd or even inedible.

Dry herbs on window screens. Don't throw out those old window screens. Give them a good cleaning, and use them to dry newly harvested herbs instead. To set up "Herb Drying Central," just find a dark, dry place that is well-ventilated and free of pests. Next, place the screens so air can circulate above and below them. Then bring on those herbs.

Dill seed, coriander seed, fennel, lemon balm leaves, summer savory, winter savory, and sage are just some of the herbs you can spread out to dry on these cost-free drying screens.

Enjoy a truckload of fragrant dried herbs

Park your car in the sun on a hot day, and you have a great "oven" for drying herbs.

Tuck your fresh-picked herbs loosely inside brown paper bags on the seats of your car, or lay the herbs out on newspapers or cleaned window screens spread on the seats. Leave two windows cracked open about 1 inch for ventilation. Check once every hour, and remove the herbs when they become brittle or crumbly.

And here is a bonus — even after the herbs are removed, your car will still smell heavenly.

Hang herbs to dry without nail holes. Pioneer women had plenty of rafters to use for hanging herbs to dry, but most people do not. Try these options to avoid putting nail holes in your walls and ceiling.

- Use a spring-loaded curtain rod or shower rod. The curtain rods come in many sizes and are often expandable.

- Hang multiple bundles from discarded refrigerator, oven, or outdoor grill racks.

- Suspend hardware cloth or old window screens between two chairs or sawhorses.

Easy reminders to use your herbs. You carefully picked your herbs at the peak of freshness, stored them in the refrigerator, and promptly forgot about them. Make sure the next batch of herbs does not suffer the same fate.

Pour an inch of water in a vase or glass. After harvesting the herbs, make a diagonal cut to trim the stems, and drop them in the vase. Cover with a plastic bag, and put the vase at the front of the refrigerator shelf. These herbs will keep for a week if you change the water every day.

If that still doesn't remind you, separate out a small bunch of herbs each week, and keep them in a water-filled vase on your kitchen counter or windowsill.

3 secrets to a better herb garden. If you love having fresh herbs at your fingertips, here are a few suggestions for setting up an herb garden:

- If you want to get the most pleasure you can from your herbs, plant them along walkways and where people will brush up against them. They won't release their fragrances until something brushes or bruises them.

- Grow bay leaves and rosemary in clay pots just beneath the soil of your garden. When the weather turns cold, lift them out and take them inside. They will continue to grow, and you can enjoy their fragrance and flavor year-round.

- Remember some herbs spread — like mint, wild marjoram, and tarragon. Each year they will take more and more room. To contain their growth, confine their roots by planting them in a section of buried stovepipe.

3 ways to make fresh herbs convenient

Dried herbs from your spice rack may seem convenient, but kitchen herbs are so easy to grow — and you won't believe how much flavor fresh herbs add to your meals. To enjoy beautiful, healthy herbs that are almost as close as your pantry, follow these tips.

- Plant them in containers, and place them outdoors next to the kitchen door.

- If that spot is not sunny enough, plant the herbs in kitchen window boxes, and water often.

- During winter, plant as many herbs as you can in small containers, and keep them together on your kitchen windowsill to share moisture.

Pack a big harvest into a small space. Here's an attractive and efficient idea for growing a variety of herbs — recycle a hanging shoe caddy and have herbs handy when you want them. Pick a spot with good exposure — a wooden fence, potting shed wall, or even a door — then hang the caddy at a convenient height. It can be attached directly with nails or screws, or hung from hooks or a curtain rod for easy removal. Pour some water in the pockets to check the drainage. Poke small holes if necessary, then start planting.

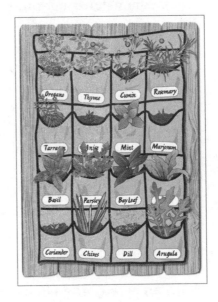

Choose the herbs you want, and the potting mix that suits each herb. Leave an inch or so between the top of the pocket and the soil, then add your seeds or plant. Finish your creation with the herbs' names on waterproof tape, pinned-on scraps of fabric, attached nursery labels, or any other attractive idea you can imagine.

The perfect spot for an herb pot. Think you can't have fresh herbs or tomatoes because you have no space for a garden? Grow oregano, mint, and parsley indoors next to a south-, west- or east-facing window. Tuck them in deep pots close to the glass, and check regularly to see if they need watering — keeping mint more moist than the other herbs.

Create a living spice rack. Even if space is tight, you can still have an herb garden in your home or on your patio. Just create a stacked herb garden with three containers.

- Find a container you like, and collect small, medium, and large versions of it.

- Fill the largest container two-thirds full with soilless potting mix, smooth the potting mix, and center the medium container on top of it. Finish putting soil in the first container.

- Fill the second container two-thirds full and center the smallest container on top.

- Finish filling the second container and completely fill the third container with soil.

Now you can plant herbs such as sage, trailing rosemary, lavender, basil, oregano, and chives. This ingenious — and attractive — idea could be just the trick for other types of plants as well.

Plant an herb garden in a wheel. Would you like a charming way to plant a small herb garden — or even create a small theme garden? Nose around at yard sales or flea markets for an old wagon wheel. Find a good spot for growing the herbs and lay the wheel on its side. Fill the spaces between the spokes with fertile soil and plant a different herb in each one. Not only will you enjoy the herbs, you'll also love the way this charming piece accents your garden.

An old wooden ladder makes an ideal herb garden organizer. Just lay it on the ground, fill the spaces with soil, and plant different herbs in each section.

Why you might need cuttings. Some herbs don't produce viable seeds, while others grown from seed don't do very well. For example, oregano from seed may not produce enough aromatic oil to add any flavor to cooking. To save both time and frustration, grow the following herbs from cuttings — lavender, pineapple sage, English thyme, lemon thyme, oregano, peppermint, and French tarragon.

Grow herbs indoors even in poor light

You'd love a window herb garden during winter, but your windows don't let in enough light. Instead of expensive grow lights, tack a fluorescent light fixture to the underside of a shelf. Stock it with one "warm" fluorescent tube and one "cool" one, and place your herbs 5 inches beneath it. Give your herbs about 16 hours of this "daylight."

If you used a fluorescent light fixture that has a cord and plug, attach it to a light timer, and you won't have to turn the lights on and off yourself. Just keep in mind that your herbs could use a few hours of real daylight, too. If you can't fit all the herbs you want under your lights, move your chives and parsley to an indoor windowsill permanently. They accept less light than other herbs.

Get your garden started with 3 easy-to-grow herbs. Sure, you can buy herbs in the supermarket. But nothing beats the freshness and convenience of a home herb garden. You don't even need a green thumb to grow your own herbs. Here are three easy-to-grow, hard-to-kill plants that will beautify any home and garden.

- Parsley. You may think of parsley as a mere garnish, but this herb adds more than just a splash of color to your plate. It also adds taste. For stronger taste, opt for flat leaf parsley rather than Italian, or curly, parsley. Parsley is very easy to grow in any soil. It doesn't need much water but does require a fair amount of sun. Plant it in a mostly sunny location, but not in direct sun. Some shade is good. You may only have to purchase one parsley plant, because it reseeds itself freely.

- Mint. You won't have any trouble growing mint, which thrives year after year with very little care. Mint grows in nearly all types of soil and in conditions ranging from partial shade to full sun. Just keep your plants well watered.

- Dill. You can use dill's seeds, leaves, and stems to season your food. Perfect for a kitchen herb garden, dill should be harvested before it begins to flower.

Score the sweet benefits of basil. A key ingredient in pesto, basil also has a magician's element of "Presto!" There's no hocus-pocus involved, but it's been known to make upset stomach, bloating, and flatulence disappear faster than you can say abracadabra. And just the aroma of basil can make you feel more mentally alert and focused. This rich and spicy herb provides plenty of vitamins K, C, and A and has shown antioxidant, anti-inflammatory, and antibacterial properties. It may also help fight blood clots by making platelets less sticky.

Basil is an annual, so you must plant it each year, choosing a spot where it will get plenty of sun. You can grow basil indoors, as long as you put it in a south- or west-facing window.

- Sow basil seeds in the spring or set out transplants after the last frost.

- Harvest leaves about six weeks after planting.

- Pinch off stems frequently so you'll have a steady supply of fresh leaves. And prune off any flower spikes or your plant will become woody.

If you have an overabundance of basil, check out these tips.

- Put sprigs in a glass of water on the kitchen counter and cover the leaves loosely with a clear plastic bag.

- Wrap leaves in a damp paper towel and store in an unsealed plastic bag in the fridge.

- Hang bunches upside down to dry. Strip the leaves — they will be brown and brittle — and store in an airtight container to use during the winter months.

- Freeze washed leaves in a plastic bag. Or freeze chopped basil with water in ice cube trays. Then just toss a basil cube or two into your saucepan. Genius!

- Make extra pesto, that delicious blend of basil, pine nuts, olive oil, and Parmesan cheese. You can even freeze pesto, as long as you add the cheese after thawing.

Preserve basil flavor with salt. Basil does not always freeze or dry well by itself, so use some of your fresh basil to make basil-flavored salt. Lay down a layer of coarse salt followed by a thin layer of herbs and another layer of salt. Let sit until the herbs are brown and completely dry. Discard the herbs, store in an airtight container, and use the basil-flavored salt in your favorite recipes.

Make a little time for thyme. Besides adding flavor to a variety of dishes, thyme can really spring into action when it comes to fighting bronchitis and coughs. The key is a component found in the plant's leaves called thymol. To soothe your cough, make a tea by adding 2 teaspoons of crushed fresh or dried leaves to 1 cup of boiling water. Steep for 10 to 15 minutes, then strain. Interestingly, the same tea may also fight dandruff. Wash your hair, then, while it's still damp, massage the cooled tea into your scalp. Do not rinse.

A low-growing, wiry-stemmed perennial, thyme does best in light, well-drained soil. It prefers full sun, but can also grow in light shade.

Stevia is a South American herb you may be able to grow as an annual. Plant it in good soil after the last frost. Water frequently and feed it occasionally with a low-nitrogen fertilizer. Harvest the leaves before flowers bloom. The leaves can be dried and used as a sweetener for tea and other beverages.

- You can start your own thyme plants from seed, or get a cutting or division from a friend.

- Outdoors, it works well as an edging plant, as a ground cover, or in rock gardens.

- For your indoor herb garden, buy a small thyme plant and keep it on a sunny windowsill.

- Start new plants every few years, because older ones get too woody.

Arthritis remedy from a flower. Arnica, one of the best medicinal herbs, has been used for centuries to treat arthritis pain. These yellow, daisy-like flowers grow in much of the United States, blooming in midsummer.

To make an ointment to rub on painful joints, crush and blend flower petals with vegetable oil. Arnica can, however, cause a skin rash on some people and is poisonous if swallowed.

Reap the benefits of potted mint. Ready to join the herb "move-mint"? Place your plants in pots rather than in your garden and reap three cool benefits.

- Close by when you need 'em. Potted mint plants are easy to move to your porch or deck. That's handy when you want to grab a few leaves to make tea or toss in a favorite recipe.

- Contains the love. Mint loves to spread. Give it lots of water and sun, and its long runners can take over your garden. Put it in a pot, and you're good to go.

- Repels irritating pests. The ants go marching home again when they encounter this sweet-smelling spice. Bees and mice also dislike mint. You can move the plant around where you need it the most.

If you suffer from migraine headaches, plant feverfew in your herb garden. Some people get pain relief from chewing three fresh leaves a day. If you have plant allergies, are pregnant or nursing, or are taking a blood thinning medication, don't use feverfew without talking with your doctor.

Dangers in the herb garden. Some herbs can put your life or health in serious peril. Avoid these seven herbs no matter what the supposed benefits are:

- aconite
- belladonna
- chaparral
- sassafras
- comfrey
- hemlock
- ephedra

Celebrate cilantro for cultured cuisine. Popular in Mexican and Thai dishes, cilantro boasts a strong flavor you either love or hate. But you may learn to love it simply because, thanks to a compound called dodecenal, cilantro can kill *Salmonella*, a common cause of foodborne illness.

In animal studies, this member of the carrot family also boosted memory, lowered cholesterol and blood sugar, and fought inflammation. It may even keep your skin looking young. In one study, an extract of fresh cilantro helped prevent sun damage.

Like basil, cilantro is an annual. For best results, grow it in full sun, although it can tolerate some shade.

- Cut leaves when they are 4 to 6 inches long. In two to three weeks, you'll get a second cutting.

- Plant a small handful of seeds every few weeks for a steady supply of fresh leaves.

- As a bonus, when cilantro goes to seed, you end up with the spice coriander.

But hang on to your hat — does cilantro taste like you just had your mouth washed out with soap? Your aversion to the herb may be genetic.

6 healing herbs help you fight infections	
Health-promoting herb	What it does to help you fight colds and flu
Astragalus	Revs up your immune system so you're able to fight off infections.
Echinacea	Eases your cold symptoms and shortens the number of days your cold lasts.
Elderberry	Clears up stuffy sinuses, boosts your immune system, and makes colds last less time.
Ginseng (American)	Prevents colds, keeps miserable symptoms to a minimum, and shortens the duration.
Goldenseal	Fights infections by battling bacteria and viruses and helps keep your mucous membranes moist.
Thyme	Safeguards against infections and pumps up your immune system.

Embrace echinacea — an immune-boosting bloom. Feel a cold coming on? Then feel free to reach for this healing herb. Of course, you can buy echinacea herbal supplements — but wouldn't it be more fun and economical to grow it in your backyard?

Also known as purple coneflower, this perennial adds a healthy dose of color to your garden while it provides a healthy dose of cold and flu protection. Clinical results are mixed, but many think echinacea can help you feel better sooner. Experts looked at 14 studies and found, overall, echinacea reduced the odds of developing a cold by 58 percent and shortened the length of a cold by 1.4 days. Sounds like some serious misery-stopping flower power.

Commercial products often use echinacea root, but you can make a tea with the flowering tops. Brew some at the first sign of a cold to soothe your symptoms and speed up recovery.

But watch out! If you're allergic to ragweed, you're more likely to have an allergic reaction to echinacea, as well.

Crack down on cholesterol with garden goodies. Fenugreek and hawthorn are cholesterol busters you can grow right in your yard or garden. They might even help you slash your cholesterol without drugs. Dried hawthorn berries and leaves can be used to make a cholesterol-lowering tea. Just remember it takes a while to work and can be toxic if taken in large doses. Play it safe and check with your doctor before trying hawthorn or any herbal remedy.

Bask in a lemony fragrance. For the fresh scent of lemons without the lemon tree, grow lemon-scented herbs. Gardeners recommend lemon verbena (*Aloysia triphylla*) for its fragrance. Lemon balm (*Melissa officinalis*) also has a lovely citrus aroma. For a delicious touch of lemon, add leaves from either one to tea. You can also grow lemon grass (*Cymbopogon citratus*) or the lemon-scented varieties of thyme, basil, catnip, or mint to add a delightful scent of lemon to your home or backyard.

Even though it's a kitchen herb, marjoram can pull its weight in aromatherapy, too. It could help lower high blood pressure, relieve anxiety, and bring on restful sleep.

Happy, healthy houseplants

Tips to pick the healthiest houseplants. Dying houseplants may not be your fault. They could have been doomed from the start at the store. Learn to bring home healthy plants with the best shot at surviving and thriving. Shop for plants that look full, even bushy, and have plenty of leaves. Also, make sure they have buds just beginning to open, instead of in full bloom. Avoid plants with:

- tightly closed green buds, which usually don't open indoors.

- yellowed leaves, or leaves with brown tips.

- leaves that have been polished to a high gloss with leaf shine.

- dry soil shrinking away from the walls of the container.

- dark spots on leaves, or holes in leaves.

- webs or cottony material at the base of leaves.

- pots that feel too lightweight, since this can signal drought stress.

Foolproof foliage anyone can grow. These babies love to be neglected. For most, overwatering is about the only thing that will kill them. Pot them up and let them go.

- Cactus — pot in well-drained soil, and place in a sunny window.

- Bromeliad — pot in loose, well-drained soil, and water when soil begins to dry out.

- Rubber plant — use regular potting soil in a pot with drainage hole, and repot when it begins to need daily watering.

- Snake plant — give it bright but indirect light, and water occasionally.

- Chinese evergreen — grow in regular potting mix with extra humus added, and keep soil moist.

- Cast iron plant — give it low light, and let top two-thirds of soil dry out before watering.

Find the perfect spot for your new plant. All houseplants love light, but some need more than others. To make sure your plant gets the right amount of light, do a shadow test in the spot where your plant will live.

First, check the plant label to see whether it recommends low, medium, or high light. If the label doesn't have that information, search for it on the Internet or at your local library.

Grab a sheet of white paper and go to the spot where your plant will dwell. Do this on a sunny day when the light in the room is at its brightest. Hold the paper where the plant will be and angle it so it faces the nearest source of natural light. Now place your other hand between the paper and the light source, keeping your hand roughly a foot away from the paper.

If your hand's shadow is sharply defined on the paper, the plant can expect a high amount of light. If the shadow is dimmer and fuzzy around the edges, the light is medium. A faint shadow means this is a low light location.

Keep in mind that different seasons bring different levels of brightness. Test the spot again in early winter and in early summer to make sure your plant still gets the right amount of light.

If the light isn't right, notice which way the windows in the room are facing. You can raise or lower the light available to a plant by moving it to a window that faces in a different direction. If not shaded, south-facing windows provide the most light, while north-facing windows offer the least. Unshaded windows that face east and west fall somewhere in between, but plants get hotter near a west-facing window. You can also try moving the plant closer to the window for more light or farther away for less light.

14 houseplants that love low light. If you have a room that just cries out for beautiful plants, but gets little sunlight, check out this list of 14 attractive houseplants you can grow in rooms that sometimes seem almost as dark as a cave.

- Chinese evergreen (*Aglaonema*)

- cast-iron plant (*Aspidistra elatior*)

- pothos (*Epipremnum aureum*)

- heart-leaf philodendron (*Philodendron scandens*)

- snake plant, mother-in-law's tongue, or sword plant (*Sansevieria*)

- zz plant (*Zamioculcas zamiafolia*)

- parlor palm (*Chamaedorea elegans*)

- dumb cane (*Dieffenbachia amoena*)

- Swedish ivy (*Plectranthus nummularius*)

- corn or cornstalk plant (*Dracaena fragrans* — Massangeana)

- arrowhead vine (*Syngonium*)

- spider plant (*Chlorophytum comosum*)

- German ivy (*Senecio mikanioides*)

- grape ivy (*Cissus rhombifolia*)

Keep in mind that no plant can grow in complete darkness. To test whether your low-light plants get enough light, sit next to them and try to read during daylight. If the light is too dim to read by, consider placing the plants near fluorescent lights for 12 to 16 hours a day.

Diagnose houseplant woes

Symptom	Problem	Solution
Yellow leaves	Too much or too little water, nitrogen deficiency	Water when soil dries out. Improve drainage. Add fertilizer.
Brown tips	Salt burn from too many minerals in the soil or from hard water	In the bathtub, flush the soil until the water runs clear.
Stunted growth, small, brittle leaves	Too little water	Water right away, then again as soon as the topsoil dries out.
No growth, dull leaves	Too much water	Wait for topsoil to dry before you add water. Improve drainage.
Tan or brown splotches	Sunburn, too cold	Move to a sheltered spot.
Curling leaves	Too hot	Water and move to a sheltered spot.
Leaf drop	Too much water or too much fertilizer	Water sparingly and fertilize only during the growth period.
White crust on the soil	Salt buildup from too much fertilizer	Flush until water runs clear. Reduce fertilizer.
No blooms	Too much or too little light, high temperatures	Move to a dark spot during the rest period. Bring out into light when ready to bloom.
Bud drop	Too little light, humidity, or food; room too hot or too cold	Fertilize and move to sunnier spot. Mist. Stabilize temperature.
Flies appear when you water	White flies	Hang sticky traps and vacuum the plants.
Speckled, yellowing leaves	Spider mites	Wash off the leaves in the shower.

Watch out for symptoms of light deficiency or overload.
Feeding your plant or giving it more water won't help if your
plant is ill from a lack of light. Learn to recognize the signs of
too much or too little light, so you'll know when to move your
plant to more appropriate lighting.

Your plant may not be getting enough light if:

- new leaves are smaller than older ones.

- leaves drop off.

- the plant stops growing or grows very slowly.

- a flowering plant stops producing flowers or produces far
  fewer flowers than usual.

- the plant leans toward the light.

- growth is spindly and elongated.

Your plant may be getting too much light if:

- the leaves become faded, develop brown burn spots, or
  dry out and drop off.

- growth is stunted.

- new growth turns yellow.

- the plant wilts during the hottest part of the day.

Surprising secret to better blooms. Want healthier house-plants? Give them aspirin. Scientific research has shown that the active ingredient in aspirin can:

Mellow yellow leaves with this common dessert food. Sprinkle a packet of unflavored gelatin around the base of your yellowing houseplant. The nitrogen will help put the green back in its leaves.

- prompt some orchids and lilies to bloom.

- counteract the growth-stunting effects of stress, plumping up foliage and fruit.

- help make plants more resistant to viruses, bacteria, and fungal infections.

Simply dissolve 1 1/2 aspirins in 2 gallons of water, and spray directly on plants. Don't make the solution any stronger, though, or you could actually slow plant growth.

Household cleaner to the rescue. Need a quick solution to a stunted plant? Mix a tablespoon of ammonia into a gallon of water. Ammonia is an instant source of nitrogen that can jump-start the plant without sticking around to harm it.

4 ways to winter-proof plants. Even indoor plants like to "hibernate" a bit in winter. Switch to this easy care schedule to keep them lush and healthy.

- Don't bother fertilizing houseplants unless they are in bloom or actively growing. They generally don't get enough light or warmth in winter to do either.

- Cut back on watering. With less growth, plants need less water. Let the soil dry out between drinks.

- Group plants together to boost humidity and protect them from the dry, indoor heat.

- Consider setting plants in a pan filled with pebbles and a little water to generate more humidity.

Replenish dry soil for a successful soak. When plants in pots dry out, the soil pulls away from the sides. Then, when you water them, the water races quickly down the sides and out the bottom, leaving the soil dry as a bone. The solution? Set the pot in a bucket, tub, or sink half-filled with lukewarm water, and let it slowly soak up the moisture it needs.

> Never fertilize a dry plant. They need water in order to move the fertilizer up into their roots. Without water, fertilizer can come into direct contact with roots, burning them and potentially killing the plant. Water the plant thoroughly both before and after adding fertilizer.

Put a stop to leaky pots. Before potting your plant, lay down a drainage layer of gravel or packing peanuts, then throw in a handful of tea bags before adding the soil. Most plants will love you for this and here's why. When you water, the layer of tea bags will absorb excess water. Not only does this prevent leakage, it also holds in moisture so roots will thrive. Nutrients from the tea bag may even help nourish your houseplants.

Rescue your houseplants from softened water. You've finally installed a water softener, but now your potted plants are struggling. That's because softened water is saltier than hard water, even if you can't taste the difference. To fix this salty problem, find out whether your outdoor hose faucets are attached to the water softener line. If not, collect hose water for your houseplants. Otherwise, try one of these.

- Buy gypsum from your garden center. Before watering your plants, thoroughly mix one-half teaspoon of the mineral into a gallon of softened water.

- Replace the soil once a year and scrub away any salt deposits you find on the pot.

- Collect rainwater to water your plants.

Water while you're away. Water your houseplants while visiting Europe or enjoying the beach in Jamaica. You can do it if you start a few days before your departure. You'll need a bucket, a stool or crate, and an old mop head made of rayon or another synthetic fabric.

Fill the bucket with water, put it on the stool, and place your plants in a tight circle around it. Turn the mop head upside down and put it in the water. For each plant, take one mop strand and bury its end deep in the soil near the roots.

Keep the plants lower than the mop head so water can seep down the strand. Also, make sure that part of the mop head will stay beneath the water while you're gone.

Check your plants once each day until you leave to be sure they are getting enough water. If they are, just add extra water to the bucket before you go. Your well-watered plants will be waiting when you come home.

The secret to watering air plants. Air plants need watering, just like normal plants. They live in the air, but they don't feed off of it. Water at least twice a week by soaking the entire plant — leaves and all — in a bucket or sink filled with water. You can tell when it's thirsty by touching its leaves. Thirsty leaves will feel soft, while happily watered leaves will feel stiff.

Turn unusual plants into eye-catching art. Tillandsia, or air plants, can grow almost anywhere, except in soil. Get creative with where you mount them.

- Sit one inside a conch shell.

- Mount several along a piece of driftwood.

- Glue a variety of air plants to a piece of lattice, and hang it on the wall like living artwork.

Soak the driftwood in fresh water for a few weeks to dilute the ocean salt trapped in it. Otherwise, the air plants may not thrive. If you put them in something that catches water, like a seashell, be sure to dump out the excess after watering them. Air plants can't stand wet feet.

You can mount an air plant to an object with almost anything — including floral wire, waterproof glue, and even Velcro. Don't try mounting them with copper wire, super glue, or a hot glue gun, though. These could damage the plant.

New life for takeout chopsticks. Don't throw away those simple wooden chopsticks that come with your Chinese dinner. Keep them ready whenever you have a seedling that needs help. A chopstick poked into the soil makes a perfect stake to help support a small plant. A piece of string or a rubber band gently looped around the seedling helps keep it upright. Or just let it lean on the chopstick as it grows.

3 little-known African violet secrets. These beautiful plants can sometimes be tricky. If you have struggled with African violets in the past, don't give up. Just remember these tips to help your plants thrive.

- Don't touch. Researchers from Oklahoma State University discovered that touching African violet plants, even briefly, causes damage and stunted growth. The problems become even worse if you use lotion on your hands.

- Plant your African violets in a mix of pine bark and sand. These ingredients give you a slightly acid soil that has excellent drainage — qualities that make African violets thrive.

- Learn how to water. Watering the wrong way can cause white spots on your African violet leaves. If you water from above the plant, pour the water directly on the dirt, not the leaves, and always use room temperature water. Remove any extra water that drains through to the bottom of the pot. To water from below, put the pot in a dish containing about an inch of water. When the top of the soil becomes damp, remove the pot from the water and let it drain.

Perfect poinsettias — year after year. Don't toss them out and buy new ones next Christmas. Keep your holiday cheer alive and growing. In May, chop your poinsettia within 8 inches of its base. Water, feed, and prune it to maintain a compact shape through the summer. To get red bracts by Christmas, fake shorter days starting in October. Move your plant into a darkened room every evening, or gently cover it from 5:00 p.m. to 8:00 a.m. Don't forget — one well-lit night can delay the blooms indefinitely. With bright sun during the day, and dark nights, your poinsettia should bloom brightly in eight to 10 weeks.

Strategies to beat ficus leaf drop. Buy your ficus young to give it the best chance at survival. These trees don't like changes in location, light, or humidity. Young plants, however, will ride out the move from greenhouse to your house better than older specimens. And since they cost less, you'll have less money on the line if they die. Bring it home in late spring or early summer to minimize shock.

9 best natural air cleaners. Houseplants not only convert carbon dioxide to oxygen. Some super-flora can actually remove dangerous chemicals like benzene and formaldehyde from the air. These compounds are a staple in cleaners, plastic, cigarette smoke, car exhaust, paint, glue, and insecticide. In other words, your home is likely full of them. University of Georgia researchers tested 28 common houseplants. These nine were tops at removing pollutants.

- *Hemigraphis alternata* (purple waffle plant)

- *Hedera helix* (English ivy)

- *Hoya carnosa* (variegated wax plant)

- *Asparagus densiflorus* (asparagus fern)

- *Tradescantia pallida* (purple heart plant)

- *Fittonia argyroneura* (silver nerve plant)

- *Polyscias fruticosa* (Ming aralia)

- *Sansevieria trifasciata* (snake plant)

- *Guzmania* species (certain bromeliads)

Having just one type of plant won't do much good, however. Invest in a combination to really clean the air in your home.

Stop allergies cold with a green purifier

Are you breathing in mold, or something even worse? Chuck the air purifiers and pot some English ivy instead.

When researchers put ivy in a sealed container with mold and dog feces, this beautiful plant removed 78 percent of airborne mold and 94 percent of dog fecal particles in the air. And that was after just 12 hours.

Make English ivy your houseplant of choice, and you could cut back on allergies and keep the air in your home fresh for free. It's a simple, natural trick to keeping allergens to a minimum. Remember to keep the plant away from small children and pets because it's toxic if eaten.

Discover the perfect bedroom plants. Every plant "breathes." Some simply do it at night, cleaning the air while you sleep. Leaves and stems contain tiny "pores" that allow plants to absorb carbon dioxide and release oxygen. Most plants open their pores during the day, but certain bromeliads and orchids, and many agaves and cactuses, do so at night.

Beware of polluting plants. Not every plant helps clean the air. Some may actually release harmful compounds. In a study at the University of Georgia, peace lily, weeping fig, and areca palm all released volatile organic compounds (VOCs) into the air. The plants themselves weren't the only source. Plastic pots, pesticides sprayed on them by growers, and microorganisms in the soil all gave off VOCs. You may be able to cut back on these toxins by potting plants in natural containers, like clay, and resisting the urge to treat them with chemical pesticides.

Grow your own air freshener. Trash those store-bought air fresheners in favor of natural fragrances. One study discovered that scented air fresheners and laundry products released more than 100 chemicals into the air, 10 of which are toxic or hazardous. Freesia, cyclamen, garden petunias, fairy primrose, and white calla lilies are just a few houseplants with sweet-smelling blooms.

Banish mold without burning your plants. Fuzzy, white mold growing on the soil of your potted plants is more than unsightly — it's dangerous. It introduces harmful allergens into your home, all while robbing your plants of their nutrients.

Some treatments will kill the mold, but they might kill your plants, too. Fortunately, the cinnamaldehyde in most

> The Icahn School of Medicine at Mount Sinai in New York suggests this attractive way to prevent mold on your houseplant soil — cover the soil with shells or aquarium gravel. Your plant will look lovely and its soil will stay free from mold.

commercial cinnamon has potent antimicrobial and fungicidal properties that can help you fight back against the mold without losing your favorite flowers.

- Scrape up all the mold you can see and throw it away.

- Add a fresh layer of potting soil to replace what you took out.

- Sprinkle the new soil with a layer of ground cinnamon to keep your plants mold-free.

Dust leaves in double time. Your knickknacks aren't the only things that need dusting. Plants need clean leaves to breathe easier and absorb sunlight. To clean them, simply hold a soft, damp rag in each hand and gingerly clasp each leaf near its base. Gently pull your hands over the sandwiched leaf to clean both sides at one time.

Simple way to get rid of fungus gnats. Those little black bugs that love to fly around your houseplants and constantly hover around your face may be fungus gnats. They love wet soil, so try waiting until the surface dirt dries to water your plants. If you can allow the first inch or two of dirt to dry out, that's even better. To check, poke your finger in the soil near the edge of the pot.

Or spread cedar chips over your houseplant soil. Most insects don't like the smell. Then coat the surface of a yellow sticky note or small squares cut from yellow poster board with petroleum jelly. Hang these near your plants to catch the gnats.

Encourage damaging gnats to scat. Gnats and fruit flies aren't just a nuisance. Their larvae feed on plant roots, stunting a houseplant's growth and causing its poor leaves to yellow and wilt. But getting rid of these pests can be easy. Just add a spoonful of honey and a teaspoon of dishwashing liquid to either a cup of warm water or a cup of apple cider vinegar.

This bait mixture draws gnats and fruit flies and often drowns them. If a few stragglers seem to be escaping, sit by the jar with a spray bottle of rubbing alcohol and spray the gnats as they appear. Do this daily until the tiny troublemakers vanish for good.

> Many houseplants are poisonous. Philodendrons, dumbcane, Swiss cheese plant, Jerusalem cherry, ivy, and the peace lily can cause swelling or burning of your tongue and throat. Oleander can be deadly.

Sticky solution to cat problem. To keep your feline friends out of your houseplants, spread double-sided carpet tape across the rim of your pot. Cats don't like the sticky surface and will go back to their litter box.

If that doesn't work, try covering the dirt with pine cones, small rocks, low-growing plants, or anything unpleasant to dig through.

As a last resort, spray the soil with a pet repellent, like Bitter Apple. Cats hate the taste on their paws and will soon leave your plants alone.

Container gardening: small space, big rewards

Tricks for choosing the right receptacles. Got houseplants or a container garden? For healthier, prettier plants, make sure you choose the best containers.

- Plastic is usually the least expensive choice. It's lightweight and provides good drainage. It cools quickly, keeping plants from overheating — but it's not very sturdy. Cold weather can make plastic brittle, and you don't want your container to break.

- Ceramic, or glazed clay pots, have good stability and retain moisture well. They come in a beautiful variety of colors and styles, which makes them more expensive. Something else to consider — heavy glaze can cause these pots to heat up and possibly damage roots.

- Terra cotta is also heavy and stable, with traditional good looks. It's porous, which is good for air circulation and absorbing moisture, but that also means your plants will need more frequent watering. Terra cotta can break easily, so it may not be the best choice if it's likely to get knocked over or moved around.

- Wood is versatile, natural, and helps warm the soil. You can paint it to coordinate with your decor. Or you can combine it with other garden furniture to make functional features, such as planters that double as a bench. Unless it's rot-resistant cedar or redwood, it may need to be treated to prevent decay. Beware of chemicals that could be toxic to your plants.

- Metal containers are sturdy, and they look modern and trendy. However, they can really heat up in direct sunlight and damage your plants.

Freebie frenzy — make your own planters. Plants aren't picky, unlike people. They will grow in almost anything that holds soil. Don't blow your gardening budget on fancy planters. Make your own simple planter for free.

Old bread bags work great. Double them up for added strength, or use a gallon-size zippered plastic bag. Fill with potting mix to within a few inches from the top. Seal the bag and staple it shut. Lay the bag on its side in a waterproof tray, like an old baking sheet. Punch a few holes in the underside of the bag for drainage. Carefully slit it open across the top, insert your seeds or seedlings, and water thoroughly.

Lettuce, spinach, and radishes do best in these small self-made containers. For bigger plants like potatoes, pick up free feed bags, bulk food bags, or burlap bags at feed stores or farms that raise livestock.

Before you hunt down castoff tires to use as a planter, contact your local government to make sure you won't break any laws or ordinances. Some communities restrict or forbid the use of old tires for any purpose.

Clever containers help you pot plants for pennies. Don't spend all your fun money on fancy containers for your garden. There's a treasure-trove of potential pots all around — if you just know where to look. Here are a couple of ideas for turning household items and yard sale finds into charming planters.

For each project, prevent your potting soil from spilling out the bottom by lining the container with a piece of fine mesh screening, a bit of moss, or even a large coffee filter.

- Glass lampshades. Turn the shade upside down so the narrow opening is at the bottom. Add soil and your plants. What a bright idea.

- Cinder blocks. These hollow building blocks are perfect for filling with plants. But don't stop with just one. Build a wall or tower by stacking them into any shape or design that fits your space. Leave as many blocks exposed as you like and fill with  your favorite flowers. For tall structures, consider securing the blocks to each other with a concrete adhesive.

Grow a movable garden. Put that old wagon that the kids outgrew a long time ago to use. Drill holes in the bottom for drainage and fill with garden soil. Plant flowers, vegetables, or maybe even a small strawberry bed in it. You can leave it in one spot, or move it during the day to take advantage of morning sun or afternoon shade.

Choose the perfect container. Walk into a garden center and you'll find all kinds of containers made of different materials. Use this table to help you find out which one is right for your needs.

Material	Advantages	Disadvantages
concrete	durable, can grow moss and lichen on their sides	heavy
glazed ceramic pots	retains moisture well	may dry out too slowly or be too airtight for root growth
hypertufa troughs	durable, can grow moss along their sides	hard to find
metal	durable and attractive options include cast iron, aluminum, copper, or steel	small ones heat up too much, especially in the sun; poor insulators in cold weather
plastic and fiberglass	lightweight, inexpensive, durable, and resistant to staining	dry out slowly
stone and artificial stone	durable	expensive and may be heavy
terra cotta	great for root growth and good air exchange	heavy, dries out rapidly
wood	keeps soil temperature from fluctuating too much, good insulator in cold weather	wood rots

Turn old gutters into gorgeous flower boxes. Just hang them from your porch or deck railing. Decide how long you want your flower box to be, then take a pair of tin snips and trim the gutter to size. Run a bead of silicone caulk along the inside edge of each gutter end cap. Fit it onto the gutter and hold it in place for five minutes, until the caulk sets up.

Don't forget about drainage. Drill a hole in the bottom of the gutter every 4 inches with a quarter-inch drill bit. Sprinkle a thin layer of small pebbles or pottery shards in the bottom of the gutter before adding soil to stop the dirt from washing out through the holes.

Attach sturdy brackets to the back of the gutters about every 4 feet, then bolt these to the deck railing.

Add a hanging basket for pennies. Turn an old colander into a hanging basket. Any colander can work — enamel, metal, or plastic. All you need is a hanging basket liner and some fishing line.

Clean the colander and, if you like, decorate or paint it with waterproof paint. Once the paint or glue from decorating is completely dry, place the hanging basket liner in the colander.

Choose three holes near the top edge of the colander. Make sure each hole is equal distance apart. Cut three equal lengths of fishing line and thread one length through each hole. Loop each length over the rim and through the hole again a couple of times before you tie the end. Then tie the tops of the lengths together. Fill the basket with soil and plants, and it will be ready to hang.

Easy vegetables and herbs to grow in small spaces. You can be your own grocer, and harvest your own delicious foods even in a small yard or patio. In fact, you can grow vegetables in planters, pots, and hanging baskets, even if you only have a sunny window, sun room, or concrete balcony. Just be sure to place your plants where they will get enough sunlight, and keep them watered. To help everything fit into your small space:

- select varieties that keep their growth compact.

- choose bush varieties of vining vegetables like tomatoes.

- train sprawling or large plants on trellises.

Also, stick with the best veggies and herbs to grow in pots and planters. These include carrots, lettuce, peppers, onions, tomatoes, chard, eggplants, cucumbers, pole beans, summer squash including zucchini, and dwarf varieties of sweet corn. Good herbs to grow in small spaces include basil, rosemary, sage, mint, and parsley.

Combine flowerpots for charming, healthy plants. Terracotta pots have a natural appeal most plastic containers lack. But they also dry out faster, and the soil temperature changes more than with plastic. A combination of the two, however, may be ideal. Plant in a slightly smaller plastic pot, and slip it inside a clay pot.

Or maybe you have an attractive container you'd like to use as a planter but don't want to put soil in it directly. The solution is the same — a plastic pot that will fit inside. And if the planter is taller than your plastic pot, place an empty, upside-down flower pot below the filled one.

Choose pots that retain moisture. If you live in a dry climate, consider other containers besides clay pots. Clay is porous, so moisture can escape easily. That means more trips with your watering can. Glazed, plastic, metal, and sealed wooden containers are nonporous, on the other hand, and will keep moisture in the potting soil.

Lighten heavy containers the easy way. "You can use plastic grocery bags to fill space in the bottom of a large flowerpot or window box, which will save you soil and make the container lighter and easier to move," says Colleen Vanderlinden, freelance writer and author of *Edible Gardening for the Midwest*. If you're short on plastic bags, use leaves or packing peanuts instead. Fill the bottom third of the container and then add soil. Your back and your wallet will thank you.

Make sure to soak clay pots in water for a few minutes before you plant in them. This will saturate the clay, so it won't absorb water from the potting mix.

Get gorgeous displays, no repotting necessary. Cut back on the amount of repotting you do, and instantly amp up the "wow" factor. Leave plants in their plastic pots when you combine them in baskets or planters. Arrange them the way you like, pushing the pots close together. Then tuck moss over and around to hide them from view. When the season changes or a plant loses its blooms, simply take out that pot and replace with something else. No dirt under your nails and no hassle.

Keep soil in and pests out. Cover the drainage hole in the bottom of plant pots with a clean coffee filter. Extra water will still drain out, but the soil won't go with it. It will also prevent pests from entering the plant through the drainage hole. Don't drink coffee? An unscented dryer sheet will do the same thing.

Think twice before using gravel in pots. Gravel is actually bad for drainage if you put it in the bottom of your pot. It can cause water to pool, which keeps the roots wet. Try using crushed aluminum cans instead.

Secret to season-long blooms. Want blooms that last all season long? Work granules of slow-release fertilizer into the soil before you put the plant in. Fill the pot with soil, and sprinkle the fertilizer on top. Massage it into the top 6 inches or so of soil evenly and thoroughly. Then put in your plants. If they look like they need an extra boost midseason, apply a little liquid fertilizer.

Prevent container stains on your deck. Before you put containers on your deck, try this inexpensive stain preventer. Check recycling centers, yard sales, flea markets, and other secondhand stores for burner grates from old gas stoves. Ask friends and family to keep an eye out for these, too.

Once you collect a few, you'll have charming "stands" to rest your containers on. Even if the containers drip on the wood, the water won't stay long enough to cause a stain.

Need to plug the holes in the bottom of a garden pot, but you're fresh out of cork? Try a few old candle stubs instead.

If the grates look unattractive to you, check your local home improvement store for spray paint that can be used on metal. Turn your grates a bright, modern silver; a country-style copper; or any other color that suits your taste.

Stop window box soil splatter. Keep your windows clean and the soil in your flower boxes where it belongs. When you plant flowers in your window boxes, add a layer of gravel, marbles, or pebbles on top of the soil. It will keep the dirt from splashing out of the box and onto the glass when it rains or when you water your plants. Plus it gives a nice, clean look to your window boxes.

Raise hard-to-grow flowers with ease. Finally, you can enjoy flowers that are high maintenance or hard to grow. Here's how. Select containers large enough for several flowers. Plant one or two varieties that you already grow successfully without much work, but leave open space for other flowers.

Next, buy silk versions of the flowers you wish you could grow. Choose only those that can easily pass for the real thing. Insert these into the spaces between the live plants.

Place small pieces of sponge in the bottom and along the sides of your pot before putting in your plant and soil. Sponges soak up water and prevent it from flushing out of the bottom of the pot. The roots can "drink" from the sponges whenever they're thirsty.

The casual observer will never know the difference, and you'll get to appreciate plants you thought you could never have. Plus, you'll get the opportunity to try different flower varieties, such as plants usually killed by a freeze or heat wave every few years.

Just be sure to replace your silk flowers every few years to keep them from becoming tattered.

Brighten woeful winter windows. By the time fall rolls around, your window boxes can look pretty sad. Replace those dried-up summer flowers with branches of evergreens. Fill the boxes with wet peat moss and sand, and insert the branches. Keep them watered, and they should stay pretty throughout the winter.

Colorful kale looks wonderful in winter. Ornamental flowering kale, not the kind you eat, is a terrific source of winter color. And it makes a showy flowerpot or window box, especially when mixed with pansies. It's easy to grow, and with leaf rosettes that vary from white to cream to rose to purple, it becomes more dazzling as the weather gets colder.

Ornamental kale is usually sold as a spring bedding plant, but it actually does better in cooler fall weather or in winter temperatures above 20 degrees. Start this plant from seed in early spring or late summer, or transplant seedlings.

Plastic Bubble Wrap makes a great insulation for potted plants left outdoors during the winter. Just line the inside of your pots with it.

Lawn care: first aid for greener, healthier grass

7 secrets for a super-lush lawn. Follow these tips for the best-looking lawn in the neighborhood.

- Select the best grass for your climate and conditions.

- Remove vegetation and loosen, enrich, and level the soil to prepare for a new lawn.

- Lay sod if possible. It's more expensive but more reliable than seeds.

- Water new grass often and thoroughly. After roots are established, water deeply but less frequently.

- When mowing, remove no more than the top third of the grass.

- Use a mulching mower and leave the grass clippings to enrich the soil.

- Rakc leaves to prevent disease and allow sunlight to get to the grass.

Lawn lore steals money right out of your wallet. Don't get your lawn care advice while standing by the water cooler or your neighbor's fence. Chances are you'll hear some wild and weird ideas — like chewing gum gets rid of moles or you can just mow over crabgrass to kill it. Notions like these may not necessarily harm your lawn, but others can truly cost you money. Take this myth for example — you must water every day.

Lawns require only 1 inch of water per week," says Kim Toal, Fayette County Cooperative Extension Agent with the University of Georgia Extension Service. Soaking your grass frequently can cost you in two unexpected ways.

- "If you water too much, you increase your chances for disease," warns Toal. And that means spending extra money on remedies to cure the problem.

- In addition, overwatering can actually change how your grass grows. "Your turf could develop a shallow root system," Toal explains, "which will cause problems during drought periods."

So what happens if you stick to the 1-inch limit? Toal says you'll not only reduce your water bill, but you'll have a healthier lawn, to boot.

Don't keep your lawn golf-course short. Sure, you can mow your lawn low enough to roll a golf ball across it, but get ready to say hello to weeds, which will thrive in the extra sunlight. On the other hand, keep your grass around 2 1/2 to 3 inches high, and it will shade your soil enough to keep most weed seeds from sprouting. As a bonus, you can mow less often.

Miracle medicine for tough turf problems. A single all-natural treatment can both aerate and dethatch your lawn while conditioning your soil. And you won't spend hours on these otherwise backbreaking tasks. Just apply a light top-dressing of crumbly, finished compost to the lawn.

- The microorganisms in compost help break down thatch.

- Organic matter in compost helps clay soil particles clump together. This aerates the soil, improves drainage, and makes the dirt easier to work.

- Compost acts as a natural fertilizer, putting nutrients back into the soil.

Because it improves both the nutrients and physical structure of the soil, compost is considered a top-notch soil conditioner. Make a spray-on treatment by steeping a sack full of finished compost in a large bucket of water. Cover for several days, then remove the "tea bag." Dilute the liquid until it looks like weak tea, and spray on your lawn at a rate of one quart per 1,000 square feet.

Top-dress your lawn twice a year with a light layer of compost. Put down half an inch in the spring and fall to improve drainage and prevent drought damage. Compost helps dirt hold more water, soaking it up like a sponge. This makes your grass more likely to survive dry stretches.

Get to the root of soil problems. The reason your grass won't grow may have nothing to do with nutrients, pests, or diseases. The soil itself could be to blame. Sink a sharp shovel in the dirt. Dig straight down several inches and look at the soil layers. If you're lucky, you'll see nothing but dark, loamy soil. Most of the time, however, you'll see 2 or 3 inches of loam atop a bed of sand, gravel, or clay.

- Sand or gravel means your lawn dries out fast and struggles to survive during droughts.

- A bed of clay means just the opposite, that your soil holds too much water, making plants prone to root rot.

Build up the good soil on top gradually, adding a light layer of compost each year.

Stop the spread of lawn diseases. Give your grass a better chance at beating a disease, and prevent its spread at the same time. Raise the height of your mower blades. Sick grass needs more leaf blade, so it can make more energy to fight off the illness. Mow the diseased area last, and hose off the underside of the mowing deck afterward to blast away infected clippings.

> Wearing cleats outside results in an aerated lawn. Wear them anytime you are fertilizing or gardening.

Take the guesswork out of watering. Established lawns need about 1 inch of water a week. Instead of guessing how long you should run the sprinklers, put some empty soup cans to work in the yard.

- Spread the cans around the lawn.

- Run the sprinklers for 15 minutes.

- Measure the water in each can with a ruler.

- Add the amounts and divide by the number of cans to get an average.

- Divide 1 inch by the average amount of water in the cans.

- Multiply the result by 15.

Say the cans capture an average of 0.2 inches of water in 15 minutes. Divide one by 0.2 to get five. Then multiply five by 15 to get 75. The answer — run the sprinkler for 75 minutes to put 1 inch of water on the lawn.

Cut back on mowing. Fed up with grass? Get lucky with clover. These hardy plants make thick, cushy ground covers just perfect for choking out weeds. Clovers are drought tolerant and never need fertilizing. Best of all, the low-growing varieties, such as white Dutch clover, rarely require mowing. Plus, the roots aerate compacted soil and add nitrogen back into the ground.

Or go low-maintenance with a no-mow herbal lawn. Many low-growing plants are fragrant, not to mention flowering. Try violets, creeping thyme, mazus (*Mazus reptans*), or pearlwort (*Sagina subulata*). For front yards where you rarely walk, consider yarrow, oregano, and phlox. If your lawn area is damp and doesn't get direct sunlight, you might want to go for a lush, green moss. Sheet moss (*Hypnum sp.*) and fern moss (*Thuidium delicatulum*) are fast-growing and adapt well. Remember, moss likes water — the more it gets, the more it grows, but unlike grass, it needs only shallow watering. Your high-maintenance lawn care days could soon be over.

Low-tech check for dry soil

Want an easy way to tell when you've watered enough? Stick a screwdriver in it.

You can buy fancy water sensors that test moisture below the soil's surface. Or you can test it yourself for free.

After watering, push a long screwdriver into the dirt until you feel resistance. It will slide easily through wet soil but stop when it hits dry dirt. Pull out the tool and check the dirt line to see how far the water has penetrated your lawn. Soil should be damp 6 to 8 inches deep after watering.

Protect your family from dog germs. Be sure to clean your lawn daily of any "deposits" your dog has made. If you don't, he could track germs into your home, and you and your family could get sick. Bury the doggy-do in the woods or in a garden. And if he waters the lawn in the same place every day, spread some gypsum on that area to keep your grass from dying.

Telltale signs of too much fertilizer. It's easy to go overboard with fertilizer. These symptoms say you've overdone it.

- dark green streaks in the lawn that eventually turn brown

- irregular yellow spots bordered by dark green

Don't fret if you see these signs. Your lawn can still recover. Simply water the area thoroughly to dilute the fertilizer.

No-guess guide for feeding your grass. Check this chart to find out how much nitrogen your lawn needs for the whole year. Notice the range for each grass. Where you fall in that range depends on where you live. For instance, if grass has a long growing season in your climate, then feed it at the higher end.

Grass type	Pounds per 1,000 sq ft
centipede grass	1 to 3
bermuda grass	2 to 6
tall fescue	2 to 4
fine fescue	1 to 3
St. Augustine grass	3 to 6
Kentucky bluegrass	3 to 6
zoysia grass	2 to 4
buffalo grass	0 to 2
bahia grass	2 to 4

Feeding lawns makes them thirsty. Fertilizing your lawn every second Sunday may be the reason it's so green — or it may be all that extra water you have to splash on fertilized ground. To make better use of your resources, add a slow release, water-soluble plant food only once a year, when you aerate. You might be surprised how much water you save.

Top turfs for the least amount of work

Get a low-maintenance grass, and say goodbye to expensive fertilizers, wasteful watering, and weekly mowing. These grasses thrive on neglect.

- Fine fescues grow great in places where the summer doesn't get too hot. They love dry, nutrient-poor soil and hate being fertilized. They don't need much water, either, although drought conditions are not ideal.

- Centipedegrass grows low, so it doesn't need much mowing. Fertilize only once a year, twice at most. It's a good grass for acidic, nutrient-poor soil.

- Buffalograss tops the list of tough turf. Once established, it needs very little water. You don't even have to mow it, although it looks better when you do. Don't plant it if you live in a hot, humid climate, though. It prefers dry, windy weather.

Select the best grass for your region. In the South, single-seed grasses tend to work best. Most warm-season grasses just look better planted by themselves. And even if you try planting a mixture, there's a good chance the strongest variety will kill out the others.

All northern cool-season grasses, on the other hand, are grown from a mixture of seeds. If one kind of grass fails, the conditions might be just right for another to flourish. What's more, diseases that attack one will often leave another alone.

Pick the perfect grass for your yard. When sinking a bunch of money into a new lawn, don't plant the wrong seed. Instead, consider what conditions your grass can expect to face and choose a variety that's built to handle those conditions.

Problem	Grass variety
Heat	zoysia, Bermuda, bahiagrass, bluestem
Cold	Kentucky bluegrass, Supina bluegrass
Drought	buffalograss, blue grama, chewings fescue, bahiagrass, zoysia, bluestem
Shade	creeping red fescue, St. Augustine, chewings fescue, bahiagrass
Wear	zoysia, Bermuda, bluegrass bahiagrass

3 signs of good grass seed. Make sure you aren't wasting your money on the next bag of grass seed. Look for these numbers on the label.

- The noxious weed percentage tells you how many weed seeds are mixed in with the grass seeds. Don't settle for any amount other than zero.

- The germination rate on a bag of good-quality seed should be at least 80 percent. That means for every 100 seeds you plant, 80 of them will sprout.

- The test date tells you how old a bag of seed is. The germination rate goes down as the seed gets older. Buy the bag with the most recent test date. Never buy one more than nine months old.

Simple plan to sow grass seed evenly. This trick works for both fertilizer and grass seed. Mix flour into your fertilizer or grass seed before you spread it. The flour acts like a highlighter pen for your yard, showing where you have already put down the fertilizer or seed. Even if you get distracted, you won't have to worry about missing — or overloading — any part of your yard.

Overseeding does more harm than good. It's tempting to put down more seed than the bag recommends. After all, more seed means a thicker turf, right? Wrong. Too much seed actually gives you thin, spindly grass. The seeds end up too close together, competing for nutrients and water. As a result, most of the sprouts will die. Overseeding also attracts disease. Putting down too much fescue, for instance, can lead to pythium blight. Play it safe and stick with the suggested amount.

Right time to mow new lawns. Mow newly seeded lawns once the grass plants reach 3 inches tall. By then, they'll be firmly rooted enough to withstand the wheels of a mower. Set your blade at its highest height for the first few mows. As the lawn begins to fill in, you can gradually lower the blade to the level you want.

Sodded lawns need slightly different care. Wait three weeks before walking on or mowing new sod, even if the leaf blades are more than 3 inches tall.

Get better results by mowing less

Want a beautiful lawn? Then stop cutting it so short. Scalping is the number one mowing mistake you can make. It will cost you more time and money in the long run.

- Longer grass needs less frequent mowing. Short grass grows fast to make up for the loss of so much leaf blade. Taller grass grows slower, saving you time and sweat.

- Routinely cut the grass too short, and the roots will never grow deep. Shallow roots leave your lawn vulnerable to drought and less able to fight off weeds, diseases, and insect infestations.

End your mowing pains. Lawn mowing is aerobic exercise that can cause sore muscles, sore joints, and even back pain, a recent study says. But mowing should be light to moderate exercise, not an exercise in misery. If your lawn mower requires strenuous effort to move and steer, look for a lighter mower. Also, look for features you can tailor to your needs. Good examples include wheels that make the mower easier to turn or adjustable handles to prevent arm, hand, and shoulder strain.

Push for a calmer, cleaner cut. Are you losing your patience because your lawn mower is hard to start and difficult to maintain? Are your tired of smelling fumes and listening to the noisy roar of the motor? It might be time to switch to a push mower — no fumes, gentle exercise, and cleaner cuts for healthier grass.

It's cheaper to operate than a regular mower, and it helps keep the environment clean. Plus, you can mow your grass on Sunday morning without disturbing your neighbors.

The right height for your turf. Every grass has an ideal height. Check this chart to find the perfect mower height to make yours healthy and more water-efficient.

Grass species	Ideal height (inches)
tall fescue	2.5 to 3.5
fine fescue	2.5 to 3
Kentucky bluegrass	2 to 3
perennial ryegrass	2 to 3
zoysia	1 to 2
common bermuda	1 to 2
centipede	1.5 to 2
St. Augustine	2.5 to 4

Simple strip cuts trimming time. Line raised sidewalks, retaining walls, and fences with a buried stone border. Dig a shallow strip along the edge. Then lay inexpensive brick pavers in it deep enough so only the top 1 inch sticks up from the ground. This forms a perfect mow strip. You can mow over the pavers without tearing up your blade, and spare yourself hours of string-trimming these otherwise tough-to-cut areas.

Sprig your lawn for big savings

Here is one way to plant a lawn without a lot of money. All you need are cuttings of a spreading-type grass, like bermuda, zoysia, or centipede.

You can buy a bushel of sprigs from a nursery or cut some from the grass already growing in your yard. Cut runners about 12 inches long. Then make a furrow in the ground with a spade or hoe. Stick half the runner into the furrow, and leave the other half on the surface. Heel it in, pressing the soil back over the buried runner. Water it twice a day to keep it from drying out.

Smart and cheap lawn repair. Lawn-patching mixes and kits can save time because they combine grass seed with products that help retain moisture and fool hungry birds. But making your own lawn-patching mix may be cheaper if you already have the ingredients on hand. Just blend grass seed with peat moss.

If you need to buy those supplies, check their prices and compare the total cost to the prices of lawn-patching kits. Buying a package of peat moss and a small 1-pound bag of grass seed can cost around $10. Some grass-patching mixes cost less than $5 while others cost $10 or more. If a cheap grass-patching kit is available with seeds that grow well in your area, then you may be better off buying the kit.

On the other hand, if the product contains the wrong grass seed or if you already have good seed on hand, buying peat moss may be the cheapest way to go. This is one case where it pays to compare.

Warning signs for a malnourished lawn. You can spot a lawn that is low in nutrients even without a soil test. Just watch for these warning signs.

- Nitrogen. Sparse yellow to yellow-green grass with stunted growth. Weeds, particularly clover, are taking over the turf.

- Iron. Grass grows well but is yellow to yellow-green.

- Phosphorus. Dull, blue-green grass. The blades turn purple along the edges, then develop a reddish tinge.

Grass clippings will add nitrogen to your lawn as they decompose, so try leaving them on the lawn when you mow if lack of nitrogen is the problem. Also, there are fertilizers, both organic and conventional, specially made to provide whatever is missing in your lawn. If one of these problems comes up, ask for the right fertilizer at your local nursery or lawn care department of your favorite home improvement store. The experts will be able to give you specifics that are right for your area's soil.

Defend your turf against drought. You may not be able to end a drought, but you can arm your lawn against it. To help fortify grass so it recovers from drought quickly, start with five simple steps.

- Adjust your standard mowing height upward. Add a half-inch if your mowing height is 2 inches, three-fourths inch if it's 3 inches, or a full inch for 4 inches. You'll encourage a deeper root system and natural chemical reactions that help your grass tolerate drought stress.

- Avoid shallow and frequent watering. Instead, wait until the first signs of wilt show up and then water deeply.

- Keep off the grass whenever possible. The less people and pets walk on it, the better off your lawn will be.

- Keep your mower blade sharp. The rough cut made by blunt mower blades causes grass to retain less water.

- Avoid using pesticides on your grass until the drought improves. They'll just add stress to an already-weakened lawn. By simply storing your pesticides until the drought breaks, you'll buy fewer containers of pesticide and your lawn will be more resilient.

DIY fix for bare areas. Lawns are like carpet, and you can repair them the same way. Cut a patch of grass from a hidden part of the yard to repair a very visible bald spot.

- Sink a sharp, square-bladed shovel all the way around a section of grass. Make sure the cuts go a few inches deep.

- Slide the shovel blade under the soil and lift out the grass, roots and all.

- Move the square immediately to its new home, and water regularly until the roots take hold.

Shield grass seed from pesky birds. Before you reseed a small patch of lawn, look in your basement or garage for an old window screen — or one that's not being used. Use it to protect your newly seeded area while the grass grows. Place the screen over the seeded patch, and weigh it down with a few stones to keep it secure. Birds won't be able to move it, and your seeds will be safe.

Protect grass from gas. Move your lawn mower onto pavement before refilling the gas tank. Gas spilled on grass will kill it within a few days, and there is not much you can do. Clear out the dead grass. The lawn will most likely fill in on its own. You can help it along by sprinkling a little grass seed or cutting a sod patch from a hidden spot in your yard.

Keep a salt shaker full of grass seed in your pocket while mowing. After you mow over a bald spot, simply sprinkle some seeds onto the bare soil. Some types of grass seeds are too big to fit through salt shaker holes. Recycle an old Parmesan cheese shaker for these.

Send moss packing. If you're determined to get rid of the moss in your yard, your best bet is to use lawn sand. But keep this in mind — although lawn sand will kill the moss, it will come back again if you don't change the conditions that encouraged it to grow in the first place.

Moss grows in shady, damp areas, especially those that are poorly fed and mowed too closely. So set your mower at a high level and aerate the soil frequently with a garden fork. Fertilize twice a year, and use lawn sand once a year. Cutting back low-hanging branches on nearby trees to let in more light could also help.

Weed control: safe solutions that really work

Kill every weed in your yard. All it takes is this four-step, easy-to-follow plan:

- In spring, spray with a pre-emergent weedkiller to limit weed growth.

- When summer comes, apply a different herbicide. Many herbicides are limited, meaning each herbicide only kills certain kinds of weeds. That is why switching herbicides helps get rid of weeds your spring herbicide could not eliminate. After the summer herbicide has done its work, pull any remaining weeds by hand.

- As autumn takes hold, apply a general herbicide.

- Give the newly treated weeds time to die off completely, and then pull up any weeds that are left.

Don't water unwanted greenery. Sprinklers water weeds right along with your prized plants. So lay soaker hoses or drip irrigation very close to your plants, and cover with mulch. The plants will get plenty of water while nearby weeds suffer from drought. This even helps prevent many new weeds, because weed seeds need water to germinate. But take these steps to prevent new problems.

- Check your mulch to make sure it does not remain damp long after a rain. This happens when mulches are too finely textured or too thick to dry easily, creating the perfect place for weed seeds to germinate.

- Keep an eye out for powerful, deep-rooted weeds like nutsedge and bindweed. These can grow through most mulches — including landscape fabric — so they may pop up in well-watered, mulched areas. Get rid of these weeds the moment you find them.

10 terrific nontoxic ways to kill weeds. You wouldn't expect a common household ingredient from your pantry to work like an expensive weedkiller, but white vinegar does. Just heat it up, pour it in a spray bottle, and take aim. It's cheap, easy, and poison-free.

Expect young weeds to die quickly, but stubborn or well-established weeds may require another round or two of spraying. If that's a few sprays too many for you, try a single dose of pickling vinegar. It's more potent than household vinegar and hits weeds harder.

Stop problem plants naturally. Spread corn gluten meal on bare ground wherever you want to keep problem plants, like crabgrass, dandelions, and purslane from popping up. Check your local nursery and garden supply store for this nontoxic product.

Just remember to spray weeds when they are small. Older, taller weeds may need more than one spray of vinegar to take them down. Plus, keep in mind, vinegar can kill any plant it touches.

Here are nine more ways to nix weeds without harmful herbicides.

- Send off weeds with sand. You've finally killed the weeds that set up housekeeping in your driveway and sidewalk cracks, but they'll grow back if you're not careful. Fill the cracks with sand, so the weed seeds can't get enough light to grow. For smaller cracks, try masonry sand, or stone dust.

- Boil them away. Here's another no-cost tip — wipe out weeds in the cracks of cement or flagstone walks by pouring boiling water on them.

- Use powerful partners. Make your neighbors green with envy and save money, too. Mix together vinegar and salt, pour in a spray bottle, and spray directly on weeds. Just don't catch your flowering favorites in the crossfire. And avoid spraying it on weedy sidewalks since it can corrode the concrete.

- Rub out weeds with alcohol. This homemade spray puts weeds down for the count. Combine 1 tablespoon of rubbing alcohol with 1 quart of water, pour into a spray bottle, and douse weed leaves. For tougher plants, add more alcohol — up to 5 tablespoons.

- Give impostors a gin bath. Knock 'em dead with this powerful recipe. Add an ounce of gin, an ounce of vinegar, and a squirt of baby shampoo into a spray bottle full of water, then give weeds a good soak.

- Offer a sip of soda. Need another use for flat soda? Try pouring straight Coca-Cola on the weeds in your sidewalks. This sticky soda kisses weeds goodbye.

- Stamp out intruders with salt. Rock salt isn't just for ice cream anymore. Sprinkle it in cracks and crevices for instant weed relief. It sterilizes the soil, so keep it away from beloved plants and areas you plan to grow in later.

- Clean up poison ivy. You can kill poison ivy without expensive, toxic chemicals. Pour 3 pounds of salt into a gallon of soapy water, stir, and spray it on the leaves and stems.

- Chalk up one more use for baking soda. Sprinkle it directly on crabgrass, but avoid getting it on the surrounding lawn. This solution seems to work best in warm climates where warm-weather grasses, like St. Augustine, Bermuda, and Bahiagrass flourish. Baking soda may not work as well on crabgrass in colder climates. In fact, it could harm cold-weather grasses. Test it on a small, hidden spot in your yard before going gung-ho. You may have to apply it more than once to kill a patch of crabgrass entirely.

Defend other plants from toxic sprays

Whether you're spraying your weeds with vinegar or something more toxic, you don't want to damage the surrounding plants. Here's a simple solution.

Trim off the bottom of a plastic 2-liter bottle and do the same to a 16-ounce bottle. Store them both with your garden supplies. When you're ready to spray a weed, pick the appropriate size bottle. Place the bottle over the weed, slip the sprayer nozzle into the mouth of the bottle, and spray. Give the chemicals 30 seconds to sink in and then move on to the next weed. Your plants will remain safe, but your weeds won't live to tell the tale.

Use the power of the sun. Solarizing is an organic, chemical-free technique that harnesses the heat of the sun to get your garden ready for planting. It not only kills weeds, but also gets rid of pests and diseases. You'll need to plan for your plot to be idle for 4 to 8 weeks, then follow these four steps for success.

- Cultivate. After you've chosen your plot, till it thoroughly and remove debris. Take out any bits and pieces that could contain weed seeds.

- Level. Get your rake and break up any clumps left over from tilling. Smooth out the ground, making it as flat as possible. This will allow the plastic a tight fit later.

- Irrigate. Give the plot a good soaking — ideally down to about a foot deep. Be ready to place plastic on top as soon as possible after watering.

- Cover. Use clear plastic — thinner is better for heating, but if you're in a windy area, use slightly thicker so it doesn't get disturbed. Then weigh down the edges using soil or stones, and wait. How long? Usually, 4 to 6 weeks are enough if it's hot, but if it's cooler, windier, or cloudier where you are, leave the plastic on for 6 to 8 weeks.

Try to disturb the soil as little as possible after removing the plastic. This will help avoid stirring up any weed seeds that could be lurking. Your soil — weed-free and nutrient-rich — is ready for your plants.

Free wiper aims to kill. A weed wiper applicator lets you paint herbicide directly on the weed. This gives you the most bang for your herbicide buck, while protecting other plants.

But instead of paying for a paint-on weed wiper, make your own from an old roll-on deodorant container.

- Use pliers and a pen to pop or tease the roll-on ball out of the container.

- Put on rubber gloves, and pour herbicide into the container.

- Put the roll-on ball firmly back in place.

- Roll herbicide on the weed leaves.

Either label the deodorant bottle and store it in a locked container, or clean out the bottle and throw it away.

Fight weeds with common household tools. Weeds are a persistent problem. There's no getting around it. But there's also no need to go out and spend money to solve the problem if you already have a simple toolbox. Use these common household and handyman helpers together with a little bit of elbow grease.

> Pour your homemade weedkiller in a portable spray bottle and carry it with you as you work in the garden. Label the bottle clearly so you don't mistake an herbicide for a fertilizer and accidentally spray your prized plants.

- Hammer. Dig the clawed end of a hammer into the soil, grab the weed at the base, and pull it out just like you would a nail.

- Pliers. Take a hint from your dentist. When persistent weeds won't come out by hand, get your pliers and go to work. You'll get a grip on the worst of weeds.

- Screwdriver. Use the flat-bladed kind. It's perfect for prying weeds out of cracks in driveways and between paving stones. It's also great for loosening tough weed roots before pulling them out by hand.

- Tweezers. Perfect for plucking tiny weeds and handy for getting hard-to-reach weeds out of tight spaces.

- Fork. The tines of an old but sturdy fork make great grippers for pulling out unwelcome garden guests.

- Apple corer. An old, serrated apple corer digs down deep and cuts the roots at the same time, and it's small enough to reach into tight spaces.

Save your plants from poison ivy vines. If you've just discovered a poison ivy vine wrapped around one of your favorite plants, don't panic. The Louisiana State University Agricultural Center recommends this method for saving your plant. Instead of spraying — and killing — your plant and the poison ivy with herbicide, break out your loppers and buy an herbicide made from triclopyr. Garden center staffers can help you find this herbicide.

Use your loppers to clip the poison ivy vine near its base and then treat the base with the triclopyr. The vine will wither away, and the triclopyr will kill the base and roots. Unlike some poison ivy treatments, you can try this one any time of year. Just remember to clean your loppers thoroughly afterward and don't try to remove the dead vine without wearing protective gloves and clothing. Wash yourself, the gloves, and the clothing as soon as you're done.

Boost the potency of your herbicide. All you need is a secret ingredient from your kitchen — dishwashing liquid. This soapy liquid is a surfactant, meaning it helps the herbicide stick to the leaf. It can also break down the waxy coating protecting weed leaves, so the plant is more susceptible to herbicide. Adding this cheap kitchen liquid may keep you from doing extra spraying or buying additional weed busters, thus saving money on lawn maintenance.

Experts recommend you add anywhere from one drop to one tablespoon of dishwashing liquid for each gallon of herbicide. But remember, dishwashing liquid may burn the grass around the weed, so use the smallest effective dose.

Read the label of any herbicide before you add dishwashing liquid to it. If the instructions say you should add a "nonionic" surfactant to the herbicide, don't add dishwashing liquid, which is ionic. Mixing dish soap into this type of herbicide may help your weeds survive.

Guard against trunk damage. Save yourself the heartache of damaging saplings and shrubs when you're whacking weeds or mowing. Cut off the bottom and top of a plastic bottle, and slit it up the side. Wrap it around the base of young trunks while you are working in the area, and slip it off when you're done.

Give your back a break. Use this simple technique when weeding the garden, and you could prevent a bad back in the future. Instead of bending at the waist, squat down to weed. This makes your knees and thighs do the work instead of your back. But if your knees and back are already a problem, try one of these.

- Create raised beds at waist height, so you no longer need to bend. For even better results, attach a board or bench along the top edges of the bed, so you have something to sit on while you weed.

- Use a long-handled trowel, long-handled weeder, or a grabber to help you weed without bending.

Make weeding fun. Let young grandchildren gather your weeds. Make a game of it, or pay them a penny per pull. Dandelions are perennial favorites with children. Ask your grandkids to pick a yellow bouquet for you before the weeds go to seed. You'll have fresh color in your house, fewer unwanted plants in your yard, and a wonderful time with children.

Show big weeds who's boss. Cut them back to the ground, and wait for them to sprout again. As soon as you see signs of new foliage, nail it with weedkiller.

Slow and steady wins the race. Don't try to weed all at once. Spread it out to make it more manageable. Pull a few plants each morning or evening, or set small goals, like weeding the garden a foot at a time. Tackle them early in the season, and you'll have less work later on.

Grow dandelions for good health. Don't think of dandelions as just a nuisance in your lawn. Herbalists have used them for centuries to treat illnesses ranging from acne to gallstones. The leaves are a great source of potassium, which helps you stay both mentally and physically healthy. So leave a dandelion patch in a corner of your lawn, but be sure it's free of pesticides before you cook up a batch.

Prevent weeds with a newspaper. Put layers of newspaper in your garden to block the sunlight so weeds can't grow. When you're ready to plant, just cut slits in the paper. It's porous enough for water to soak through, yet holds moisture in. For a more attractive appearance, you can cover it with mulch.

Keep out trespassers by your garden fence. You put up a garden fence to keep pets and wildlife out, but make sure you don't invite weeds in as a result. Weeds that spring up along your garden fence can invade your garden by spreading either their seeds or underground runners. If you would rather not spend hours weeding, spraying herbicides, or using a string trimmer, try this instead. Lay pavers, bricks, or a thick layer of bark mulch underneath the fence or along both sides of its base.

Pave garden paths with sawdust. No more walking on weeds! Dig up your garden walkways several inches deep, then fill them in with a thick layer of sawdust. This material acts as a natural herbicide by tying up the nitrogen in soil so weeds can't grow. For this same reason, don't use it around plant beds.

Lay overlapping pieces of cardboard on unused beds, cover with 3 or more inches of bark, and let the bed rest during winter. The cardboard should turn to rich mulch come spring, and you'll have a weed-free, well-rested garden.

Mulched beds keep unwanted sprouts at bay. Lay a thick blanket of mulch to keep weeds from sprouting. A layer of grass clippings, bark, straw, leaves, or other natural material blocks sunlight and air weeds need to grow. Plus, mulches return rich nutrients to the soil as they decay, so they feed your plants while protecting them from competing weeds.

Make winter weeds work for you. Give weeds like chick-weed, clover, and medic a stay of execution if they pop up in your vegetable or flower garden during winter or late autumn.

Chickweed (*Stellaria media*) makes a good cover crop and can help prevent the ground from becoming waterlogged. Winter clover (*Trifolium sp.*) and medic (*Medicago sp.*) can also be good cover crops because they return nitrogen to the soil.

Just be sure to till or shovel these weeds back under the soil before they flower and go to seed — and make certain they are well buried. Otherwise, you will fight extra weeds all summer.

Prevent weeds from a surprising source

A study of 10 retail brands of birdseed found that each one contained at least three kinds of weed seeds — and the seeds sprouted into weeds when tested. But that does not mean you should stop feeding the birds to save your yard. Just use one of these methods to bake your birdseed, and the weed seeds will never sprout.

- Conventional oven. Spread the seed out on a long, flat pan. Bake at 300 degrees for 30 minutes.

- Microwave oven. Microwave one gallon of seed in a paper bag for five minutes on high. To bake less seed, place 1 or 2 pounds of seed in a bowl, cover with a paper towel, and bake one minute for each pound of seed. Do not place microwaved birdseed back in storage.

Don't forget to let the seed cool before putting it in your bird feeder.

Roll out the red carpet. Or beige, or blue, or brown. Cut leftover carpet into long runners and lay them between the rows of your garden. The carpet will keep weeds from sprouting, and the cushioning could make kneeling easier on your joints. Choose carpet without foam backing. Otherwise, you'll find yourself "weeding" bits of plastic out of your garden for years to come.

Keep invasives under control. It's tempting to stick an invasive plant in the yard. They grow fast and need little care. That's also what makes them invasive. Experts warn against letting these loners into your landscape. But if you still want one of these plants in your yard or garden, take these steps to keep them contained. That way, your quick-growing greenery doesn't become a hard-to-kill weed.

- Slide a large kitchen knife into the soil every few weeks and cut around the plants. This severs the spreading roots and tendrils, so they don't sprout elsewhere.

- Cut the bottom out of a plastic planter and sink it, or a wide piece of pipe, into the ground at least 10 inches down. Then plant inside the walls. This will keep your plant from laying down roots where it doesn't belong.

Trees and shrubs: make your foliage flourish

Defend your shrubs against winter. Instead of buying a whole load of products to protect your shrubs against winter's onslaught, perhaps you can use items you already have. Check with your local cooperative extension agent for the shrub protection tactics that work best in your climate. Then see if these tips can help you save money.

- Create a wind screen. If your shrub is small enough, a teepee of branches tied off at the top may do the job. Use evergreen branches, if they are available. For a larger bush, pound three or four wooden stakes into the ground so their tops are a little higher than your shrub. Grab an old sheet or blanket you no longer want. Make sure the sheet can reach from the top of the stakes to the bottom, then staple it to the stakes so you surround your bush. For a temporary wind shelter, you can use Bubble Wrap instead.

- Place evergreen branches, a thick layer of raked leaves, or another inexpensive mulch around the base of your shrubs. This retains moisture, helps resist foliage browning, and helps prevent root damage from frost heaving.

- To protect shrubs from frost, cover them with unwanted drapes, old sheets, tarps, fabric, burlap, or even an old car cover. Use stakes or a frame to keep your cover from touching the buds, blooms, or leaves. And make sure the bottom edge of the cover rests on the ground, so the plant is fully enclosed. Don't forget to remove your cover the next day if warm daytime temperatures are expected.

Give flowering shrubs an encore. When the show is over for another season, your flowering bush doesn't have to look dull. Just add a later-blooming vine near the base and train it to run up the branches.

Plant the vine in good soil, far enough away that its roots don't have to compete with those of the shrub. And be sure both plants get plenty of water.

Send damaging tree roots deeper. Your watering practice could be what's causing tree roots to do damage, like breaking up your driveway. Water less often but more thoroughly, and roots will go deeper searching for a drink, leaving the surface unbroken.

Be kind to azaleas. Don't plant these flowering shrubs too deep. The upper roots, in fact, should be right at the soil line or just a little lower. If you are transplanting an azalea, be sure to spread the roots out if they have been growing in a circle inside the pot.

For lots of blooms, apply 2 inches to 4 inches of mulch and keep them well watered — at least an inch every seven to 10 days. But go very light on fertilizer, feeding them only in early spring. Too much fertilizer can burn them.

Beat iron deficiency with tea. Acid-loving shrubs grown in alkaline soil can end up low in iron. Watch for yellowing leaves on rhododendrons, azaleas, and blueberries. At the first sign, give them a sip of tea. Steep used tea bags and pour the cooled liquid around the base of these plants for an instant boost.

Wrong way to amend your soil. It's one of the biggest mistakes you can make — amending the soil in the hole where you plan to plant a tree. Experts once recommended it. Now they know it's a bad idea.

Amend only the hole, and the roots of woody plants like trees may not grow beyond it. Instead, they'll act like container plants, becoming root-bound over time. If you need to enrich poor soil, don't just amend the hole. Amend the entire bed to encourage the roots to spread out.

Terrific tips for transplanting. The best time to transplant trees and shrubs is when they are dormant, from late fall to early spring. Transplanting is a traumatic experience for plants. Trees seem to stand it better in late autumn when they lose their leaves. Just remember to wait for a good, hard freeze. You can successfully move a tree from then until it leafs out in the spring. You're usually OK even when the buds turn green but wait until fall once the leaves start to develop.

Invest in fruit trees. Having your own fruit trees can save you money at the grocery store, and they are a good, long-term investment on your property. But a full-grown apricot tree,

Pecan trees provide lots of shade and add to the value of your property. But if you are dreaming of pecan pies, don't delay planting. The trees take five to eight years to produce nuts.

for example, needs at least 15 to 25 square feet of space. If you don't have that much room, consider planting a dwarf variety. Although the tree is smaller, the fruit is the same size as that of regular trees.

Isolate black walnut trees

You may know about the heavy stains black walnuts can leave on your hands and clothing. But did you know black walnut trees produce a substance, called juglone, that is harmful to many plants? These trees are especially a problem for plants that love acid, like azaleas, rhododendrons, and blueberries. And put your vegetable garden with tomatoes and potatoes far from the root zone of these trees — that means at least 50 to 60 feet from the trunk.

Grow your own citrus fruit. Citrus trees are pretty easy to sprout from seed. Best of all, you don't have to live in a hot region to grow them. But you do need to plant them in pots that can be moved inside in cold weather. That's not so hard to do with the smallest varieties, which can be grown in a pot as small as 18 inches deep.

Produce fruit in a warm pocket. If you live in a cool zone, don't be too quick to decide you can't grow some fruit trees and other plants suited to a warmer region. You may have pockets in sheltered areas of zone 4, for example, with conditions more like zone 5.

Flowering trees for next to nothing. Every year cities around the nation give away free flowering trees to plant in your yard, often as part of Arbor Day celebrations. Check with your local Parks and Recreation department or nearby botanical garden to see if they're participating. Even if they aren't, you can still take advantage of a great deal. Join the Arbor Day Foundation for $10 and get 10 trees free. Choose from flowering trees, Eastern red cedars, oaks, redbuds, or other trees suited to your hardiness zone.

Show support for weak trees. The experts say most trees and shrubs become stronger if you don't stake them. But a tree with a weak trunk might need some extra support. Place a stake in the hole before you plant the tree, and tie the trunk to it with strips of cloth or pantyhose. These will be easy to loosen as the tree grows, and they are less likely than wire to cut into the trunk.

Move a mighty oak. Oak trees sprout easily from acorns, but not always where you want them. Like other nut trees, they have long taproots and should be moved while they are small. Fortunately, some oaks tend to grow slowly. White oaks, for example, grow about a foot a year, giving you some time to decide where you want to transplant it. But you'll have to move more quickly with a pin oak, the fastest-growing variety. It shoots up more than twice as fast.

> Ropes or wires tied around trees won't cut into the bark if you first line them with a section of old garden hose.

Pick the right tree every time. Buy the wrong tree and you could waste a lot of money on a plant that can't survive. To bark up the right tree, remember this advice from Wayne Juers, horticulturist and plant doctor for Pike Family Nurseries headquartered in Norcross, Georgia.

- Decide whether you want quick shade or a slower grower. "Fast growth always provides a fast shade, but at the same time, it provides a very brittle tree that is easily blown over or breaks in strong winds and ice," says Juers. Slow-growers are more likely to survive bad weather.

- Figure out how much sun and shade your tree will get. Do a little research to determine which tree varieties grow well in that light and then eliminate the ones that grow too fast or too slowly for your needs.

- If you're planting the tree yourself, choose a tree with a trunk diameter — called a caliper — of 2 inches or less. Trees with larger calipers can be tough to plant on your own. "You need a professional or you need a crew to help you dig the hole and get it in," Juers explains.

- Only choose trees with a straight trunk.

- Bypass trees with scars, exposed bark, or peeled bark. These are signs of damage during unloading.

- Avoid any container tree that has very loose dirt or looks as if it fell out of its container. And check balled-and-burlapped trees closely, too. "Make sure it has a nice size ball," says Juers. "It shouldn't be square or odd-shaped, and the ball must be firm. If the ball is loose, that means it was dropped and soil has moved away from the roots, and the tree probably won't live."

Best flowering trees to shade your patio. These five trees are perfect for planting near your patio. Their gorgeous flowers and foliage are stunning year-round, and they won't grow too large.

- flowering dogwood (*Cornus florida*)

- sourwood (*Oxydendrum arboreum*)

- autumn-flowering Higan cherry (*Prunus subhirtella 'Autumnalis'*)

- Eastern redbud (*Cercis canadensis*)

- Snowdrift crabapple (*Malus 'Snowdrift'*)

Wood rot puts trees in a bad spot. Heart rot is a serious disease of hardwood timber in the South, and it also affects shade trees. It's caused by fungi that destroy the dense core, or heartwood, that supports the tree.

Although the damage takes place inside the tree, there are some outward signs of trouble. One is the appearance of a cavity in the trunk, usually near the ground. Others are too many woodpecker holes, carpenter ants coming and going from a hole in the tree, shelf-like mushrooms growing on the side of the trunk, sunken or flaking bark, and dark ooze dripping from the trunk after a rain.

You can't fix heart rot, so watch out for damage to outer layers that lets water, boring insects, and fungi get to the inside of your trees. Damage can come from broken limbs, lightning, improper pruning, or running into the tree with a tool or a truck. Make sure those little wounds heal properly, or you could lose the tree.

> Beware of invading aspen. When planting a tree near a sidewalk, sewer, or septic tank, avoid the aspen. Its roots produce suckers that can cause damage.

Bring more birds to your feeder. Give birds plenty of safe cover, and they will flock to your feeder. Plant trees around the feeder that do double duty as hiding place and food source, like serviceberries, redbuds, dogwoods, and flowering crabapples. Use trees that birds naturally love, and you'll draw more feathered friends to your buffet.

Shape a tree from a bush

Topiaries look beautiful, but they can be intimidating for the beginning gardener. Here's an easy way to shape your own.

Buy a 5-gallon boxwood and invert a tomato cage over it. Tie any loose wire ends together at the top to form a cone. Trim the bush to match the outlines of the cage. As the bush grows through the cage, use the wire sides as a clipping guide. In a few seasons, your "tree" will be ready to show off. Remove the cage and decorate your boxwood with Christmas lights for a welcoming holiday touch.

Simple trick for lush, full foliage. Force evergreen shrubs to bush out. Pinch off the buds on the ends of new branches as they appear. The plant will then put more energy into growing side buds on those same branches. The result will be a fuller-looking plant with lush, thick foliage. Just be careful not to mistake a flower bud for an end bud when you're pinching. For deciduous shrubs, cut new shoots to half their length during growing season. They'll react by sending out more side shoots.

Easy leaf-bagging for the one-person yard crew. Leaf-bagging has always been a two-person job, but now two clever tricks can help you go it alone. If you only need to fill one plastic bag, loop the bag's ties over your wheelbarrow handles so the mouth of the bag faces into the wind. Now the bag is rigged for hands-free operation. Just scoop the leaves in, and you'll soon be done.

If you expect to fill several plastic bags, lay out a tarp or shower curtain and rake the leaves onto it. When you have enough to fill a bag, roll the tarp up like a sleeping bag. Put one end into the bag, turn the tarp up on that end, and shake it so the leaves fall into the bag. When you've emptied the tarp, remove it from the bag and repeat the process for the next bag. No fuss, no muss, and no help needed.

Make an ugly tree stump fade away. Get rid of an unsightly tree stump without digging it up. This no-fuss method works wonders and saves you a boatload of cash. Drill large holes deep into the stump, especially near the edges. Fill them with sugar and soak the stump and its holes thoroughly with the hose. Cover with a foot of mulch and wait. Your tree stump will simply decay away. Or drill a few holes in the center of the stump and dump your leftover coals from the barbecue grill after every cookout. You'll burn the stump away from the inside out.

Get pine pitch off your hands with Crisco. Rub it gently on the sticky spots, then wash well with soap and water.

Trim and train your vines for garden drama

Cut creepers to avoid costly repairs. Your home's exterior is just as important as its interior. And since an exterior paint job costs between $2,000 and $4,800 for a 2,000-square-foot home, it literally pays to take care of the outside now, before it needs a complete redo. Extend the life of your current exterior and boost your curb appeal with this simple step — cut down vines.

They may give your house a rustic, cottage look, but vines crawling up your home's walls can do hidden harm. Vines trap moisture, causing wood siding to rot. They also break down the mortar on brick walls, creating tiny nooks and crannies that let moisture seep indoors.

Better to keep vines on trellises away from your house. Leave enough space between the trellis and your home for air to circulate.

Slash your cooling bills in summer. Shade trees take time to grow, so it could be years before they actually lower your cooling bills. Get relief in the meantime. Plant a fast-growing annual climber, like moonflower, morning glory, or scarlet runner bean, under south- and west-facing windows in spring.

Give them a trellis or other structure to climb, and they'll block the intense summer rays that heat your home. Live in an apartment or condo? Plant them in window boxes, instead. Come autumn, cut them back or let them die back from the cold to let in warming winter light.

Save your money. Don't bother fertilizing vigorous, fast-growing climbers like wisteria and trumpet vine. Feeding them once a year actually results in fewer blooms. They'll put the extra nutrients into growing stems rather than flowers.

Give climbing plants extra oomph. Fertilizer isn't just for leaves and roots. You can spray it on the wall, too, to give climbing vines a boost. Once you've planted your climbers, or after you've pruned them back, spray their wall support with a liquid foliar fertilizer. The plants will absorb it as they climb.

Easy-to-make supports for wall climbers. Not all vines are built for climbing. Some lack tendrils that twine or suckers that stick. They need help going vertical, but setting supports in brick, stucco, and wood can be a lot of work. Simplify things with some silicone sealant and twist ties.

- Head to the hardware store for a tube of clear, 100 per-cent silicone caulk.

- Fish out the extra twist ties you've saved from packages of garbage bags.

- Dab a spot of caulk in each place you want your climbing vine to cling.

- Bend the twist tie in half, and stick the bottom into the caulk.

- Do this up the length of wall you want the climber to cover.

- Let the caulk dry, then begin tying your vines. Place a vine into each tie and twist it closed.

You can spray-paint the ties green or black, so they blend in with the plant. When it's time to prune back the climber, simply untie the vines.

Avoid trellis damage by tying. Tie vines and canes loosely to a trellis or fence rather than threading the stems through the structure. If you simply weave a stem in and out of trellis bars, it will tear the frame apart as it grows and push it away from supporting walls.

Support vines that don't cling naturally. Grapevines attach themselves to the base they are climbing on with tendrils. English ivy clings with hold-fast rootlets. Twiners, like clematis and morning glory, wrap themselves around a post or a tree trunk. But some vines need your help to stay off the ground. For support, screw metal cup hooks into a fence post or trellis. If you need to tie the vine to the hooks, use soft green yarn so it won't show or hurt the vine.

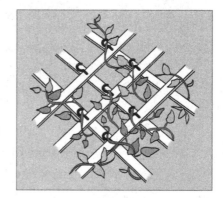

Become a topiary master. Wire hangers become garden art when you recycle them into beautiful topiary frames. Just bend the hanger into whatever shape you like, then unbend the hook and drive it into the ground. Plant dwarf ivy around the base and keep an eye on its vines, making sure they attach themselves to the wire. Before long, the ivy will have transformed your old hanger into a little green man, or animal, or your favorite letter of the alphabet.

Dress up mailbox with the ideal vine. Vines twining 'round your mailbox may look romantic, but the wrong ones can easily take over. Ensure your mailman can open the box by choosing dwarf varieties of your favorite climbers. Dwarf clematis and miniature roses are just the right size for a short support, like a mailbox post.

Relax among fragrant flowers. Twine fragrant, flowering plants on an arbor, trellis, or pergola, and you'll gain a serenely scented spot that tempts anyone to linger. Jasmines and honeysuckles are sweet selections. So are variegated kiwi vine, evergreen clematis, and mountain clematis. Rose lovers can plant "New Dawn" for fragrant pink roses or "Wedding Day" for aromatic white roses.

Perennial vines take time to fill out and fill in. Bulk them up by interplanting with annuals for almost-instant greenery. Mix in a few sweet pea, morning glory, or nasturtium climbers amongst your slower-growing woody perennials for the first few years.

Camouflage your compost bin. Plant shrubs to screen your compost bin from offended neighbors. Sunflowers, tomatoes, or pumpkins will also do the trick. If your compost bin is made of chicken wire, you can even plant flowering vines to climb it. Whatever living camouflage you choose to plant should spring up in no time, thanks to all the nutrients leaching into the soil from the compost pile.

Pruning: 'shear' genius tips to clip and snip

Simple rule of thumb for right-time pruning. The best time to trim your trees and flowering shrubs depends on when they bloom. Follow this rule for the most abundant blooms ever.

- Shrubs that bloom in the spring, such as azaleas and rhododendrons, flower on old growth. Prune them just after their flowers fade.

- Shrubs that bloom in the summer and fall, like rose of Sharon, flower on new growth. Prune them in the early spring when they are still dormant from winter.

- Deciduous trees, including elms and oaks, do best when pruned late in the winter.

Following this schedule lets shrubs recover from pruning before it's time to bloom again.

Wash tools to stop diseases. Clean the blades of your pruning tools after each use either with denatured alcohol or a mild solution of one part bleach to nine parts water. This is especially important after trimming diseased plants. Be sure to wash the bleach mixture off the metal blades with soapy water. It may be a hassle, but cleaning your tools can help stop the spread of plant diseases and save you heartache later.

The best way to hold shears. Check your grip before clipping valuable plants. Hold pruning shears with the thin, narrow blade toward the part of the plant you are keeping, and the thick, heavy blade toward the branch you are pruning off. The branch you remove will take the brunt of any messy, crushing damage done by the lower blade, while the thin blade will leave a clean cut on the part of the plant that stays.

Feed plants after pruning. Pruning makes plants hungry, especially hard pruning. Feed pruned plants in spring with a general fertilizer and mulch around them with the compost of your choice. This dose of nutrients will help it put out fresh growth triggered by your pruning.

Expert advice for crape myrtles. Some people think these trees won't bloom without a hard pruning every year. Not true. In fact, cutting them back severely actually invites pests and disease. You can prune them, but you don't have to. They will thrive without it. If you want to trim them, simply prune them for health like any other tree, removing dead limbs, crossing branches, and low-growing suckers.

Hard prune plants to get more growth out of weak greenery. The more you cut it back, the stronger it will return. On the other hand, a strongly growing plant needs just a little light pruning to keep it healthy.

First aid for ailing shrubs. Neglected shrubs need tender loving care. Hard prune them after their growing season with an aim to remove dead, choked, or unhealthy branches. This opens up the center to let in more light and air. You can rehabilitate these special patients all at once in a single year, but not all plants do well with hard pruning. If your plant doesn't, spread out this work over two or three years.

Level hedge tops with ease. Cut a foolproof straight line across the top of your hedges with two sticks and a string. Drive a tall stake into the ground at each end of your hedge, and tie a string between them at the height you want to clip the hedge. Make sure the string is taut. Use it as a guideline while pruning, and you'll have a straight line every time.

To cut or not to cut

Prune a tree's limbs for one of three reasons — first to ensure safety, second for the health of the tree, and third to make it look beautiful. Next time you do maintenance pruning on a tree, use this branch-size decision guide to figure out what to cut off.

- For a branch less than 2 inches in diameter, go ahead and cut.

- Between 2 and 4 inches in diameter, think twice before you cut.

- More than 4 inches in diameter, be sure there's a good reason to cut.

Trimming protects wind-blown trees. Strengthen your trees with proper pruning, especially if you live where high winds are common. Take out small, inside branches that can catch the wind and break off the larger limbs. Then the wind can pass through the tree instead of blowing it down. No matter where you live, keep dead and damaged limbs pruned to reduce the energy load on your trees. Good pruning practices will also pay off when snow and ice storms add undue weight to limbs and branches.

Avoid mistakes that disfigure trees. Don't make the unkindest cut of all. Prune your trees skillfully so you won't lose the extra branches — or the whole tree — to disease. Before you cut, find the node, the place where one branch or twig connects to another. Cut near the node, but don't cut too closely or peel bark off the tree.

These mistakes — called bark ripping, flush cutting, and stub cutting — can leave the tree open to damage, disease, and dead branches. But if you prune correctly, the neatly pruned branches make great stakes for flowers and vegetables. Not only do they provide a charming, natural look, they also help you spend less money on stakes.

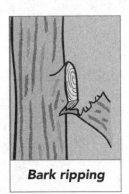
Bark ripping

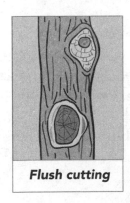
Flush cutting

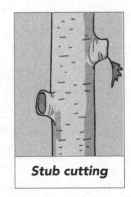
Stub cutting

The latest news on dressing wounds. Skip the wound dressing and pruning paint for most trees. Research has shown that applying it to cuts only makes you feel better, not the tree. It won't cure an existing infection or stop decay. It may even slow the healing process and keep the wound from closing.

The only time you should use wound dressing — when treating a pruning cut or other injury on an elm or oak. Applying pruning paint during the elm's growing season or to the oak in spring can help protect these species from Dutch elm disease and oak wilt.

Bring a lopsided shrub or tree back in balance with wise pruning. Cut back the weakest shoots hard, but only prune the tips of the strong branches. Continue doing this each year until the weak stems have filled in enough to balance the plant.

Secret to safe offseason pruning. The correct time to prune your favorite tree was months ago, but dead and low-growing branches are a problem now. Fortunately, you may not need to wait. Experts say you should avoid pruning 15 percent or more of the top of the tree except during its correct pruning season. But light pruning — less than 10 percent of the plant — can be done any time of year.

Be careful if the tree is an oak or elm because pruning these hardwoods at the wrong time of year can lead to tree-killing diseases. Play it safe and contact your local cooperative extension agent for advice before pruning these trees.

Pick the method for best effect. There's no way around it — if you have rosebushes, they will need pruning. You may need to prune a larger bush to keep it within bounds, and you should remove rootstock suckers if they appear. These are easy to recognize as light green and typically covered with lots of thorns. A healthy bush can be pruned to a couple of feet from the ground. Decide what results you want, then choose the pruning method to produce a variety of brilliant blossoms. Here are three ways you can prune.

- Light pruning will lead to lots of small flowers on short stems.

- Moderate pruning leaves more canes on the bush.

- Severe pruning will produce longer canes and a few larger flowers.

Get the most blooms from your rosebushes. Before you snip that gorgeous rose, be sure to cut at the right spot. Otherwise, your plant will produce tiny, weak stems that won't hold up your stunning rose. When you're pruning or clipping, cut back to a stem with at least five leaves. Your rosebush will thank you by putting out a stronger stem that can support the weight of more rose blossoms.

Know when to cut straight. You can't cut all stems at an angle. Some plants produce buds side-by-side. In these cases, making a sloping cut at one bud would damage the other. Compromise — make a pruning cut straight across just above the two buds. Although generally not recommended, a straight cut is the only way to prune these stems without harming the buds.

Pinch for amazing flower displays. You know pinch pruning prompts a plant to bush out with side growth. Did you know you can use this technique to create incredible displays of blooms? Pinching out shoots delays flowering. If you stop pinching them during their blooming season, the shoots will all set buds and flower at the same time — about one to two months after you stop pinching.

Root prune rather than repot. Root pruning is a good alternative to repotting overgrown houseplants. Slip the plant out of its pot, grabbing it by the root ball rather than the stems. Gently pull out the roots to ease compaction, and shake out some of the old soil. Prune about a third of the smaller roots with a pair of sharp shears, but leave the larger, feeder roots untouched. Repot it in fresh soil, then cut back about one-third of the top growth. Never remove more than a third of the total roots on a plant.

> Don't pinch off more than one-third of the leaves at a time when training your climbing topiary. Otherwise, the plant may go into shock. To remove all the leaves along a stem, prune gradually over several weeks.

Clip to help transplants survive. Tired of transplants dying? Scale back their top growth to give them a better chance in your yard. A container-grown plant may have more leaves and stems than its roots can support after the shock of being transplanted. Prune off some of this growth after planting to help it gain a foothold in its new home.

Cut ornamental grasses without the mess. It's time to trim your ornamental grass, and you're not looking forward to picking up cut blades of grass off the ground. But this year will be different because you will do less clean up. Here's how. If your garbage collectors allow you to dump trimmings in your trash can, bring the can near the plants you will be working on.

Before trimming each plant, grab a bungee cord, rope, or some duct tape, and wrap it around the grass above where you plan to cut. Make sure this "holder" won't come loose and then start trimming. When done, you should have a neatly wrapped bundle on the ground, and you can dispose of it easily in the nearby trash can.

Pick the right pruner for the job. When it's time to cut branches from trees or large bushes, pick a cutting tool based on the size of the limb so you don't damage the plant or ruin your tool.

- Hand pruners work for branches less than one-half inch in diameter.

- Lopping shears are best for branches between one-half inch and 1 inch in diameter.

- A pruning saw is ideal for branches larger than 1 inch in diameter.

    If you need to make a cut on a branch high off the ground, look for a pole pruner with a lightweight fiberglass pole.

Earth-friendly ways to wipe out creepy-crawlies

All natural bug repellents and insecticides — straight from your kitchen. Repel ants, mosquitoes, and other pests without a drop of toxic chemicals.

- Coffee grounds. Coffee perks you up — and so will this news. Ants hate coffee grounds. Sprinkle coffee grounds around your plants, yard, garden, and the outside of your house to keep ants away.

- Cloves. Snip an old pair of pantyhose into sections, tie off one end of each section, fill it with whole cloves, and tie off the other end. Tuck these sachets into drawers and closets to get rid of moths.

- Dish soap. Mix one tablespoon of mild dishwashing liquid — not dishwasher detergent — in a gallon of water. Apply this to your plants to repel or kill red spider mites, thrips, mealy bugs, and aphids. Like store-bought insecticidal soap, this may burn the leaves on some sensitive plants. Test a small area before applying to the whole plant.

- Garlic. Put two cups of water and one garlic bulb in your blender. Blend, strain, and pour into a spray bottle. Coat the leaves and stems of plants under attack from white-flies, beetles, deer, or aphids. This only stops pests for a week, but it may last longer if you add a few drops of mild liquid soap, like pure Castile soap.

- Tea leaves. Surround a plant with a circle of tea leaves and coffee grounds to keep slugs away.

- Crushed eggshells. Crush some eggshells, and spread them around a plant that needs protection from slugs. The slugs can't handle those sharp edges.

- Citrus rind. Halve a grapefruit, scoop out the pulp, and place the rind, round side up, near a slug-damaged plant in your garden. Check this trap once a day for slugs.

- Rosemary. Grow rose-mary in your yard or in a pot to help repel mosqui-toes. Sprinkle rosemary and sage on barbecue coals when you cook out-side to keep the annoying pests away.

> Make your own insectici-dal soap for pennies. Mix three-fourths teaspoon of Murphy's Oil Soap into 1 quart of water and then show insects who really owns your plants.

Garlic clears out garden pests. The wonderful smell of cooking garlic can draw a crowd in your kitchen. Fortu-nately for your garden, garlic isn't as tempting to deer, insects, and mites. You can use this fragrant herb to keep garden pests away.

- Dust some garlic powder directly on your plants.

- Plant garlic between rows of vegetables or near roses, raspberries, and fruit trees. Garlic keeps aphids away from roses, red spiders away from tomatoes, and Japanese beetles away from raspberries. It also repels weevils, carrot flies, moles, and fruit tree borers.

- Spray your plants. Some commercial deer repellents use garlic as an active ingredient, but you can make your own garlic spray. Just blend six cloves of garlic, an onion, and one tablespoon each of cayenne pepper and biodegradable dishwashing liquid. Add a quart of water, let it steep for 24 hours, and strain.

Clever combos for a pest-free garden. Some herbs and flowers give off strong odors that confuse pests or drive them away. Sage, carrots, and plants in the cabbage family all produce odors that ward off each other's pests. French marigolds drive greenflies and black flies away from tomatoes. Here are a few more clever combinations.

Plant this	To repel this
basil among tomatoes	tomato hornworms
nasturtiums near squash	squash bugs
tomatoes among asparagus	asparagus beetles
marigolds, mint, thyme, or chamomile	cabbage moths
carrots with leeks or onions	onion flies, leek moths, carrot flies

Prickly plant serves two garden purposes. The stinging nettle is a mysterious plant. It attracts beautiful butterflies to your garden and repels pests. Royal Admiral butterflies lay their eggs on the underside of the plant's leaves so their young can chomp on the leaves as soon as they hatch.

If you look long enough, you'll probably spot some beauties. But you can also turn the stinging nettle into a powerful pesticide. Steep the stems and leaves in a bucket of water for 24 hours. Remove them and use the water, which now contains formic acid from the stinging nettle, to kill mites and aphids on your plants.

> Sick of seeing your tomatoes being eaten by tomato hornworms? Plant marigolds around the tomato plants in your garden. It's an easy and natural way to keep those crawling green caterpillars away.

Wipe out bugs with milk jugs. Turn a harmless, plastic milk jug into a deadly bug killer. Just toss in a cup of sugar, a cup of vinegar, and a banana peel. Leave the jug open, and hang it from a tree or set it in your garden. All the bugs that have been munching on your fruits and vegetables will be lured to the milk jug — and their doom.

Stop cutworms with 3 clever tricks. Pick your favorite or try all three.

- Draw the outline of a comma around the plant using a small amount of cornmeal. The worms will die when they eat it.

- Make a protective collar to fence out cutworms. Cut the bottom half off a 3-ounce or 5-ounce plastic cup, and use the top half as a collar. For smaller plants, cut a toilet tissue roll into two rings, or make a similar ring from stiff paper. Press the collar 1 inch deep into the soil.

- Sink a nail into the soil beside the stem of each tomato plant, leaving the head 2 inches above the ground. This prevents the cutworm from wrapping itself around the plant's stem, so it cannot ravish your tomatoes.

Grow this natural pest control every year. These delightful flowers actually deter harmful bugs from your tomatoes, roses, peas, and more. That is why French marigolds were probably in your grandmother's garden. Rediscover what they can do for you today.

Plant these marigolds among roses or tomatoes — or plant roses or tomatoes where French marigolds grew last year. Scientists have discovered the roots of French marigolds produce compounds that can repel or kill nematodes — a type of worm — that love to munch on roses, beans, spinach, tomatoes, and celery. French marigolds may help protect potatoes from eelworms.

Here's a sweet solution to your nematode problem. Till in 3 pounds of sugar per acre in early spring and again in late fall. You'll find no more damage from nematodes.

For best results, plant them throughout your garden.

Bug-busting combinations. When you're planning your next garden, consider these "companion plantings" to help keep down the bug population:

- Plant radishes with your squash plants to keep away squash bugs.

- Marigolds repel aphids, Colorado potato beetles, whiteflies, and even rabbits.

- Grow basil around your eggplants and tomatoes to keep away pests.

- Try sage, rosemary, and thyme with cabbage to repel cabbage worms.

- Onions keep bugs away from beets.

- Borage will defend your tomatoes against the dreaded tomato hornworm.

- Garlic will keep aphids away from almost anything.

Stop insects and disease with seaweed. Keep pests away from your plants with underwater vegetation. A healthy garden is the best defense against insects and disease. Seaweed contains iron, zinc, barium, calcium, sulfur, and magnesium. These trace elements make it wonderful for promoting growth and giving plants the strength to fight off enemy attacks. Apply seaweed fertilizer either as a mulch or a spray and watch your garden grow strong.

Invite pest eaters to patrol your garden. Imagine a garden where you never need pesticides because your own personal pest police constantly sweep it clean. You can have that garden if you attract bugs and animals that eat your pests — and you can grow charming plants to do it.

- Plant holly, elderberry, dogwood, barberry, or cotoneaster to invite insect-eating birds for a snack.

- Grow borage or sweet alyssum among your flowers or vegetables. Aphid eaters love them.

Just remember that pesticides will harm your insect eaters, so avoid using them.

Simple way to summon pest-eating bugs. Some people fight fire with fire. You can fight bugs with bugs. Although some bugs eat or damage garden plants, others eat those plant-eating pests. Pest-eating bugs are called beneficials, and you can invite them to dinner by growing plants that produce plenty of pollen and nectar.

For example, attract ladybugs to your garden by planting flowers like zinnias, yarrow, aster, daisies, and sunflowers, or herbs such as parsley, coriander, anise, or fennel. Grow these near your pest-plagued plants, and the ladybugs will reward you. They will eat the aphids, mites, scale, thrips, and other pests right off your plants.

Spined soldier bugs defend your garden. Don't go to war with the spined soldier bug, a stink bug that feeds on the larval forms of many beetles and moths. It's pale brown, shield-shaped, about the size of your thumbnail, and feeds by sucking out its prey's internal juices with a long beak it keeps folded under its body.

The helpful spined soldier bug is quite sensitive to pesticides. So if you see them around, don't spray. Let them kill your pests instead. Their prey includes the Mexican bean beetle, diamondback moth, corn earworm, cabbage looper, Colorado potato beetle, and flea beetle.

Halt home invasion by lady beetle. The multicolored Asian lady beetle eats aphids, just like domestic ladybugs. But she ranges in color from bright red-orange to pale yellow-orange and can also make a pest of herself — she likes to come inside your house for the winter.

When the Asian lady beetle is excited, she emits a sticky, yellow substance that smells awful and gets all over your things. Don't use pesticides on these good bugs, but seal up cracks and windows where they might gain entry. If they get inside anyway, use a vacuum or a broom and dustpan to gently gather them up and take them back outside.

> Foil an insect's plan for your garden. Use strips of aluminum foil as mulch in your garden, around corn, cucumbers, and squash. The reflective ability of aluminum foil repels many types of insects.

Frogs help garden pests croak. Frogs feast on many of the same bugs you're probably trying to chase out of your garden. In fact, if you stop using pesticides and herbicides, frogs could help wipe out your pests for pennies. Here's how to invite these helpful hoppers in for a snack.

- If you have a pond, add native plants around the sides to give frogs a place to hide from trouble. Let some algae grow to nurture baby frogs. Don't add goldfish, or your frogs won't live long.

- Make frog houses from piles of rock, wood, or leaves. Be sure to leave a doorway and frog-size space inside.

- If you don't have a pond or water nearby, tuck a few water-filled terra-cotta saucers under bushes or other shady, protected spots. Be sure to include a little dirt in the bottom to make them more pond-like. These saucers give your frogs a watering hole to visit. Just remember to keep them filled.

Turn to toads for pest control

Make toads feel at home in your garden, and they will make unwanted pests disappear. A toad can gobble up 50 to 100 insects each night. That means fewer mosquitoes, flies, and slugs in your backyard. It's not difficult to lure toads to your garden. Just provide them with a place to live.

While you can buy commercial toad houses, broken clay flowerpots work just as well. Turn the pot upside down, so the broken rim acts as a doorway. Or set it on its side and partially sink it into the ground. Place the pot in a damp, shady location and wait for a toad to show up.

To make it safer for toads, avoid using pesticides or other chemicals in the area. You'll quickly discover that toads make good neighbors — warts and all.

Amazing tricks to make ants disappear. Ant problems? Learn how to foil, trap, lure, repel, and kill the little pests — keeping them out of your home and yard for good. Dozens of solutions can be found right in your own pantry. Here are a few of them.

- White vinegar. Don't let ant colonies build condos on your lawn. Pour this simple solution on the hills and watch them vacate the premises. Spray full-strength vinegar near doors and windowsills to keep ants out of your home, as well. Repeat if needed.

- Water. Pouring boiling water on anthills also works. Make things even hotter by adding several drops of hot chili oil to the water. Just as with vinegar, you may need to do this more than once, but it will eventually get the job done. Spray soapy water on your countertops and sinks to keep ants away or spray it directly on ants to kill them.

- Salt. Seasoned ant fighters know that ants won't cross salt. Sprinkle it around doorways, windowsills, and anywhere else ants may enter. Ants also won't cross a line of chalk, flour, or baby powder. To fight fire ants, switch to Epsom salts. Pour an inch over their mounds and another inch around the mound.

- Baking soda. Leave some baking soda in areas where you've seen ants. It should kill them. You can also mix equal parts baking soda and salt, and sprinkle the mixture in problem areas.

- Cream of Wheat. Sprinkle dry Cream of Wheat around the perimeter of your room or pour it on an anthill. When ants eat it, it expands in their stomach and kills them. Minute Rice works the same way.

- Orange peels. Citrus fruits contain natural pesticides. Put orange peels and water in your blender, and blend until smooth. Then dump the mixture on anthills early in the morning, before ants leave their nest.

- Borax. Mix borax with powdered sugar or maple syrup. The mixture will lure and poison ants. Don't use this method if you have kids or pets.

Spray away unwanted guests. If black pepper is nothing for garden pests to sneeze at, a few cayenne peppers will really burn them. Ants, spiders, caterpillars, and cabbage worms are just a few of the bothersome friends who won't appreciate the extra spice in their lives. To make an effective spray, just blend up a few dried cayennes with water in a blender.

Plants that keep away ants. Keep ants away from your house and garden with plants that have natural defense systems against insects. Ants particularly don't like three members of the mint family — peppermint, spearmint, and pennyroyal.

Southernwood, a fragrant and shrubby relative of sage brush and wormwood, is another ant repellent. Also try onions,

Herbs and spices make ants vanish. If you know where ants are coming into your home, sprinkle cinnamon, black pepper, chili powder, bay leaves, or dried mint to block their trail. Ants don't like to cross these substances.

chives, sage, and catnip. And plant tansy next to your peonies. It rejects the little sugar ants that crawl all over peonies and kitchen cabinets. If the mints and tansy are too aggressive for you, grow them somewhere else and spread cuttings to shoo the ants.

Foil fire ants the old-fashioned way. All ants are annoying, but fire ants are also dangerous. These vicious pests boast a painful bite. A swarm of them could even kill a small child. Luckily, you can stop them with an ancient Chinese secret — diatomaceous earth.

The Chinese have been using this nontoxic powder for 2,000 years. Diatomaceous earth, or D.E., is a natural powdery substance that pokes and dehydrates ants as they walk across it. It's perfect for indoor ant trails. You can find D.E. in garden shops and hardware stores.

Diatomaceous earth doesn't work as well when applied directly to an ant mound. But it may help other pesticides work better because it penetrates ants' bodies. In fact, some formulations of insecticides called pyrethrins include D.E. to boost their effectiveness.

Protect your plants from aphids with tea. Just follow these instructions:

- Bruise two large handfuls of basil leaves and stems, and drop them in a gallon jar.

- Pour in one gallon of water, and let sit in the sun for four to eight hours.

- Strain through a mesh strainer, or use a section of pantyhose if you don't have one. Add several drops of liquid hand soap, and shake to mix.

- Spray this tea remedy on your plants to fight aphids, leafhoppers, grubs, squash bugs, mites, cabbage loopers, and cucumber beetles.

Try this low-cost milk mixture that spells the end to an aphid infestation. Just prepare nonfat dry milk according to the package directions, pour in a spray bottle, and coat your plant leaves with it. This may also prevent viruses spread by aphids.

Solve aphid problems naturally. To drive away aphids, combine 2 tablespoons of minced garlic, one-half cup of parsley flakes, and 3 cups of water. Boil it down to 2 cups, then strain the mixture and let it cool. Take 1 cup of the mixture, put it in a hose-end sprayer, and spray your plants.

Invite lacewings to an aphid feast. Lacewings are bugs that love to eat aphids, but they need a place to sleep off those heavy meals. Make one of these homes to tempt them to stick around.

- Cane cabin. Tie a bundle of hollow bamboo canes and twigs together with twine. Secure it with more twine near each end of the bundle. Create a rustic look by tucking pine straw or twigs beneath the twine.

- Tubular townhouse. Cut the top and bottom off a 2-liter soft drink bottle so only a plastic tube remains. Measure the length of the tube. Cut a piece of corrugated cardboard slightly shorter than that tube. Roll up the cardboard, and insert it into the tube.

Hang your new lacewing house outside. Make sure it is protected from rain and will not blow away in the wind.

Scare off mosquitoes with the power of flowers

Enjoy grilling out this summer without swarms of biting insects or toxic chemical insect repellants. A natural plant chemical derived from flowers repels mosquitoes, fleas, deer ticks, houseflies, and fire ants.

It's called geraniol, and it's made from geraniums, lemon grass, and other plants.

Researchers in Florida spent 17 years testing nearly 4,000 natural chemicals to find one to rival the pesticide DEET. Vegetable gardeners already know to plant geraniums to ward off pests like beetles and cabbage worms. So they probably wouldn't be surprised to learn that geraniol was five times as effective as citronella candles at keeping away mosquitoes.

You'll find geraniol in the form of sprays, granules, infused wristbands, and towelettes from BugBand.

But since geraniol has also been used to attract bees for pollination, it may attract bees to you as well, so beware.

Mighty methods to minimize mosquitoes. Itching for an easy way to keep mosquitoes away? Look no further than marigolds. To repel mosquitoes and other flying insects, plant this flower in your garden. It's beautiful and functional. That's because the unpleasant smell of marigold flowers drives away pests. You can also place potted marigolds on your porch or deck to defend against mosquitoes.

Marigolds aren't the only plants that discourage mosquitoes. But for the others to be effective, you need to crush the leaves or stems and rub them on your skin. Catnip, rosemary, and lemon thyme can ward off mosquitoes this way. Test a small patch of your skin first to make sure it's not too sensitive.

Check out these other simple tricks to get rid of annoying mosquitoes.

- Sidestep standing water. Remove any unnecessary puddles in pots, drainage ditches, gutters, and anywhere else water may accumulate in your yard. Change the water in your birdbath, vases, or pool frequently. Standing water serves as a breeding ground for mosquitoes.

- Defend yourself with dryer sheets. Dryer sheets act as a natural bug repellent. Hang a dryer sheet on your patio or tuck one into your cuff or neckline to drive away mosquitoes.

- Slather on a scent. Keep mosquitoes away by making yourself smell horrible to them. Dab some lavender oil on your wrists and elbows. Or rub a slice of onion on your skin. Orange and lemon peels also do the trick. You can also dilute some vanilla extract in water, and wipe the mixture on your skin.

- Vex mosquitoes with vinegar. Add two teaspoons of apple cider vinegar to a glass of water and set it on your deck or porch. You can also use a cotton ball to rub white vinegar on your skin.

Battle mosquitoes with bats. In the comic books, Gotham City flashed the Bat Signal to summon Batman to the rescue. You don't need a superhero to fight mosquitoes, but you can still summon some winged help. Just build or buy a bat house to lure bats to your property.

Why do you want to lure bats? Because bats gobble up mosquitoes and other pesky insects. In fact, a bat can eat up to 1,000 mosquitoes an hour.

For cheap, nontoxic mosquito control, install a bat house. Also known as a bat box, a bat house is open at the bottom with a roof on top. It's very narrow, unlike a birdhouse, because bats like tight spaces. They also like it warm, so you should paint the box a dark color to absorb the sun's rays. However, if summer temperatures regularly exceed 95 degrees where you live, a lighter color will do. The inside of the box should be rough to simulate the bark of a tree and to give bats something to cling to.

Hang your bat house on a tree, a pole, or a building. Place it in a sunny spot about 15 feet high. Your mosquito problem should be solved. As a bonus, providing bats with an alternative roost will keep them out of your house.

Repel mosquitoes with fragrant plants. You may love the fragrance of basil growing in your garden, but mosquitoes have a different take. They dislike the smell and will stay clear of your garden or patio where it's growing. And the tansy plant, with its pretty flowers, also smells bad to mosquitoes. So plant it, as well, to keep your yard a pest-free zone.

Think twice about bug zappers

Don't believe the claims that electronic bug zappers will rid your yard of mosquitoes. They actually kill more good insects — the ones that eat the eggs and larvae of the bugs that bite you — than they do 'skeeters. They also attract insects to your yard that wouldn't normally be there. You'll do more good by getting rid of standing water and other places in your yard where mosquitoes breed.

Wage war on annoying mosquitoes. There are many ways to deter mosquitoes, but not many are chemical-free. Tell them to buzz off with these clever ideas that are safe for you and your family.

- Sandalwood incense sticks. The scent of sandalwood is an effective mosquito repellant. An Australian study found that this natural method was up to 73 percent as effective as DEET, a chemical insecticide that can affect your nervous system. What's more, sandalwood smells better and has none of the side effects. Place the incense sticks in the ground — start with one in front of you and one behind. Light them and you're ready to work in your garden. You can buy these sticks inexpensively online or at a local flea market.

- Battery-powered fan. A breeze of just 2 mph will stop a mosquito from getting where it wants to go. Let that portable fan on your desk do double duty in your garden. Place it on the ground and tilt it, or raise it up on an overturned bucket. You'll keep cool, and those pesky critters will be blown away.

- Sticky bug bat. Staple a plastic lid to a paint stir stick and smear it with petroleum jelly on one side. When mosquitoes — or other unwanted flying visitors — come calling, you'll be ready to stop them in midair. Or try an old ping pong paddle or a fly swatter covered with a plastic bag. Just make sure the sticky stuff is on the up side when you rest your bat on the ground.

What really works against mosquitoes. Victoria's Secret has a "secret" that may surprise you. Douse yourself with its perfume Bombshell, and you can kiss bothersome mosquitoes goodbye!

A recent study discovered that the perfume works almost as effectively as the repellent DEET. Instead of attracting mosquitoes, as researchers expected, the fragrance repelled the insects for over two hours. They think it's because Bombshell masks natural body odors, which attract mosquitoes.

You'll need more than a light spritz, though. Try these other products for proven-to-work protection.

- Defeat bugs with DEET. DEET has long been the king of bug repellents, but many people are concerned about harmful side effects. Products containing between 7 percent and 30 percent DEET seem to be the safest and most effective, say scientists. Anything higher than 30 percent can trigger health problems like skin irritations and seizures. And anything below 7 percent won't protect you for very long.

- Put on pretreated apparel. Clothing manufacturers like Burlington make shirts and pants pretreated with the insecticide permethrin. The chemical works by killing mosquitoes when they land on you or by keeping them away from you. You would still need to treat exposed skin, including face and hands, and any untreated clothing.

- Another option is to buy a can of permethrin and spray on your outdoor wear. The insecticide remains effective after several washings.

- Spray on semi-natural substitutes. Sprays containing 20 percent picaridin or 30 percent oil of lemon eucalyptus performed as well as DEET in a *Consumer Reports* test. Picaridin contains compounds similar to the piperine found in black pepper. The gum eucalyptus tree produces oil of lemon eucalyptus. Both products have less serious side effects than DEET.

Banish bees with herbs and spices. Garlic, cinnamon, and peppermint — three very different flavors with one thing in common. Bees hate them.

Make a spray adding a few squirts of dishwashing soap to water. Add either cinnamon, crushed garlic, or peppermint oil to the solution, and spray it around your house. Or better yet, place pots of peppermint on your porch or patio.

To rid your pool or garden fountain of honeybees, mix one-fourth cup dishwashing soap with about a quart of water in a spray bottle. Spray the bees directly while they're buzzing around near the water. They will die in an environmentally friendly way. When they don't return to their colony, the rest of the bees won't know where to find the water source.

Is Avon's Skin So Soft legit?

Some people swear by it, but does it really work? Yes, but only if you use the right product. Both Skin So Soft Bath Oil and Skin So Soft Bug Guard offer protection, but they work on different types of mosquitoes.

In one study, the bath oil protected against the *Aedes aegypti* variety of mosquito, but was ineffective against *Aedes albopictus*. The bug guard had the opposite results. If you're a fan of Skin So Soft products, you may want to experiment to see which works best in your neighborhood.

Put the sting on wasps and bees. Banish wasps, bees, and yellow jackets with an easy homemade trap. Just use a 2-liter bottle about half full of sugary water. The flying invaders will crawl in and drown. It works even better if you cut off the top and invert it back inside the base. Secure it to the top with tape. Punch holes in the sides and hang your trap about 4 feet off the ground for best results.

Learn to like wasps. Several varieties of small, stingless, parasitic wasps feed on the eggs of other insects. Even the dreaded yellow jacket can bring over 225 flies an hour to a nest to feed its young. It also drags caterpillars home from your garden. Other wasps lay eggs among the larvae of leaf-eating caterpillars, aphids, flies, and beetles. When they hatch, it's the baby wasps that win. Attract good wasps to your garden by growing flowers from carrots, celery, parsley, and Queen Anne's lace.

Give your wasps a house-warming present they won't forget. Attach a hose-end spray bottle filled with ammonia onto your garden hose and turn on the water. Then soak the wasps and their nest. The ammonia shower will kill the wasps at once and eventually topple the nest.

Head off cicada damage in prized plants. Cicadas may not show up every year, but they can still damage some of your best landscaping plants. To lay their eggs, female cicadas split open branches in your small fruit trees, small yard trees, and shrubs, causing them to brown and wilt. In fact, some plants may lose most of their branches. Here's what to do when you hear cicadas are coming.

- Cover threatened bushes and trees with cheesecloth, tulle, or another netting with holes less than one-half inch wide.

- Tie the bottom of the netting with twine to close it off, and secure it around the trunk with clothespins.

- Skip large, mature trees or any plants that lack woody stems or branches. These plants can either avoid or recover from cicada damage.

- Unwrap your netted trees when local authorities give the all-clear, usually in July or August.

Scents-ible ways to repel flies. Make your home smell wonderful while making it less welcoming for flying pests. A little peppermint or lavender should do the trick. Tell pesky flies to "buzz off" with these scented oils. They smell lovely to people, but keep flies far, far away. Soak some cotton balls with these oils, and leave them around your house to discourage insect intruders.

You can also shoo away flies with other pleasant scents. Plant mint around the outside of your home or place sachets of crushed mint inside to repel flies. Potted sweet basil plants also keep flies at bay. Cloves work, too. Hang clusters of cloves or small bags of ground cloves in your home. Flies hate the smell of citrus. For a natural repellent, scratch the peel of an orange and place it where flies like to hang out.

> Say goodbye to fruit flies. Grow basil in window boxes and in pots near your doors to keep fruit flies from entering your house.

Send spider mites packing. You think your plants have spider mites because they have bronzed, scorched, or distorted leaves — or even webbing. Hold a piece of white paper under a leaf and tap the leaf with a pencil. Examine the paper with a magnifying glass. If small spots appear on the paper and move around, you may have spider mites. Here's how to fight back.

- Add peat moss around the base of outdoor plants and set potted plants on plates of water. Mist or spray the plants several times a day. Spray the undersides of leaves with a strong stream of water to dislodge the mites.

- Move plants out of direct sunlight or shade them during the hot, late afternoon hours.

- Mix equal parts water and rubbing alcohol together and either spray it on the plant or pour it on a cotton ball and wipe down the leaves. Rinse the plants a few hours later. Before using this on the entire plant, test a small area first.

Make horticultural oil spray at home. Common household ingredients can defend roses and hydrangeas from disease-causing bugs and mites. Mix 1 tablespoon of biodegradable dishwashing liquid with a cup of corn oil, safflower oil, peanut oil, sunflower oil, or soybean oil. Then add 2 cups of water. This horticultural oil spray will snuff out pests so your flowers can flourish.

Cabbage, broccoli, cauli-flower, and Brussels sprouts are all defenseless victims of the cabbage moth. Well, maybe not so defenseless. Add a little spice to the garden and a little protection against the cabbage moth by planting some mint, sage, dill, or thyme.

Enjoy a flea-free yard without harmful chemicals. Grow plenty of the plants fleas hate, and grow them throughout your yard. Try favorites like pennyroyal, fennel, rosemary, and basil. Chrysanthemums may also help because they are the source of pyrethrum, an insecticide used against fleas. For extra coverage where no flea-fighting plants grow, harvest some fennel or rosemary, or crush pennyroyal or dried basil leaves. Then spread these herbs around your yard. You can also scatter eucalyptus, cedar shavings, or ground red pepper.

Stop slugs without paying a penny. Capture slugs by putting cabbage leaves or old pieces of board in your garden. Since slugs like to hide under these during the day, visit your slug traps during sunset or early evening. Flip the boards or cabbage leaves over, swipe the slugs off, and dump them where they'll never reach your garden again. If you're short on boards and cabbage leaves, surround your plants with a barrier of crushed eggshells instead. Slugs don't like to crawl over the eggshells' rough edges, so they'll stay away.

Tempt slugs with beer. Beer attracts slugs, and slugs can't swim. So if you have some beer in your garden, slugs will leave the tomato plants, crawl into the beer, and drown. Bury a plastic butter tub or similar container to hold the beer. Only fill it about half full so they can't climb back out. It's the yeasty smell they like. To brew your own concoction, combine 2 cups warm water, 2 tablespoons flour, one-half teaspoon brewer's yeast, and 1 teaspoon sugar.

Crawling through sand is no day at the beach for slugs and snails. They can't stand the feel of coarse substances. Guard your garden by spreading a bed of sand around your plants. You can also use sawdust, or human or animal hair. Slugs and snails will stay away.

Slug slugs with a cup of coffee. When your morning coffee gets cold, throw it on your garden. Caffeine deters slugs and snails, killing the small ones and scaring off the larger ones. It

attacks the central nervous system of all kinds of insects, but
works really well with slugs
and snails because it is water-
soluble and seeps in through
the mucus membranes these
slimy creatures get around on.

> Add onions and marigolds to your garden, and you will subtract slugs. These common plants act as natural slug deterrents.

Stymie snails with garlic spray. Garlic wards off snails,
caterpillars, and aphids. Make a homemade garlic concoction
to protect your garden. Mix three heads of garlic and 6 teaspoons of mineral oil in a blender, and let the mixture sit at
room temperature for two days. Then add the garlic mixture
to a combination of 1 pint hot water and 1 tablespoon oil-
based soap, and refrigerate it in screw-top jars. When you go
to spray your garden, combine 2 tablespoons of the refriger-
ated mixture with 4 pints of water. It should do the trick.

Scare off slugs with sandpaper. When you are finished
with those sandpaper disks in your workshop, give them a
second life in your garden. Cut them open to make a collar
that you can slip around the base of your plants. Slugs won't
crawl over them.

Ban bad bugs from blooms and seedlings. "If you cut the
bottom off of small yogurt containers, you can slip the bottomless yogurt cup over any tender seedlings in the garden
to protect them from slugs and cutworms," says Colleen
Vanderlinden, freelance writer and author of *Edible Gardening for the Midwest*. "Just slide it over the plant, press it about
an inch into the soil, and your plant will be protected."

Magnolia helps keep bugs in check. Consider yourself lucky if you have a saucer magnolia in your yard. This beautiful tree is one of the best pest-control clocks. Each phase of blooming tells you when to treat for different bugs.

When the magnolia	Start controlling for
sets pink buds	eriophyid mites on hemlock and spruce, European pine shoot moth, pine bark adelgid, spruce needle miner, Cooley and eastern spruce gall adelgid
transitions into early bloom	eastern tent caterpillar, leaf crumpler, spruce spider mite, and Zimmerman pine moth
blooms	Juniper webworm, Fletcher scale, ash plant bug, and spring and fall cankerworm
drops its petals	gypsy moth, hawthorn mealybug, willow aphid, European sawfly, honey locust pod gall, and spruce budworm

Wildlife woes: protect your garden from four-legged vandals

Grow plants that drive back deer. Gardeners often complain that deer eat their plants even though they are on the "deer hating" lists. But reports also suggest three plants nearly always remain untouched — lantana, oleander, and any variety of salvia.

But those are not the only plants deer hate. Deer rarely eat powerfully scented herbs such as rosemary, catnip, dill, garlic, lavender, mint, oregano, and thyme. They also stay away from flowers like bee balm, cleome, coreopsis, daffodils, heliotrope, lily of the valley, and verbena. So consider growing these plants in place of the ones your deer have been devouring. Some people have reported that growing a border of strongly scented herbs around a deer favorite is enough to protect the plant.

3 ways to stop deer in their tracks. You've always wondered why some people can keep deer out of their gardens while you can't. Now you can learn their secret. "If you're going to try to do any kind of pest control with one tool, you're doomed to failure," says Stephen Tvedten, author of a free nontoxic pest control manual at *stephentvedten.com*. So don't try one way to block deer. Try three.

- Grab your blinking Christmas lights. "Christmas lights that are set up on a motion detector will keep things out," Tvedten explains.

- He also recommends spraying fruit trees, shrubs, and flowers with a mixture of several egg whites stirred into a gallon of water.

- But if your deer are too hungry or too numerous to be stopped by these tricks alone, place netting over smaller plants. Or surround your garden with lightweight plastic mesh fencing tall enough to keep leaping deer out. This nearly invisible fencing won't be an eyesore to you — but deer will hate the sight of it.

Try different tricks to deter deer. When it comes to driving deer out of your garden, you have plenty of options. Everyday items you can use to deter deer include cayenne pepper, baby powder, dog hair, and aluminum pie tins. You can also blare your radio or play a recording of a barking dog to frighten the deer away. The key is to use a variety of these tactics. Switch things around every now and then. Otherwise, the deer will catch on.

Mix 2 tablespoons of hot pepper sauce and 2 teaspoons of mild dishwashing liquid into a gallon of water. Spray this mixture on plants to keep deer from eating them.

Scare stags from your garden. Want to keep deer out of your garden without hurting them? Run a string around the perimeter, about 3 or 4 feet off the ground. Then tie strips of white sheets along the string every few feet. A flash of a white tail is a warning signal to deer, so the white strips, hung about tail height, should frighten them away from your peas and corn.

Strong odors keep deer on the run. Smells are important danger signals to deer. You can use certain odors to keep them away from your garden and orchard. Bars of soap — especially heavily scented deodorant soaps — mask a deer's ability to smell other danger and encourage them to flee. If you want to try something more exotic, visit a local zoo and buy coyote or mountain lion urine or tiger dung. Scatter it around your garden, and the deer will make a hasty retreat.

> If you use an egg-white spray to repel deer and it clogs your sprayer, try this. Either strain the spray before pouring it into the sprayer, or switch from regular egg whites to an equal amount of liquid egg whites such as Egg Beaters. Either one should end the clogs.

Visit your barber to intimidate deer. Deer shy away from the smell of human hair, so the next time you get a haircut, ask if you can gather up the clippings from the floor. Take them home and scatter them about your garden. They'll also help keep rabbits away. Another way is to hang several handfuls of hair in a mesh bag or piece of old pantyhose about 3 feet off the ground. Hang a bag every 3 feet and refresh them once a month.

Wily ways to keep your garden raccoon-free. Pesticides can be both expensive and toxic. But using safer remedies like these may keep raccoons out of your garden, protect your health, and help you spend far less.

- "If you have bright lights that come on when something moves in the garden, they're not going to like that," says Steve Tvedten, pest control expert. So pick up a flashing light that's activated by motion detectors and put it in your garden.

- You can also surround your plants or garden with a yard-wide perimeter of chicken wire laid flat on the ground. Raccoons won't cross it. "They don't like the way it feels," Tvedten explains.

Repel critters with Epsom salt. Keep nosy raccoons and woodchucks out of your garden or garbage can. Just sprinkle a few tablespoons of Epsom salt around those areas. The critters hate the salt and will steer clear of it. Plus, the salt acts as food for your plants. Don't worry — it won't harm the animals, either. To make sure the Epsom salt trick keeps working, you'll have to replace it every time it rains.

> Raccoons sure are cute, but not in your garden. To keep them from eating your produce, spread dog hair around the edges. Raccoons will think a fearsome beast lives there and think better of eating his food.

Force out hungry moles. These small, burrowing animals have to eat all the time. Fortunately, they prefer insect pests, like cutworms, grubs, and slugs — not roots and bulbs. Even so, they can make a mess of your lawn. If you want them to vacate the premises, get rid of their food supply. With no grubs and slugs to munch on, the moles won't stay around, and you'll be free of two sets of pests.

New way to win the war on diggers. Pesky moles may be the enemy of neat yards and undamaged plants, but getting rid of them is tough. So here's how to make them your allies instead.

First, protect your plants with a barrier. This is usually best for beds and rows of plants. You need sheet metal or hardware cloth that is long enough to surround the area and is at least 25 inches wide. Dig a trench that is 10 inches wide and between 15 and 24 inches deep. Make sure it surrounds the bed or row.

Shape your barrier into an "L" that points away from the plants it protects. Rest the barrier in the bottom of the trench so several inches of metal remain above the soil. Refill the trench.

Now you can start reaping the benefits of moles. This old-time gardener's trick still works today. Collect the molehill soil, mix it with some compost, and you may not need to buy potting soil. Not only is molehill soil almost completely weed-free, but mole tunneling also helps loosen and aerate the soil and mixes deep soil with surface materials. The end result is a higher-quality, fertile soil your plants will love.

If you don't need potting soil, you can still put molehill soil to good use. Just spread or scatter the soil over your lawn as a top-dressing. Moles may also help if you have a grub or Japanese beetle problem because they will eat up those pests.

You can also manage moles by burying the drum from an old washing machine with the top even with the ground. Plant your bulbs inside. The metal keeps underground pests away from their feast. And since the holes in the drum allow for drainage, your plants won't rot in soggy soil.

Easy potion persuades moles to leave. Make moles move out of your yard when you give them this nontoxic soak.

- Pour 6 ounces of unflavored castor oil and 1 cup of water in the blender.

- Add 3 ounces of unscented liquid hand soap, but do not use the antibacterial kind.

- Run the blender until the mixture is frothy.

- Put a cup into a 15-gallon hose-end sprayer, and apply to your yard and garden.

This coats the mole food in your yard with castor oil, lending a particularly vile flavor to every possible item on the mole's menu. The mole does not like castor oil any more than you do, so he will go elsewhere to hunt for food.

Make your own mole trap. Catch moles alive with a pit trap made from a large can or wide-mouth jar. Find an active runway by stamping down a section of tunnel. If the mole reopens it, dig a hole deep enough to bury the container so the top is just below the bottom of the tunnel. Gently cave in the tunnel on each side of the trap, and cover the top with a board or a piece of cardboard and dirt from the hole. When the mole opens the tunnel again, he'll drop into your pit trap. Check the trap several times a day. When you've caught a mole, release him where he won't ruin your lawn.

Try surrounding your garden or yard with a ring of daffodils or oleander. These plants have a reputation for keeping gophers away.

Scare off gophers, mice, and moles. The Animal Humane Society suggests a spicy sauce remedy to repel these types of rodents. Mix together 1 tablespoon of peppermint oil, 1 tablespoon of Tabasco sauce, 1 teaspoon of chili powder, and 2 cups of cold water. Soak several cotton balls in the mixture until drenched, and drop them down the mole or gopher hole.

But don't throw out this sauce if you have any left over. Mice also do not like these ingredients. In fact, experts say remedies containing either peppermint oil or chili powder make mice scurry away. So you can imagine what happens when you put these ingredients together. Give it a try and see for yourself.

Trap mice with a tasty treat.
Is your garden overrun with pesky mice? Make them an offer they can't refuse — put pumpkin seeds in your mousetraps for bait. Mice can't resist this yummy treat.

> Plant your bulbs with crushed oyster shells so little voles, relatives of mice, won't eat them anymore.

Build a better mousetrap. Make a cheap, humane mousetrap from a bare garbage can or 5-gallon bucket. Simply rest a board against the rim so the mouse can climb, and place a dollop of peanut butter in the bottom. The mouse will fall in the bucket while trying to reach the peanut butter. Release the mouse as far away from your home as possible. If this does not work, upgrade your trap with a used plastic bottle.

- Drill holes just below the rim on opposite sides of the bucket.

- Drill holes in the lid and bottom of a 16-ounce soda bottle or large plastic pill bottle.

- Thread the bottle on a dowel or wire coat hanger.

- Thread the dowel or hanger through the bucket holes.

- Smear peanut butter around the middle section of the bottle.

When the mouse attempts to get the peanut butter on the bottle, the bottle will spin, dumping him in the bucket.

Repel rodents without poison. Don't want to put poison around your house? Here are three alternatives.

- Mothballs. Make use of those old mothballs by scattering them around your garden and flower beds to keep rodents and cats away. On top of that, toss a few in your tool chest to prevent rust on your tools.

- Peppermint oil. Soak a cotton ball in peppermint oil or peppermint extract, and place it where mice have been visiting.

- Black pepper. To repel rodents, try sprinkling black pepper around your garden plants and on your compost pile. If you know where they live, sprinkle pepper in and around there, too.

Block furry nibblers from digging. You just put your new plants in the ground yesterday, and chipmunks or squirrels are already digging them up. Make sure that does not happen again. From now on, surround every new plant with hardware cloth or a double ring of 3-inch-wide, flat river rock. When you lay down your barrier, be careful to cover virtually all the soil near the plant, so your furry nibblers have no place left to dig.

Pepper your plants to stump squirrels. Turning squirrels away from your garden is a breeze. Make that a sneeze. Just sprinkle some cayenne or black pepper around anything the bushy-tailed pests might eat. They'll think twice about coming back.

Say "so long" to skunk smell. Ah, the distinctive aroma of skunk. You know it when you smell it, whether it's in your car, on your dog, or hanging around your patio. Here's a simple way to make it go away.

Mix a quart of 3 percent hydrogen peroxide with 4 tablespoons of baking soda and 3 teaspoons of liquid soap. Use this solution to wipe down your smelly pet or the patio tiles — wherever the odor lingers. Don't forget to wear rubber gloves to protect your hands, and rinse off the solution when you're done.

Sneaky way to keep uninvited animals away. Don't let cats and squirrels trash your yard or garden. Fight back. In a large bowl, mix 5 tablespoons of flour, 2 tablespoons of cayenne pepper, and 2 tablespoons of powdered mustard. Slowly add 5 cups of water and 5 cups of vinegar and continue mixing. Use a funnel to pour the mixture into a spray bottle and label it. Squirt the mixture wherever animals are disturbing your yard. They won't be back for seconds.

Pamper felines with special outhouse. If you want your outdoor cat to keep out rodents and, at the same time, keep out of your garden, consider making her a spot where she can dig and defecate without disturbing your prized plants. Cats like to dig in soft material, so a big sand pile or an area with loose dirt or small bark mulch ought to make her a luxurious restroom. Plant some miscanthus grass for her to chew on, or maybe a little catnip would keep her coming back.

Use tomato cages to keep out kitties. If you're tired of raking up cat poop every spring, take your flat, collapsible tomato cages in the fall and lay them down in your garden. Cats like to have room to scratch around, and there's not enough space between the wires. You can also lay out bamboo poles or the thorny clippings from your rosebushes. Chicken wire works, too.

Cats turn up their noses at the smell of citrus, so sprinkle orange peels, lemon peels, and lime peels around plants that need protection. This keeps unwelcome cats away naturally.

Deny cats a place to dig. Cats like to dig in soft, dry dirt before they go to the bathroom, which is why your garden often becomes their toilet. Be unwilling to give them a place to dig by using attractive river rock to fill up empty spaces and hold in moisture. Space larger rocks so there's not enough room to stretch out and dig.

Discourage tabbies with a water gun. Want an excuse to buy one of those great big water rifles the kids play with in the swimming pool? It's a great way to chase cats out of your garden. Cats don't like getting wet, so discourage trespassing with a blast of water. Put a little vinegar in the chamber for even better results.

Surprise shower keeps cats away. Scare cats and dogs away from your yard and garden with a motion-activated water sprinkler. You'll have to get your movement and watering zones set up just right, but it won't take too many trips for pesky pets to learn to stay away. Don't forget it's there, or you might get soaked, too.

If your cat constantly digs up your garden, try planting some rue. This strong-scented shrub, which grows 2 feet tall, can deter cats from trespassing.

Clever ways to pet-proof your garden. Your lovable pets can turn into destructive pests when they enter your garden. Follow these tips to keep your dog or cat from harming your beloved plants — and vice versa.

- Protect pets from poison. Some plants are poisonous to pets. Avoid growing them or keep them out of your pet's reach. You should also avoid using harmful chemicals in your garden. Keep fertilizer away from pets, as well.

- Establish boundaries. Fence off areas of your garden to keep pets out. Stone or brick paths will help steer your pet out of the soil. Raised beds may also deter pets from making mischief.

- Point out the potty. Train your dog to go in an area away from your garden. Set up an outdoor litter box for your cat. That way, they won't use your garden as their toilet.

- Provide distractions. If your dog loves to dig, designate an area where digging is encouraged. You can even hide toys or treats in a pile of sand. Put a scratching post outdoors to give your cat something to claw. You could even plant some catnip away from your other plants to keep your cat pleasantly occupied.

Keep dogs from doing their business in your yard. Doggy-do messing up your garden? Mix up a brew that will keep Fido and friends — with their sensitive noses — out of your yard for good.

Chop up a clove of garlic and the most pungent onion you can find. Mix these and a teaspoon of Tabasco sauce, a tablespoon of cayenne pepper, 4 teaspoons of dried oregano, and a quart of warm water in a large pail. Let sit overnight, and then sprinkle in areas where dogs like to rest or dig. Once they smell this concoction, you won't see them in your yard again.

If you think this mixture will be too strong for your human nose, here's an alternative. Brush or spray a mixture of 2 cups rubbing alcohol and a teaspoon of lemon grass on the areas you want treated. This also repels cats.

Frighten away pests with fake snake. A beaten-up garden hose takes on new life with a little paint job. Many pesky animals are terrified of snakes, so make one. After you've finished creating your reptile, lay him out by the garden as a low-lying scarecrow.

Snakes are good for your garden. They eat mice, grasshoppers, slugs, and other pests. If you want to attract one to your garden, provide pools of water and a few planks, rocks, or other hiding places.

Fight back against rascally rabbits. Try these tricks to help keep rabbits from wreaking havoc in your yard and garden.

- Send old tennis shoes and other old shoes to a happy retirement in your garden or lay down some dog hair. Rabbits may be fooled by the scent and stay away.

- Rabbits love cover, so take inventory of places rabbits can hide. Clean out brush piles and debris, get rid of tall weeds, and remove or relocate any potential hiding place.

- Dust a sprinkling of talcum powder on your plants and rabbits will steer clear of your garden. Be sure and reapply after rain.

- Put a quart of water in a sprayer. Set the sprayer aside. Drop four fresh jalapeño peppers in your blender. Add enough water to make a slushy liquid. Blend the water and peppers, strain, and add your "jalapeño juice" to the water in the sprayer. Add one drop of multipurpose glue, like Elmer's, close the sprayer securely, and shake it. Spray this on plants to protect them from rabbits.

Keep bunnies at bay for good. Sprinkle blood meal on the soil to keep rabbits out, recommends Steve Tvedten, pest management expert. But if you have unusually persistent rabbits, head for the hardware store and ask about hardware cloth. "Plant" a cylinder of hardware cloth around each small tree or shrub you need to protect.

Bury the bottom 2 to 3 inches in the soil, but make sure it's tall enough to rise at least 2 feet above the ground or future snowfalls. To protect an entire garden or bed, check the area for rabbits first. Then put up a fence of either chicken wire or hardware cloth.

Keep rabbits from eating your plants. After you empty a spice dispenser or salt shaker, soak a cotton ball with vinegar and drop it in. Put the hole-covered top back on, and leave it near the plants you want to protect.

Solve the case of the vanishing pond fish. The fish in your garden pond can be very attractive to hungry raccoons, herons, and other backyard wildlife. Persuade fish-eating predators to take their appetites somewhere else.

- Create hiding places. Give your fish a place to hide when predators come for dinner. Sink sections of sewer pipe or wide, black PVC pipe into the bottom of the pond. Or build an emergency shelter in the deepest part of your pond. Use bricks for the sides and a large patio paver stone for the roof. Repurpose open weave, stackable, plastic storage crates as underwater stands for potted plants so they can provide an extra shelter. Include plenty of underwater plants for the fish to hide behind, too.

- Fortify the edges. Place loose stones, thick and wide border plantings, or boulders around the edges to make reaching the pond much tougher for predators.

- Block it off. Stretch fine nylon netting over the top of the pond to keep predators from reaching in, wading, or swimming.

- Scare them away. Use blinking Christmas lights or an item attached to a motion detector, such as a radio or a sprinkler.

- Fence them out. Install an electric fence around your pond.

- Make it steep and deep. Give your pond steep sides and make it at least 3 feet deep.

Use scare tactics on invading birds. After a lot of hard work, you might think gardening is for the birds. But that doesn't mean you want the birds to eat all your crops. Take some precautions to scare birds out of your garden.

It takes more than a simple scarecrow — unless it can sing and dance, like the one in "The Wizard of Oz." Try a variety of devices. Pinwheels, aluminum pie plates, and ribbons all work well. Stretch ribbons between two poles so they'll make a roaring noise when the wind blows.

Make sure to alternate the devices and change their location every few days. And hide the devices that aren't being used. Otherwise, the birds will just get used to them. Keep things unpredictable.

Here's another idea. Save some of those plastic grocery bags you get from the supermarket. Fill the bags with air, and tie them shut with a twist tie. Then attach the inflated plastic bags to tall stakes around your garden. When the wind blows, the plastic bags will move and make rustling noises, scaring the birds away.

Start using the scary props about two weeks before your crop will start tempting the birds. If you start too soon, the birds will be too familiar with your props to be scared. If you start too late, the birds will be too familiar with the taste of your crops to be driven away.

Scare away birds with computer castoffs. Collect damaged or outdated computer CDs from friends and neighbors and you may finally get to eat your tomatoes before the birds do. Just be sure nobody will ever need those CDs again. Here's how to use them.

When you plant tomatoes, tie string between the tops of your tomato stakes and thread a CD onto each section. When you're done, all your tomato stakes should have a shiny CD hanging between them. If you don't have CDs, don't worry. Just use pie plates or wide strips of foil with a hole poked in the middle. For extra protection, stick a few children's Mylar pinwheels into the surrounding ground.

Cut long strips from a plastic garbage bag and staple them to the rim of a paper cup. Glue the cup to the top of a 5-foot bamboo stake or other pole. Stand it in your garden where the breezes will flutter the plastic. Birds won't come near.

Ward off woodpeckers with balloons. Decorate your house with colorful balloons. Not only will they make your house look festive, they will also scare off woodpeckers. Hang the balloons close to where the woodpecker usually taps, and make sure they can blow in the breeze. If regular balloons seem too friendly, you can also find inflatable owls, hawks, or snakes at some garden shops.

Best ways to attract, feed, and house your feathered friends

If you build it, they will come. Birds are attracted by the terrain and plants on a property. Landscaping for birds involves nine basic principles.

- Food. Every bird species has its own unique food requirements that may change as the seasons change. Learn the food habits of the birds you wish to attract. Then plant the appropriate trees, shrubs, and flowers to provide the fruits, berries, seeds, acorns, nuts, and nectar.

- Water. You may be able to double the number of bird species in your yard by providing a source of water. A frog pond, water garden, or birdbath will get lots of bird use, especially if the water is dripping, splashing, or moving.

- Shelter. Birds need places where they can hide from predators and escape from severe weather. Trees, shrubs, tall grass, and birdhouses provide excellent shelter. Even dead trees are good hiding places.

- Protection. Birds should be protected from accidental death. When choosing the placement of bird feeders and nest boxes, consider their accessibility to predators. Birds will fly directly at picture windows when they see the reflection of trees and shrubs. A network of parallel, vertical strings spaced 4 inches apart can be placed on the outside of windows to prevent this problem. Stickers and decals on the window may help deter birds. Be cautious about the kinds of herbicides and pesticides used in your yard. Apply them only when necessary and strictly according to label instructions. In fact, try gardening and lawn care without using pesticides.

- Diversity. The best landscaping plan is one that includes a variety of native plants. This helps attract the most bird species.

- Four seasons. Give birds food and shelter throughout the year by planting a variety of trees, shrubs, and flowers that provide year-round benefits.

- Arrangement. Properly arrange the different habitat components in your yard. Consider the effects of prevailing winds and drifting snow so your yard will be protected from harsh winter weather.

- Hardiness zones. When considering plants not native to your area, consult a plant hardiness zone map. Make sure the plants you want are rated for the winter hardiness zone classification of your area.

- Soils and topography. Consult your local garden center, university, or county extension office to have your soil tested. Plant species are often adapted to certain types of soils. If you know what type of soil you have, you can identify the types of plants that will grow best in your yard.

Organic gardening good for birds

Don't use chemicals on your lawn or in your garden if you want to attract butterflies and bees and have a healthy bird population. The worms and insects that thrive there provide birds with good food, while they, in turn, keep down the pests that might do damage to your plants. On the other hand, it's not just insects that die when poisons are used. The pesticides in insects also endanger the birds that eat them.

8 easy ways to attract birds to your yard. Birds will flock to your yard if you provide food, water, shelter, and safety. Here's how to start.

- Mount bird feeders on poles, and put baffles on the poles to prevent other wildlife from climbing it.

- Don't waste your money on feeds that contain canary seed, oats, wheat, corn, milo, or red millet. Choose regular sunflower seeds, black oil sunflower seeds, or millets other than red millet. If you like cardinals, include safflower seed.

- Get their attention. Birds are attracted to dripping water. Use a nail to poke a hole in the bottom of a can or milk jug, hang the container a few feet above your birdbath, fill with water, and let it drip. Once birds become accustomed to drinking from your bath, you won't need the dripper. Change the bath water every few days so your feathered friends won't get sick.

- Make your birdbath drown-resistant. It should be no deeper than 3 inches at its deepest point and have a rough surface, like concrete, that helps prevent slipping. If your bath is too deep or slippery, add pebbles or gravel to make it more shallow and improve traction.

- Choose a birdbath that sits on a pedestal if cats or other predators frequent your yard, and place it well away from bushes or hedges. Predators may use shrubbery to sneak up on unsuspecting birds.

- Place the birdbath near a tree with overhanging branches, so birds have a nearby place to shake off water and preen after bathing. Wet birds may be too heavy to fly very far or high.

- Select plants that provide food or cover for birds through-out the year, especially when little else is growing. Plants that produce berries and seeds can be good choices for food sources, while evergreens may provide cover during winter.

- Don't bother cleaning up flower seed stalks in autumn. Let the birds clean the seeds out of them instead.

Make a plan to entice birds.
Your project is to landscape your property with an assort-ment of trees, shrubs, and flowers that will attract birds. Get started by following these guidelines.

Chokeberry, serviceberry, mulberry, and elderberry shrubs are like a magnet for your feathered friends. And the red berries of the dog-wood tree are especially attractive to bluebirds.

- Set your priorities. Decide what types of birds you wish to attract and then build your plan around the needs of those species. Attend a local bird club meeting and talk to local bird-watchers about how they attract birds to their yards.

- Use native plants when possible. Check with the botany department of a nearby college or your state's natural heritage program for lists of trees, shrubs, and wildflowers native to your area. These plants are naturally adapted to the climate of your area and are a good long-term investment.

- Draw a map of your property to scale using graph paper. Identify buildings, sidewalks, power lines, buried cables, fences, septic tank fields, trees, shrubs, and patios. Identify and map sunny or shady sites, low or wet sites, sandy sites, and native plants that will be left in place.

- Get your soil tested by your local garden center or county extension agent. Find out if your soil has nutrient or organic deficiencies that fertilization or compost can correct. Make sure your soil works well with your plant selection.

- Talk to resource experts and review your plant list with them. People at a nearby arboretum can help with your selections.

- Develop your planting plan. Sketch on your map the plants you wish to add. Draw trees to a scale that represents three-fourths of their mature width, and shrubs at their full mature width. There is a tendency to include so many trees that eventually your yard will be mostly shaded. Be sure to leave open sunny sites where flowers and shrubs can thrive.

- Implement your plan and document it on paper and with photographs. Try taking pictures of your yard from the same spots every year to track the growth of your plants.

- Maintain your plan. Keep your new trees, shrubs, and flowers adequately watered. Use landscaping fabric, wood chips, or shredded bark mulch to keep your planting areas weed-free.

And finally, make sure to take the time to enjoy the wildlife that will visit your new landscape.

Bird feeding answers every birder wants to know. New to bird-watching? Here are a few common questions and answers for bird feeding success.

- When is the best time to start? Usually, whenever the weather is severe, birds will appreciate a reliable supplemental food source. In northern areas, start before the onset of cold weather so birds have time to find the feeder.

- When's the best time to stop? Although you can feed birds year-round, especially with fruit and nectar, you can stop feeding them seeds once a reliable supply of insects is available in the spring.

- How close to my window can I put a feeder? Birds will come right to your window. Sometimes it takes a while for them to overcome their initial reluctance, so be patient. Don't worry that a feeder on the window will cause birds to fly into the window.

- How long does it take for birds to find a feeder? It may take more time for birds to find window feeders than hanging or pole-mounted feeders. You may want to wrap aluminum foil around the top of the feeder hanger. Sometimes all it takes is the reflection of light on the foil to catch their attention.

- My feeder is full of seeds and I haven't seen a bird in months. Am I doing something wrong? When birds desert your feeder, it may be simply that a lot of natural food is available nearby. Or something may be wrong, such as spoiled seeds or a contaminated feeder. Throw the seeds away and wash the feeder. Look at where your feeder is placed. Be sure it's not vulnerable to predators. At the same time, make sure it is not in an open area, away from the cover in which birds usually travel.

> Make a quick, cheap bird feeder for your feathered friends. Wrap strips of tape, sticky side out, around a tree branch. Sprinkle with birdseed. Pat them a little to help them stick. The birds will flock in to feast in no time.

- Can birds choke on peanut butter? There is no evidence that birds can choke on peanut butter. However, birds have no salivary glands. You can make it easier on them by mixing peanut butter with lard, cornmeal, or grit. Your birds will appreciate drinking water, too, from a birdbath or trough.

- Do wild birds need grit? Birds have no teeth to grind their food. The dirt, sand, pebbles, and grit they eat help grind up their food. Adding grit to your feeder is helpful, particularly in the winter and spring.

Feed goldfinches upside down. If you're particularly fond of goldfinches, here's a tidbit of knowledge to attract them to your feeder. All finches love thistle seeds, but only goldfinches feed upside down, so if you put the opening for the seed beneath the perch, they'll be able to eat with no competition from other types of birds.

Shells do double duty. Crushed eggshells do the same thing as grit, and in the spring have an added benefit — they provide birds with extra calcium for producing eggs of their own.

Dinner for one, please! You can control the number of birds at your feeder by putting out smaller amounts of seed, or by using specialty seeds or restrictive feeders that will attract only certain species. If you fill your feeder only when it's empty, the birds will look for food elsewhere.

Feeders that restrict access will encourage small birds and discourage large birds. Wood feeders with vertical bars and feeders covered with wire mesh frustrate larger birds.

The most nonselective feeders are the tray, platform, or house feeders, because they allow easy access by all birds.

- Suet feeders. If starlings are a problem at your suet feeder, discourage them by using a suet feeder with access only from the bottom. Starlings are reluctant to perch upside down. Chickadees and woodpeckers don't find that a problem.

- Tube feeders. Only small birds are likely to be attracted to tube feeders without trays. Remove the perches, and you will further restrict the feeder to only those birds that can easily cling — like finches, chickadees, titmice, and woodpeckers.

- Platform feeders. Birds that visit platform feeders (doves and sparrows) favor white proso millet. Ducks, geese, and quail will eat corn. Many cereal grains (corn, milo, oats, canary, wheat, rape, flax, and buck-wheat) in mixed birdseeds are not favorites of birds that visit tube feeders.

Don't fret about birds' feet sticking to metal feeders and perches in the wet winter weather. Birds don't have sweat glands in their feet, so they won't freeze onto metal feeders. There's no need to cover any metal parts with plastic or wood to protect birds' feet, tongues, or eyes.

The most effective way to attract the largest variety of birds to your yard is to put out separate feeders for each food:

- a starling-resistant suet feeder

- a house feeder for sunflower seeds

- a bluebird feeder

- a wire mesh cage feeder for peanuts

- a nectar feeder

- a tube feeder for thistle

- a stationary or tray fruit feeder

- a house or platform feeder for millet

Be picky about your seed. You can virtually eliminate visits by birds you would rather not see by offering seeds they won't eat. If you use more than one type of seed, put them in separate feeders. This will reduce wasted seeds because birds will toss unwanted seeds out of a feeder to get to their favorites. Watch a feeder filled with a seed mix and you'll see the birds methodically drop most of the seeds to get to their favorite — sunflower.

Many birds prefer sunflower. Some prefer millet. A few prefer peanuts. Sparrows, blackbirds, doves, and juncos will eat the other grains in pre-made mixes — corn, milo, red millet, oats, wheat, and canary seed. Birds will also kick out artificial "berry" pellets, a processed seed flavored and colored to look like real fruit. Black oil sunflower is the hands-down favorite of all the birds that visit tube and house feeders.

Insects lay their eggs in burlap bags. Don't buy seeds in burlap bags or paper and plastic bags with patched holes. That may be a sign of insect or rodent infestation.

Prevent weeds and disease from fallen birdseed. Seeds that fall from your bird feeder can sprout and give you a bumper crop of weeds. Here's how you can stop them from sprouting.

- Bake your birdseed in the microwave before you put it in your feeder. Experts suggest you pour one gallon of seed into a paper bag, and microwave it for five minutes on high.

- Spread the seed on a long, flat pan and bake it in your conventional oven at 300 degrees for 30 minutes.

- Lay a small tarp on the ground under your feeder. Empty it occasionally so a heavy rain won't wash the seeds into your yard.

- Use a shop vacuum to clean up stray seeds several times during the winter when the ground is bare and dry.

Regardless of the season, birdseed that sits on the ground for even a short time can be contaminated by dampness, mold, bacteria, animal droppings, lawn fertilizers, and pesticides. It's healthier for birds to get their handouts at a feeding station or bird feeder, rather than off the ground. You can start simply with a piece of scrap wood elevated a few inches above the ground. Add a few holes for drainage and you've built a platform feeder. It won't be long before the birds find it.

> Move your feeder a few feet each season to give the ground underneath time to assimilate the seed debris and bird droppings.

Put together a whimsical teacup bird feeder. Teacup bird feeders make great gifts for family and friends — and while you're at it, make one for yourself. To make this bird feeder, you'll need:

- a pretty teacup and saucer from a flea market, garage sale, or thrift mall.

- strong glue, such as epoxy glue, Gorilla Glue, or super glue.

- 24 inches of three-quarter-inch copper pipe.

- a flat-topped pipe cap that fits snugly over one end of the copper pipe.

Choose a location for your bird feeder. Look for a place that's sheltered and easy to see from inside your house. Push the copper pipe into the ground to mark the spot.

Wash the teacup and saucer and let dry completely. Place the saucer on a flat surface and apply glue to the area where the teacup normally sits. Place the teacup in the saucer and press it in place.

Your glue directions should tell you how long to hold it in place to dry. Don't attempt the next step until the glue has dried completely.

Turn the cup and saucer over so you have access to the bottom of the saucer. Apply glue to the pipe cap and press it into the center of the upturned saucer. Hold it in place and let it dry completely.

Take your teacup and saucer out to the copper pipe and slide the pipe cap over the end of the pipe. Fill your feeder with birdseed and enjoy watching your new friends.

Create a haven for hummingbirds. Your yard doesn't offer any shade for your hummingbird feeder, and you can't seem to convince hummingbirds to visit. Fix both problems with a single, colorful solution.

Hummingbirds love red, so take an old straw hat or a red plastic plate and decorate it with red silk or plastic flowers. If you use a plate, poke a hole in the center, turn it over, and decorate its underside. Using flowers that have wire stems may make the job easier.

When the decorations are secure, attach the hat or the plate so it's centered above the top of your feeder and shades the feeder on all sides. You may be able to hang the plate from the bar that supports your feeder. Otherwise, try some combination of wire, fishing line, and florist's tape to attach the hat or plate.

The red flowers not only add shade, they help attract the hummingbirds' attention. That may be all it takes to make them regular visitors to your feeder. What's more, experts recommend shade for your feeder because the hummingbirds' food spoils more quickly in sunlight.

Make your own hummingbird nectar. Just add one-quarter cup of sugar to a cup of boiling water. Let cool before putting it in your feeder. But remember, sugar water will ferment when left in the hot sun, turning nectar deadly. Do not put out a nectar feeder if you are not willing to clean it at least weekly, preferably twice a week.

Tempt hummingbirds to visit your herbs. Fragrant herbs can attract the tiny beauties to your yard. Try hyssop, anise hyssop, comfrey, rosemary, and catmint in your garden and see if you don't gain a hummingbird or two. Also, experiment with varieties of bee balm and sage to find out which ones your local hummers like best.

Fill a hummingbird feeder without spills. You don't need to buy a special spill-proof hummingbird feeder to put an end to your refill problems. You can make any feeder goof-proof for pennies. Take your pick. These options are easy, cheap, and you won't spill a drop.

- Use a turkey baster or squeeze bottle to transfer the liquid from its original container to your feeder.

- Nestle a funnel in the mouth of your feeder and pour in the hummingbird nectar.

Watch the calendar. There is no evidence that feeding hummers after Labor Day will delay migration. Still, remove feeders in areas with subfreezing winter weather shortly after that holiday. Tempting hummers to remain beyond normal departure dates by keeping food available may be hazardous to them.

Pick the perfect house for nesting birds. In the birdhouse business, there's no such thing as "one size fits all." Decide which bird you want to attract and then get a house for that particular bird. Look through any book or catalog and you'll see birdhouses of all sizes and shapes, with perches and without, made of materials you might not have thought of, like recycled paper, gourds, plastic, rubber, pottery, metal, and concrete. The proper combination of quality materials and design makes a good birdhouse.

- Wood is just about the best building material for any
  birdhouse. It's durable, has good insulating qualities, and
  breathes. Three-quarter-inch thick bald cypress and red
  cedar are recommended. Pine and exterior-grade plywood
  will do, but they are not as durable.

  It makes no difference whether the wood is slab, rough-
  cut or finished, as long as the inside has not been treated
  with stains or preservatives. Fumes from the chemicals
  could harm the birds.

  There's no need to paint cypress and cedar, but pine and
  plywood houses will last longer with a coat of water-based
  exterior latex paint. White is the color for purple martin
  houses. Tan, gray or dull green works best for the other
  cavity-nesting species. The dull, light colors reflect heat
  and are less conspicuous to predators. Don't paint the
  inside of the box or the entrance hole.

  Regardless of which wood you select, gluing all the joints
  before you nail them will extend the life of your birdhouse.
  Galvanized or brass shank nails, hinges and screws resist
  rusting and hold boxes together more tightly as they age.

- Natural gourds make very attractive birdhouses. They
  breathe, and because they sway in the wind, they are less
  likely to be taken over by house sparrows and starlings.

  Grow your own gourds and you'll have dozens to choose
  from in the years ahead. If you don't have the space to
  grow them, a coat of polyurethane or exterior latex (on
  the outside only) will add years to the one you have.

- Properly designed pottery, aluminum (for purple martins only), concrete, and plastic houses are durable. Just don't drop them. Be sure to provide ventilation, drainage, and easy access for maintenance and monitoring. Concrete or a mix of concrete and sawdust offers protection other houses cannot. And squirrels can't chew their way in!

Build a better bluebird house. If you put up a bluebird birdhouse near a field, orchard, park, cemetery, or golf course, you might have a chance of attracting a pair of bluebirds. They prefer nest boxes on a tree stump or wooden fence post between 3 and 5 feet high. Bluebirds also nest in abandoned woodpecker nest holes.

The most important measurement is the diameter of the birdhouse hole. An inch and a half is small enough to deter starlings and house sparrows, known to kill bluebirds. Discourage other problem animals — like cats, snakes, raccoons, and chipmunks — by mounting the house on a metal pole, or use a metal predator guard on a wood post.

> Pyrethrin and rotenone insecticides are recommended for killing fly larvae, bird lice, and mites after birds have finished nesting for the season.

Keep it messy for the birds. Want to attract more birds to your yard? Don't get overzealous in your fall yard and garden cleanup. Be sure you leave plenty of plants — like thistle and milkweed — that provide flossy material for nests in the spring. One way to find out what the birds in your area like to use is to take apart a few of last year's nests and examine the building materials.

Invite birds to build. An empty onion bag is ideal for hanging out nesting supplies for your backyard birds. Fill it with straw, bullrush down, cotton, feathers, animal hair, or small pieces of bark and wood. A "builder-friendly" neighborhood will usually attract a good number of settlers.

Construct a "home sweet home" for purple martins. Many people want martins in their yards because of their reputation for eating thousands of mosquitoes a day. While it's true that they eat flying insects, don't expect purple martins to eliminate mosquitoes in your yard completely. Martins prefer dragonflies, which prey on mosquito larvae.

Martins are entertaining creatures, and you'll enjoy watching their antics in your backyard. You have the best chance of attracting martins if you put a house on the edge of a pond or river, surrounded by a field or lawn. Martins need a radius of about 40 feet of unobstructed flying space around their houses. A telephone wire nearby gives them a place to perch in sociable groups.

> Keep bees and wasps from attaching their nests by coating the inside of the roof of the birdhouse with bar soap.

Martins nest in groups, so you'll need a house with a minimum of four large rooms — 6 or more inches on all sides, with a 2 1/2-inch entrance hole about 1 1/2 inches above the floor. Ventilation and drainage are critical factors in martin house design. Porches, railings, porch dividers, and extra roof perches, like a TV antenna, make any house more appealing.

You can also make houses from gourds by fashioning an entrance hole and small holes in the bottom for drainage.

If you use gourds, it's not necessary to add railings and perches. Adult martins will perch on the wire used to hang the houses. Before you select a house, think about what kind of pole will support it. Houses for martins should be 10 to 20 feet off the ground.

Gourd houses are the easiest to set up. String them from a wire between two poles, from a sectional aluminum pole, or on pulleys mounted to a crossbar high up on a pole.

You can mount lightweight aluminum houses for martins on telescoping poles, allowing easy access for maintenance and inspection. Because of their weight (more than 30 pounds), wood houses should not be mounted on telescoping poles. You'll have to use a sturdy metal or a wood pole attached to a pivot post. The problem with this lowering technique is that you can't tilt the house without damaging the nests inside. If you put your house on a shorter, fixed pole, 10 to 12 feet high, you can use a ladder to inspect and maintain it.

The ins and outs of owls' nests. Most owls seldom build their own nests. Great horned and long-eared owls prefer abandoned crow and hawk nests. Other owls — like barred, barn, saw-whet, boreal, and screech — nest in tree cavities and birdhouses.

Barn owls are best known for selecting nesting sites near farms. Where trees are sparse, these birds will nest in church steeples, silos, and barns. If you live near a farm or a golf course, try fastening a nest box for owls about 15 feet up on a tree trunk.

Screech owls prefer abandoned woodpecker holes at the edge of a field or neglected orchard. They will readily take to boxes lined with an inch or two of wood shavings. If you clean the box out in late spring after the young owls have fledged, you may attract a second tenant — a kestrel or small falcon. Trees isolated from larger tracts of woods have less chance of squirrels taking over the box.

Birdhouses — location, location, location. Where you put your birdhouse is as important as its design and construction. Cavity-nesting birds are very particular about where they live. If you don't have the right habitat, the birds are not likely to find the house. You can modify your land to attract the birds you want to see by putting out a birdbath, planting fruit-bearing shrubs, including more trees or installing a pond with a waterfall.

> Don't worry that the adults will reject the nestlings if you handle them. That's a myth. Most birds have a terrible sense of smell.

Here are some tips on where to put birdhouses:

- Don't put birdhouses near bird feeders.

- Houses mounted on metal poles are less vulnerable to predators than houses nailed to tree trunks or hung from tree limbs.

- Use no more than four small nest boxes or one large box per acre for any one species.

- Put about 100 yards between bluebird boxes and 75 yards between swallow boxes. If you have both species, pair the houses with one bluebird box 25 feet from a swallow box.

- Don't put more than one box in a tree unless the tree is extremely large or the boxes are for different species.

- If you have very hot summers, face the entrance holes of your boxes north or east to avoid overheating the box.

Squirrel-proof your bird feeder. If you've seen squirrels in your neighborhood, it is safe to assume they will visit your feeder. Think long and hard before you hang anything from a tree limb. Squirrels are incredibly agile, and any feeder hanging from a tree is likely to become a squirrel feeder. In the long run, a squirrel-proof feeder or any feeder on a pole with a baffle is the least aggravating solution. The most effective squirrel-proof feeder is the pole-mounted metal house type.

If you must hang a feeder, select a tube protected with metal mesh. Most plastic squirrel-proof feeders, despite manufacturers' claims, may eventually succumb to the squirrels. Any wood or plastic feeder can be effective when mounted on a pole with a plastic or metal baffle, if the pole is at least 10 feet or more from a tree limb or trunk. Remember, squirrels can jump great distances.

> Never put up a birdhouse with a perch below the entrance hole. Perches offer starlings, house sparrows, and other predators a convenient place to wait for lunch.

Turn up the heat on seed-stealing critters. Squirrels love to eat, and they don't care where their next meal comes from.

One way you can fight back is with hot pepper. You can buy suet and birdseed treated with cayenne pepper, or you can add your own hot pepper powder or spray to birdseed to keep squirrels

from eating it. It coats the seeds, and leaves a nasty taste in the
squirrel's mouth. Birds aren't bothered by the heat, but using too
much can irritate their eyes. Chili flakes or seeds are also worth a
try. Use gloves whenever you handle any kind of hot pepper, and
avoid contact with your eyes, nose, and mouth.

If you don't like the idea of causing discomfort to squirrels, fill
your feeder with seeds they're not fond of — such as safflower,
nyjer thistle, or white proso millet seeds. Just one taste and
your neighborhood squirrels may be looking for somewhere
else to eat.

And don't forget the usual weapons in the squirrel war —
putting your feeder where a squirrel finds it hard to get to,
protecting the feeder with baffles, or buying a style of feeder
better at keeping them out. Squirrels are devious and determined, and multiple defenses may be your best bet.

Toy around with squirrels. Try this bargain squirrel stopper.
Instead of replacing your bird feeder with an expensive, squirrel-proof model, buy a cheap, silver
slinky. Fasten one end of the slinky to the
underside of your bird feeder and position the bottom circle of the slinky
around the top of the feeder's supporting
pole so it can drop to the ground. The
slinky should surround the feeder pole
from top to bottom. Reattach the bird
feeder to the pole. Now the squirrels can
no longer climb up to the bird feeder.

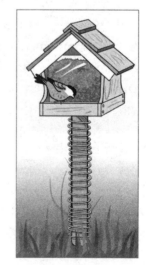

Of course, some squirrels may try to
jump down to the feeder from a nearby

roof or tree, so place the feeder well away from any potential launch platforms. If you cannot move the feeder, make sure the feeder is metal, not plastic. Squirrels can chew through plastic bird feeders.

Keep squirrels out of your bird feeder permanently. Feed the birds, not the squirrels, by using these clever tips.

• Cut the bottom off a 2-liter soda bottle or 5-gallon water bottle. Drill holes through the neck of the bottle and use part of a coat hanger to hang the bottle from the bottom of the bird feeder. The resulting umbrella shape makes pole climbing impossible for squirrels. You can also get the same effect with an old bucket. Just cut the bottom off and drill holes through the sides of the bucket near the base. Use the coat hanger to attach it to the bottom of the bird feeder, and squirrels will seek easier pickings elsewhere.

• Ask someone at the home improvement store to help you find an HVAC reducer. This is a short metal cylinder designed to connect a small duct to a larger one. You'll also need screws and small pieces of wood — called shims — to fit between the inner wall of the reducer and the bird feeder pole. Slip the reducer over the pole, jam the shims in the empty space between the pole and the reducer, and attach the entire contraption to the bird feeder pole with nails or screws.

Protect birdhouses from predators. Every bird that stops by your yard to feed or nest must keep its eyes open for danger. You can help them survive.

- Cats. Nesting birds are extremely vulnerable to cats, as are fledglings and birds roosting for the night. Bell collars on cats offer birds little protection. Nailing a sheet metal guard or cone to a tree trunk is unsightly, but may deter less agile felines. Houses mounted on metal poles are the most difficult for predators to reach, especially if you smear the poles with a petroleum jelly and hot pepper mixture. The best deterrent is for owners to keep their cats inside whenever possible.

- Dogs. Pet dogs are a hazard to nestlings in the spring and summer. Don't let your dog run loose during nesting time.

- Squirrels. Red squirrels, and sometimes gray squirrels, can become a serious menace to birdhouses and the birds themselves. If you find your nest hole enlarged, chances are a red squirrel is the culprit. Once inside the box, squirrels make a meal of the eggs and young. Adding a predator guard made of sheet metal to the entrance hole is usually enough to keep squirrels out.

- Raccoons and opossums. These pests will stick their limbs inside nest boxes and try to pull out the adult, young, and eggs. Adding a three-fourths-inch thick predator guard to the birdhouse or an inverted cone to its pole support is a simple solution.

- Snakes. Slithery predators play an important part in the balance of nature. If you find one in your birdhouse, don't kill it. Snake-proof your birdhouse by putting it on a metal pole lathered with petroleum jelly and red cayenne pepper.

- House sparrows and starlings. If you don't discourage them, these two nuisance species introduced from Europe will harass or kill cavity-nesting birds. You may destroy the nests of house sparrows and starlings, since these birds are not protected by law. However, the law does protect other birds.

- House wrens. These birds sometimes interfere with the nesting success of other birds by puncturing their eggs. But, unlike the house sparrow and starling, these birds are native to North America and are protected by law. Don't be tempted to intervene when wrens appear at your back-yard birdhouse.

- Insects. Many insects lay their eggs and grow in bird-houses. Inspect your birdhouses for signs of gypsy moths, blow flies, wasps, ants, gnats, and bees. In areas where gypsy moths abound, avoid placing boxes in oak trees, which gypsy moths love.

End the bird droppings on your deck rails. You love birds, but hate the droppings on your deck railing. To keep birds from landing, place stones or shards of brick every few inches along the railing, or string wire 3 inches above it. Before using harsh commercial products to clean off the droppings currently on the railing, try scrubbing with a stiff brush, water, and a small amount of mild dishwashing liquid.

Outdoor smarts: stay safe and healthy as you garden

Dress for gardening success. Working in your garden isn't exactly like walking the red carpet. But you should still pay attention to your wardrobe. You want to be comfortable, while protecting yourself from the sun, bug bites, and plants that can irritate your skin. You may not be a fashion sensation, but you'll be dressed perfectly for the occasion.

- Choose lightweight, loose-fitting clothing that lets you move around without getting too hot.

- Wear long-sleeved shirts, long pants, and high socks to keep your skin covered.

- Opt for sneakers or sturdy shoes rather than sandals.

Give old gloves new life.
Don't ditch your cloth gardening gloves just because they have a few holes. Pull the old switcheroo — switch hands and wear the gloves backward. You'll get some extra use out of them that way.

Here's a handy way to carry small tools or seed packets. Buy a canvas carpenter's apron with several pockets at your local hardware store. Wrap it around your waist while gardening.

The right wardrobe chases away mosquitoes. Here's what to wear to turn off mosquitoes. Choose heavyweight long sleeves, long pants, socks, and shoes as your anti-mosquito armor. Thinner fabric may be cooler, but mosquitoes can bite right through it unless you spray the clothing with insect repellent containing DEET.

Also, avoid wearing bright colors, shiny jewelry, perfume, or cologne. These bright sights and sweet smells attract bugs the same way an ice cream truck attracts kids.

Shield yourself from the sun. Gardeners should appreciate the power of the sun. Without it, your plants wouldn't grow. But you should also beware of it. Protect yourself from sunburn and skin cancer with important gardening "tools," like a wide-brimmed hat, gloves, and sunscreen.

Garden safely in summer heat. Heat exhaustion and dehydration are no laughing matter. Get your heaviest yard work done early in the day, while the air is cooler.

And don't throw yourself into gardening all at once. Build up your body's tolerance to the heat by working a little more each day than the day before. Drink plenty of water, and plan plenty of rest breaks. Skip the coffee, since it acts as a diuretic, and stick with light meals.

When it comes to gardening gloves, think like Goldilocks. Don't settle for gloves that are too loose or too tight. Make sure they're just right. Otherwise, you can end up with painful blisters.

Beware thirst-free dehydration

You can be dehydrated even if you're not thirsty — especially as you age. So drink plenty of water when you garden and watch for these signs of dehydration.

- dry lips and tongue
- rapid heart rate and breathing
- dizziness
- confusion
- dry, taut skin
- dark-colored urine

If you notice these symptoms, see your doctor right away.

Steer clear of tetanus. One-third or more of the tetanus cases each year are contracted while people are gardening or doing yard work. Tetanus is a rare but sometimes fatal disease caused by bacteria found in dirt and on tools. Small cuts and splinters are enough for transmission. It's a good idea to get a tetanus booster every 10 years, regardless of your activities.

Don't let injuries take you out of the garden. Injuries from lawn and garden tools send over 200,000 people to the emergency room every year. Make sure you never become one of them. Take these steps to protect yourself.

- Prevent surprise sprains and strains. Don't try to lift a heavy flowerpot by yourself. Fill it after you place it and get help from friends and wheelbarrows when you need to move it.

- Wear sturdy shoes to protect your feet, especially if you have diabetes.

- Any time you use poisonous sprays, wear protective gloves and clothing. Wash yourself and your clothes thoroughly afterward.

- Wear protective goggles when using power tools and equipment.

Protect yourself from sharp blades. Put your old garden hose to good use. Cut it into sections to fit over the blade of your hoe or the tines of your tiller during storage. This trick protects not only the blades of your tools but also any unsuspecting fingers that might come in contact with them.

Safe winter walkways without plant damage. De-icing salt may be absolutely necessary — to make your sidewalks, driveway, and garden paths slip-free zones.

But it can be very damaging to your plants. The sodium in most regular rock salt de-icers can hamper root growth and limit your plants' ability to absorb the nutrients and water they need. Switch to a calcium chloride de-icer, which is a little less harmful.

Protect your eyes with a tennis ball. If you use a cane while gardening, cover the top of it with an old tennis ball. This makeshift cushion will protect your eyes when you bend or stoop.

For even better results, mix one part calcium chloride de-icing salt with 10 parts sand or kitty litter. This softens or melts snow and ice while providing good traction.

If any of the frozen stuff is left after you apply this de-icing mix, just sweep or shovel it off your driveway or walkway — but make sure you don't dump it near your plants.

Make slippery moss disappear. Kill the stuff that makes your walkways a slippery hazard. Mix up bleach and water in a one-to-one ratio. Then dab it directly onto the moss with a sponge. You can spray or sprinkle it on, but the bleach may harm nearby plants. Wait a few hours for the moss to die, then hose off the walkway thoroughly.

Reduce allergies with low-pollen posies. Perhaps you like to garden, but struggle with allergies during the growing season. If so, stick with plants that produce bright blossoms. Since they attract insects to spread their pollen, they need less of it. On the other hand, plants that depend on the wind for pollination produce a lot more of the stuff that makes you sneeze.

Azalea, hibiscus, oleander, pyracantha, and yucca are some shrubs that shouldn't aggravate your allergies. Other plants you are likely to be comfortable with include cacti, chrysan-themums, crocus, daffodils, ferns, hyacinths, irises, lilies, orchids, roses, and tulips.

If you have allergies, trees to avoid during pollen season include elm, sycamore, oak, walnut, maple, birch, ash, willow, and pecan. Some trees you won't need to avoid are fir, magno-lia, palm, pear, redbud, and yew.

Some other plants you may also want to watch out for are privet hedge, Bermuda grass, bluegrass, artemisia, amaranth, and sorrel.

Rain can clear away pollen. If you are allergic to pollen, a good air-cleansing rain is your friend. On the other hand, if your allergies are caused by mold, wait until everything dries out to return to your gardening.

Breathe easy in your garden, even with allergies. With a few precautions, gardening and lawn work don't have to be off-limits even if you have allergies. Just cover your nose with a mask, wear long sleeves and pants, and wash your clothes right away when you come inside. Keep your grass short and your garden weed-free.

> Got allergies? Avoid gardening before 10 a.m. when pollen counts are highest.

Protect yourself from poisonous plants. "Leaves of three, let it be" is an old saying to help you identify poison ivy, but don't count on it to help you with other poisonous plants, like poison oak or sumac. Sometimes the leaves of these plants grow in groups of five, seven, or even nine, depending on the environment.

There's another way to identify these plants. Poison ivy has yellow-green flowers and white berries and grows as a low shrub or a vine that climbs up trees. Poison oak grows as a small tree or shrub with clusters of yellow berries and leaves that resemble oak leaves.

The sap in these plants contains urushiol, a substance that causes an allergic reaction in some people. If the plant is damaged even a little, the urushiol resin can get on your skin or clothing and set off a reaction. Urushiol can also stick to pets, garden tools, or other objects and get on your skin.

Consider these skin-saving tips before you head for the great outdoors:

- Wear long sleeves and long pants. If you're going to be pulling weeds, wear heavy-duty vinyl gloves. The resin may be able to penetrate rubber (latex) gloves. Even dead plants can contain the active resin and should not be handled without protection.

- Try a barrier cream. Although most skin creams designed to protect against poison ivy don't work very well, studies find that a product containing 5 percent quaternium-18 bentonite is effective in preventing or reducing reactions to poison ivy or poison oak exposure.

- Don't use a string trimmer or mow poisonous plants without a catcher.

- Clean clothing, shoes, and tools that may have come into contact with poison ivy. Wash up with soap and water as soon as you're back indoors.

Beware of dangerous garden plants. Curious children and pets aren't aware of the dangers of pretty but poisonous plants, so you have to be. Keep little ones safe from these potentially fatal flowers, seeds, leaves, and berries. If a pet or a child shows signs of plant poisoning after being in your yard or garden, seek medical help immediately.

Plant	Danger	Symptoms
Daphne	The berries of this ornamental shrub are highly poisonous. Eating just one can cause intense burning in the mouth and throat.	headache, delirium, upset stomach, diarrhea, and convulsions
Digitalis (also known as foxglove, dead man's bells, or witches' gloves)	A beautiful but dangerous flower with poisonous leaves.	nausea, vomiting, diarrhea, and abnormal heartbeat
Hydrangea flower	The buds are the main culprit, but the whole plant contains a poison that is similar to cyanide.	shortness of breath, dizziness, and rapid pulse
Jasmine	Eating the berries can be fatal.	nervousness and stomach upset
Larkspur or delphinium	The young plant and mature seeds are especially potent.	burning mouth, nausea, and slow heartbeat
Lily of the valley	The leaves are especially dangerous, but the whole plant is poisonous, and potentially lethal.	confusion, headache, hallucinations, and cold, clammy skin with red blotches
Mistletoe	The berries are extremely poisonous.	blurred vision, drowsiness, nausea, and diarrhea
Moonseed	The berries look like wild grapes, but don't be fooled.	convulsions

Continued

Plant	Danger	Symptoms
Narcissus	Its bulbs are the most toxic, but the whole plant is poisonous.	nausea, convulsions, and paralysis
Nightshade	The whole plant is poisonous, particularly the unripened berries.	dilated pupils, inability to speak, difficulty breathing, intense nervous and digestive upset, and convulsions
Oleander	One leaf can be fatal to a small child.	vomiting, diarrhea, circulatory problems, and seizure
Rhododendron and azaleas	Its seeds and pods are poisonous.	drooling, teary eyes, vomiting, seizures, and coma
Wisteria	Its seeds and pods are poisonous.	nausea, vomiting, and diarrhea
Yellow or Carolina jasmine	The nectar is poisonous even to honeybees.	sweating, weakness, shallow breathing, convulsions, and paralysis
Yew	The berries and especially the foliage are toxic. Death is often sudden, without warning.	coldness, trembling, staggering, and collapse

Ditch the itch of poison ivy. If you come into contact with a poisonous plant in spite of all your precautions, here's what you can do:

- Swab the infected area with alcohol. This helps remove the resin up to 30 minutes after exposure. If you are sensitive to urushiol and you don't clean your skin quickly, redness and swelling will begin in 12 to 48 hours, along with blisters and severe itching. After a few days, your rash will become crusty and scaly, and you should be completely healed in 14 to 20 days.

- Resist the urge to scratch if you can. Scratching will not spread your rash, but your fingernails may carry germs that could set off an infection. You can relieve the itching by soaking in a cool bath or applying wet compresses to the affected area. Taking an antihistamine or trying an over-the-counter hydrocortisone cream can also help. If you have a severe reaction, your doctor may prescribe steroid creams or pills. Calamine lotion can soothe itching and absorb oozing from blisters, but don't use it once the blisters stop oozing and dry up.

- For more relief, drain your blisters. Here's how — insert a needle into the edge of the blister. Gently press the top of the blister to remove the fluid. Hold a piece of tissue or gauze onto the skin to absorb the liquid. Wash the skin well and put on your anti-itch cream, but don't remove the skin covering the blister. This skin protects the delicate layer of skin underneath. And don't open any blisters on your face or genitals. Let your doctor take care of those.

Soothe poison ivy with oatmeal

Instead of prescription antihistamines or creams, soothe the itch from poison ivy with this clever trick. Run a warm bath and add a colloidal oatmeal product like the ones available from Aveeno. Enjoy a nice long soak. You'll be delighted by how economical and effective a 20-minute soak can be.

Homemade versions of colloidal oatmeal have been used for chicken pox and may work for poison ivy, as well. To make your own, put one to two cups of uncooked oatmeal in a blender or food processor and turn it into as fine a powder as you can. Stir the powder into your bath while the water is running and then soak the itch away.

Simple tricks protect your skin. Sometimes it's not convenient to wear gloves when you're weeding, planting, or pruning. But you may still want protection from dirt, lime, scratches, or poison ivy. Try a lightweight solution — slip your hand into a newspaper bag, or a bread bag from the supermarket. It will cover your arm but still provide good flexibility and touch. Put a rubber band around the top if it starts to slip off.

For more arm protection, cut off the feet of an old pair of socks to use as temporary sleeves on bare arms — combine with gloves if you want.

Gardening gives stress the slip. Put on your gardening gloves. There's something soothing about digging in the dirt.

Maybe it reminds you of days in the sandbox, or perhaps it just brings you closer to nature. However it works, gardening not only rewards you with a prettier yard but it also lets you get rid of some of those worries along with the weeds.

Karin Fleming, HTR, president of The American Horticultural Therapy Association, says, "Gardening is a great all-around exercise that can be enjoyed by people of all ages and abilities. It helps tone muscles, which promotes healthy bones, and it helps maintain flexibility, stamina, and strength. It is also a known fact that gardening helps reduce stress and lower blood pressure."

Harvest good health in your own back yard. A health-building fitness center may be just outside your front door. Whether you dream of a garden lush enough to grace a magazine cover or simply want a neat lawn, you can get great exercise from yard work.

At first glance, it might not seem like a workout, yet when you dig, rake, and plant, you are expending more energy than when you play golf or walk the dog.

The toughest gardening workouts come from specific tasks like mowing the lawn with a push mower, chopping wood, shoveling, or tilling. These activities burn as many calories as doubles tennis, fencing, downhill skiing, and playing softball.

As you can see, gardening burns calories, builds muscle, and even improves flexibility. The following numbers from the Calorie Control Council, a nonprofit association representing the low-calorie and reduced-fat food and beverage industry, show how many calories a 150-pound person can burn in just 30 minutes of yard work.

Yard or garden task	Calories burned
Shoveling snow	205
Stacking firewood	170
General gardening	170
Raking	136
Mowing lawn	136

7 strategies for pain-free gardening. If you're occasionally — or frequently — stiff and sore from gardening, now is the time to take action. Try these tips to ease the stress and strains.

- Consider lighter tools with a fatter, longer, or more muscle-friendly handle if you notice back, knee, wrist, elbow, or other strains. For example, choose a rake with a bent handle to prevent wrist strain.

- Avoid stooping or bending over whenever possible. Instead, get closer to the ground by sitting on an upside-down crate or use a kitchen step stool.

- Choose a shovel that matches the height between your arm and the ground. You can find them as short as 38 inches long.

- Plant perennials, bulbs, or annuals that reseed themselves without your help. You'll still get beautiful flowers, but you won't have to replant every year.

- Give climbing veggies their own trellis to limit the reaching and stretching you must do.

- Use duct tape to attach a broomstick onto your trowel and you'll never have to bend over again. Make sure your fork and spade have handles long enough to reach your waist.

- Kneepads aren't just for risky sports. Wear them in the garden so you won't have to move a knee cushion every time you reposition.

Get fit in your garden

Staying active is just as important as eating healthy, but you don't have to run marathons or bike 20 miles. Take it from Pat, 56 years old and an avid gardener. "I know some people think gardening isn't really exercise, but I'm here to say, 'Are they kidding?'

"Working in my garden means bending and lifting, moving and stretching, not to mention digging and hauling! Anyone who's ever had a garden knows that shoveling compost, lifting 40-pound bags of mulch, transplanting seedlings, dividing plants, and pulling weeds are serious physical activities.

"There's always something to do, from spring planting and weeding to fall raking and cleanup. It keeps a body moving!"

Have a safe garden workout. Gardening can be both convenient and fun. When you garden for fitness, you skip the hassle and cost of going to a gym. Nobody pushes you. You decide how hard and how long to work. In short, gardening is a fun workout you can do on your own terms.

To make gardening work well for you, try these tips.

- Begin your gardening session by warming up, and make sure you cool down slowly afterward.

- Rome wasn't built in a day and your dream yard or garden shouldn't be either. Set small goals. For instance, spend only 20 to 30 minutes weeding or pruning at a time.

- Try switching hands occasionally when raking, hoeing, or digging.

- If you do the same task for long periods, you're more likely to get stiff and sore. Do a few minutes of weeding here and a few minutes of planting there. Never keep at one task for too long.

- Bend at your knees, not at your waist.

- Take frequent breaks to stop and stretch, especially if you spend a lot of time kneeling. Besides, it's the ideal place and time to stop and smell the roses.

Reap big rewards with a little exercise. Make physical activity your ally against the brittle bones of osteoporosis and its dangers. Weight-bearing exercises, such as gardening or lifting weights, can help you keep and build strong bones.

Ask your doctor about exercises that will strengthen large leg muscles to help prevent falls and fractures. Even if you already have osteoporosis, walking, jogging, lifting light weights, gardening, and dancing may help.

Yard work builds strong bones. Working in your yard can do more than give you the most beautiful lawn on the block — it could help give you the strongest bones, too.

Exercise, particularly weight-bearing exercise, helps increase bone density. And a recent study found that gardening may be one of the best activities for building bones.

Researchers found that women who gardened at least once a week had higher bone density than women who did other types of exercise like aerobics, jogging, swimming, and walking. The only other activity that gave as much protection as gardening was weight training.

Even better, gardening is done outdoors, which exposes women to bone-healthy, vitamin D-boosting sunlight. But perhaps even more importantly, most women enjoy gardening. For any exercise to be effective, it has to be continued, and people are more likely to continue an exercise they enjoy.

> Just because your bed pillow has lost its fluffiness doesn't mean you should put it to sleep. Use it as a kneeling pad in your garden. To keep it clean and dry, put it in a plastic garbage bag and tape it closed.

So get out there and start digging and weeding. Your bones will appreciate it.

A sunny garden ups your vitamin D. Vitamin D plays a big role in how much calcium your body absorbs. In fact, low levels of D go hand-in-hand with weaker, more fragile bones.

Sunlight is one of the best sources of this nutrient. Your skin naturally turns sunshine into vitamin D, so a few minutes of walking or gardening outdoors could actually help build your bones.

As you age, your skin tends to make less D from its sunshine time, and sunscreens block the rays even more. But don't trade a painful burn for strong bones. Instead, rely on a variety of sources — foods as well as sunlight — to get 600 to 800 International Units (IU) of vitamin D each day.

Play in your garden to avoid arthritis. Lower your chances of arthritis without resorting to drugs. Australian researchers found that women in their 70s who did just over an hour of moderate exercise every week were less likely to develop frequent arthritis symptoms during the following three years. Women who got more than two hours of moderate exercise had even higher odds of preventing arthritis symptoms. But there's even more good news. Exercise doesn't necessarily mean running or working out at a gym. Mowing, raking, and working in your yard or garden counts, too.

Make it easy on your knees. Sew old pockets onto the knees of your favorite gardening pants. When it's time for the dirty work, fill them with old sponges. Kneeling never felt so good.

Protect your knees in the garden. You always have stuff to do around the yard, but knee pain often gets in the way.

Here are two ways to finish your to-do list while staying off your knees.

- Rather than kneeling and crouching when you do work close to the ground, borrow your grandson's skateboard or your husband's mechanic's creeper (the thing he uses to roll under the car). Sit on it and scoot yourself along as you do things like weeding or planting.

- Try raised beds in your garden, so you won't have to get down and dirty when you pull weeds and pick vegetables.

Make a garden kneeler for pennies. Buy a slab of 3-inch foam and wrap it in thick plastic bags. Some of the thinner discount store bags won't hold up well, so stick with thicker department store bags or outdoor garbage bags. Consider putting one inside the other for added durability. When you're done, use duct tape to secure the bags snugly around the foam.

Dirty trick improves your mood

Gardening can do more than boost the value of your home — it might also boost your mood. That's because soil contains *Mycobacterium vaccae*, friendly bacteria that increase the levels of the feel-good hormone serotonin in your brain. British researchers recently observed the bacteria's effect in mice. They say it changed the mice's behavior in a way similar to antidepressant drugs.

Take a seat. Use a 5-gallon bucket to carry your small gardening tools. As a bonus, you can flip it over and sit on it as you weed, plant, or just take a breather.

Sock it to knee pain. If you find yourself on your knees often, whether you're gardening or doing household chores, you might like this little trick to save wear and tear on your joints. Cut the tops off of old, worn-out socks and slip them up (even over your pants) to your knees. These stretchy tubes make great holders for all types of pads, like bath sponges or pieces of foam.

Protect your wrists from strain and pain. The pain, tingling, and numbness of carpal tunnel syndrome can come from any activity that involves doing the same thing over and over again with your hands. Even something as relaxing as gardening or woodworking can cause this physical stress.

Carpal tunnel syndrome occurs when the median nerve, which runs from your forearm into your hand, becomes squeezed at the wrist. To avoid turning a favorite pastime into a painful chore, follow these wrist-saving tips:

- Change tasks every 30 minutes.

- Keep your grip on objects as loose and relaxed as possible.

- Take a break between tasks. Try stretching your wrists and forearms, or vigorously shaking your hands for 15 seconds to relax muscles and release tension.

- Switch positions frequently.

- Don't lean your weight on your hands. Work in a position where your body weight is support by stronger joints.

- Buy tools that have padded handles or are ergonomically designed.

- Put shock absorbers on power tools.

- Try to keep your grip on objects as loose and relaxed as possible.

- Use electrical devices that will save your hands, like power tillers.

- Use as little force as possible to get the job done.

Special tools for small hands. Think small when it comes to tools. If regular-size tools are too big or heavy for you, consider buying a set of children's tools. Just make sure they are smaller, sturdy versions of real tools — not cheap plastic toys.

Soften splintery handles.
Splinters can take all the fun out of gardening. Sand your tools' handles or wrap insulating tape around them when you notice them becoming rough. Or rub them with linseed oil to take care of those splintery spots.

Go ahead. Sit down on the job. Gardening should be enjoyable and relaxing. Bring a chair or stool into the garden to cut down on the usual — and uncomfortable — squatting and bending.

Cushion your hands with handlebar covers. Don't let blisters from wooden wheelbarrow or rake handles spoil your fun in the garden. Head to the bicycle shop for some spongy handlebar covers. You may need to use a lubricant, like petroleum jelly or liquid dish soap, to get them to slide over the wooden handles. But once you get them in place, you'll love the way they protect your hands.

Clean and soften dirty hands naturally. Remove garden stains and soften your hands at the same time. Just rub them briskly with a paste of oatmeal and milk. If you don't have those ingredients on hand, try a mixture of two tablespoons of cornmeal, a tablespoon of water, and a little bit of apple cider vinegar.

Carry that bucket comfortably. If you have to carry a heavy bucket with a wire handle, you know it can dig into your fingers and make them sore. Make it a little more comfortable with a piece of an old garden hose. Just cut a short piece, slit it, and slip it over the handle of the bucket for a little cushion and more comfortable grip.

Give dirt the brushoff. Just as your current toothbrush fights cavities, your old toothbrush can fight garden grime. Use it to scrub your hands and fingernails after working in the garden.

Wheel away back pain. Your child or grandchild may no longer enjoy his little red wagon — but that doesn't mean you can't. Don't strain yourself by lifting heavy loads in the garden. An old wagon comes in

> Scrape your fingernails over a bar of soap before heading to the garden. It will block most dirt from getting under your nails and make it easy to wash away any dirt that does.

handy for transporting gardening tools, heavy rocks, bags of soil or fertilizer, bulbs, and plants.

A sharp way to avoid thorns. When pruning roses or other thorny plants, wear oven mitts rather than regular gardening gloves. Your hands will appreciate the extra protection.

Baby monitor keeps you informed. You need to work outside, but there's a breaking news story you want to follow. Use a baby sleep monitor to help you do both. Just put the monitor next to your radio or television. Take the other part outside with you, and you can keep up with the news while you rake leaves or plant your garden.

Give your hands a beauty treatment. Coat your hands with a generous layer of your favorite hand lotion before you put on gardening gloves. The lotion will act as a barrier, keeping garden dirt from sticking to your skin or getting under your nails. After you take off the gloves and rinse off the lotion, your hands will be clean and smooth.

Handy trick protects your hands. Save a clothespin or binder clip, and use it to fasten your gardening gloves when you're not using them. Clip the pair of gloves to the hem of your favorite gardening jacket so they are always at hand.

Garden treasures to create and share

Give the gift of sweet scents. Gather up some old glass jars or Mason jars and create thoughtful gifts that won't put you over budget. Scent jars let you infuse a room with the fragrance of your choice — then calm it down when you put the lid back on the jar. Select just the right scent for each recipient. Here's how to make them.

First, find a clean, attractive glass jar, preferably one with a lid. If you have saved jars that held candles, spaghetti sauce, or even peanuts, these will work. Decide what mood you want the scent jar to create — like holiday spices, garden blooms, or refreshing citrus.

For a floral scent, place a half-inch layer of rose petals in the bottom of the jar, and add a quarter-inch layer of salt. Continue alternating layers until the jar is about half full. As the salt pulls moisture from the rose petals, scented oils are released into the air. Use orange peels instead of rose petals for a citrus scent.

To create a spicier blend, cover the bottom of the jar with a mixture of cinnamon sticks, cloves, and nutmeg. Add more spices in layers for an attractive look. Sprinkle about a dozen drops of cinnamon bark essential oil onto the spices.

Pretty packages from pine cones and twine. Create elegant, rustic bows with pine cones from your own backyard. Loop ribbon or raffia into bows and secure with twine or hobby wire. Then attach the pine cones to the center of the bow, using either hot glue or wire. Tie the bow onto the gift with twine for a natural look, or with matching ribbon. Spruce up your gift even more by substituting a few sprigs of greenery like cedar twigs in place of the bow. Wire the sprigs and pine cones together, then tie to the package with twine.

Wow friends with designer leaf prints. Design your own wrapping paper, cards, and table linens with leaves of various sizes and a little paint. Start with heavy paper or pre-washed cloth. Using a small paintbrush, apply tempera paint, or fabric paint if you're working with cloth, to the veined side of a leaf. Lay the leaf, paint-side down, on the surface you are decorating. Cover it with wax paper, and gently roll over it with a rolling pin. Remove the wax paper and peel the leaf back carefully, starting at its tip. Repeat with other leaves, laying them randomly in a pleasing pattern. To "set" the fabric paint, iron the design on the wrong side for several minutes. Just be sure the paint has dried for at least a day.

> Bring the country garden look indoors. Frame and hang some empty seed packets in your kitchen. It's an inexpensive way to add a country touch.

Create leaf designs with sunshine. From your favorite shirt to your living room drapes, the sun bleaches everything. With nothing more than cheap construction paper and a few leaves or fern fronds, you can turn this bleaching effect to your advantage and make sun prints.

On a sunny day, go outside and arrange some leaves in a pleasing pattern on the paper. Hold the arrangement in place with small rocks or a piece of glass and forget about it for five hours. The sun will bleach the paper around the leaves, creating a distinct leaf design. Use this attractive paper to make cards and gift wrap.

Pick flowers to make unique place mats. If you're expecting a large crowd for dinner and don't have enough place mats, make your own with treasures from your garden. Pick small, flat flowers and leaves and arrange them artistically on a sheet of wax paper. Carefully lay another sheet of wax paper on top and iron gently in place. Your guests will be impressed with these unique place mats. You can even use this decorative paper to wrap gifts or make gift bags.

Take an old wooden shelf and cut out three to five holes large enough to hold a flowerpot. Paint the shelf to match your trim and mount it outside. Choose a variety of plants or all the same. Just remember to keep these small planters watered.

Pick a place card. Look to nature for unique place cards for your guests. Collect leaves from magnolia branches or ivy vines. Write names on the leaves with a marker. Opaque white, gold, or silver ink will stand out against the green.

Pine cones aren't just for Christmas. Painted white and decorated, they become Easter trees. With a little imagination and a few craft supplies, they are whimsical turkeys. Glued together, they form a bird's nest that you can fill and decorate for a springtime centerpiece.

And there are hundreds of ways to add them to your fall and winter holiday scheme. Make trees, wreaths, angels, and Santas. Stack them, pile them, dust them with glitter or scented oils, tie them with ribbons, or toss them in the fire. Pine cones are versatile, inexpensive additions to any decorating project.

Bring the outdoors in. For festive decorations from nature, collect sweet gum balls, small pine cones, berry clusters, and leaves. Float a little bit of gold or silver metallic paint on water in a container, like a bowl or wide-mouthed glass jar. Dip each item to coat it with a thin covering of paint. Sprinkle with glitter if you want a more glitzy look.

Attach them with clothespins to a coat hanger and hang them over layers of newspaper to dry. Add them to wreaths or table decorations, or use them to fill a colorful basket.

Make fallen trees into custom candleholders. All you need is a drill and a fallen tree. Save a few logs the next time you or a neighbor has a tree taken down. Find a limb or trunk at least 2 inches in diame-ter if you plan to light taper candles, or wider if you prefer votive candles. Cut a relatively straight piece of the wood into a variety of lengths, as short or long as you like. Try to make your cuts straight, so that your logs end up with flat tops and bottoms. With a spade (boring) bit, drill a hole in the top center of each log. Use a bit the same width as the base of your candles.

Stand up your logs and drop in your candles. For the most eye-catching effect, choose trees with interesting bark, like birch, and cluster your candle logs together in groups.

Add color to boring planters. Don't throw out half-empty paint cans. Instead, use the paint to create one-of-a-kind planters that will add a whimsical touch to your porch. Clay pots, tin cans, and even a 5-gallon bucket can be painted with stripes, polka dots, zigzags, or whatever and filled with plants. For a coordinated look, limit your palette to just two or three colors, and use different painting techniques to give them interest.

Never retire old boots. If you've got a pair of old boots hanging around, fill them with some gravel and a lot of dirt and plant pansies or other flowers in them. Just don't forget to add a few drainage holes. Sitting on a front stoop or in your garden, they'll bring a smile to your face and remind you of hours spent outside.

Creative containers make terrific terrariums. Turn old light fixtures, vases, and kitchen items into terrariums. All you need is something with a clear glass cover to let in light. Consider these creative containers.

- cake plate with glass lid

- glass apothecary jar

- old-fashioned rose bowl

- fish bowl

- upside-down clear vase

- bell jar

- outdoor lantern or porch light

- pocket watch dome

- indoor wall sconce

Set colorful saucers atop open-ended glass containers to transform them into closed terrariums. Saucers and shallow bowls also make great bottoms for holding gravel, soil, and plants under glass covers.

Make icy lights for winter nights. The bad news is temperatures won't climb above freezing for days. But that's perfect weather for ice luminaria. For each one, you'll need small rocks, a votive candle, a 16-ounce plastic or cardboard container, and a gallon or half-gallon bucket or carton. Fill the small container with rocks and put it in the larger container. Pour water into the large container until it nears the smaller container's rim. Let freeze. Pour warm water in the small container and pull it free. Remove the ice block from its container, place it outside, and drop in a candle.

Think safety while holiday decorating. Garlands and Christmas trees grace many homes from November to January. While beautiful, they keep firemen up at night.

To protect your tree from flames, make a fresh cut at its base before screwing it into the tree stand, and refill the reservoir daily with water. Keep greens in a cool spot away from radiators, heat vents, even TVs. The mantel is a natural place for a bough of mixed greens, but use a screen to protect the rapidly drying branches from sparks. Even strings of lights can cause a fire if wrapped around a dry garland.

Wrap your gift in flowers. Gifts for people with green thumbs are easy to find but hard to wrap. Whether it's a plant or a special tool, present your gift in true gardener's style. Save empty flower seed packets and seed catalogs. Cut out and glue your favorite blooms onto a plain paper bag. Use the front cover of a seed packet as a centerpiece and surround it with paper roses, daffodils, and tulips. And don't forget to make a gift tag for your earth-friendly bag.

Indoor "tree" changes with the seasons. Dress up your table or mantel for any holiday with branches from your own backyard. Find a fallen branch with an interesting shape and several twigs sprouting from it. You'll use these to hang ornaments. Brush it off and bring it indoors, then decide whether to spray-paint the wood or leave it natural. For holidays like Christmas, spraying it white or silver creates a lovely winter wonderland look.

Next, display it in a decorative bowl or vase. Fill the bowl with sand or floral foam to keep the branch upright. Hide the foam with Spanish moss or glittery garland. Use fishing line, yarn, or ribbon to hang seasonal ornaments from the twisted twigs of your indoor tree — plastic Easter eggs, small

Christmas ornaments, or whatever else strikes your fancy.
You can reuse your "tree" year-round, changing out the decorations with each season.

Be careful with candles. Fresh pine-scented garlands and
elaborate centerpieces are as much a part of Christmas as
ornaments and stacks of
gifts. But if an arrangement
you brought home from the
florist has candles in it, be
careful not to light them.
Greenery, especially pine
boughs, are highly flamma-
ble. It's better to enjoy them
unlit than to remember this
joyful season as the "year of
the fire."

> Here's a clever way to
> clean the inside of a narrow
> vase that's too small for
> your hand. Put the fizz of
> Alka-Seltzer to work. Just
> fill the vase with water and
> drop in two tablets. The
> bubbling action from car-
> bon dioxide release will
> gently scrub the vase.

Creative fillers for a clear vase. A clear glass vase is one
of the most versatile containers for a flower arrangement.
You can create different looks by using unique fillers to
anchor your flowers as well as disguise the stems. Marbles,
pebbles, sand, pine cones, fruit, nuts, shells, even Christmas ornaments make visually appealing anchors for your
flowers. Just be sure your fillers don't steal the thunder
from the real show stopper — the flowers themselves.

Extend the life of cut flowers. That little packet of powder
you get from the florist to feed your cut flowers really works
to help them last longer. In fact, you might want to ask for
an extra packet or two when you buy a bouquet.

Flower-saving packets contain three types of ingredients — a chemical biocide to kill the bacteria and fungi that feed on plants as they wilt, an acidifier like citric acid to help flower stems take up water, and sugar that the plant uses as nutrition.

Recipes for homemade cut-flower solutions contain some or all of these components. Try these when you run out of packets. Your cut flowers will last and last when you follow these florists' secrets.

- Lemon-lime soda. Adding a bit of this to the water gives your flowers sugar and some acidity.

- Crushed aspirin. This remedy provides acid, similar to lemon-lime soda.

- Vinegar and sugar. Several tablespoons of white distilled vinegar and a spoonful of sugar provide nourishment and acidity.

- Bleach. Just a few drops of this disinfectant will kill the bacteria that speed up the demise of your lovely flowers.

- An old penny. Drop a copper-containing penny — one minted before 1982 — into the vase of water. The copper works to kill fungi and extend the life of your blooms.

Whichever flower-extending recipe you choose, be sure to change the water in the vase every few days to keep it fresh.

Keep your florals from fading. Enjoying cut flowers for the longest time possible starts at the store and continues once you bring them home. Success is in the details.

You may pay more for flowers at a specialty florist, but it's probably worth it. Flower bouquets on display at a super-market are not always cared for properly. Florists take more care because they lose money when they have to toss flowers that go bad.

When selecting cut flowers, look for buds just starting to open, firm flowers, and undamaged stems. Sniff the water to be sure it smells fresh.

Prepare the flowers before you place them in a vase. Cut the stems at an angle to give them more surface area to take up water. It's best to do this job with a sharp knife, preferably while holding the stems under running water. And be sure everything that comes into contact with your flowers — knife, vase, even your hands — is clean. Bacteria on the flowers will make them wilt.

Maintain a flower-friendly environment. That means keeping the flowers out of direct sunlight, a drafty room, or high temperatures. And don't place a bowl of fruit near the flowers, since ethylene gas from ripening fruit will hasten the demise of your buds.

Snip most flower varieties from your garden in late afternoon or early evening. Not only will each flower be thoroughly supplied with water and food when you cut it, but you'll also get a longer-lasting display. Cut roses and irises while they're still buds.

Measure twice, cut once. For a lovely arrangement, measure the stems to fit your vase. They should be about one-and-a-half times as tall as your container. If your vase is 6 inches tall, your stems should be about 9 inches long.

Keep pollen from staining your decor. Avoid the mess and damage of pollen shedding from your cut flowers. When you include flowers like lilies in an arrangement, be sure to cut off the pollen-bearing anthers from the stamens and throw them out. Turn the flower upside down and use sharp scissors to snip them.

Straighten tulips with a penny. If you want your tulips to stand straight and tall, drop a few copper pennies in the vase. Though florists aren't sure how this works, the penny seems to keep them from twisting and turning in search of light.

Help blooms stay upright. Here's a tip to keep droopy flowers standing tall — use drinking straws. Thread stems through wide straws and place them in a vase. Your flowers will stand taller and last longer.

Don't be daffy with your daffodils. Cut flowers from your garden are a beautiful addition to your home. If you're lucky enough to have tulips and daffodils, here's a tip: don't bring them in from the garden and put them together in the same vase. The slime from daffodil stems can ruin cut tulips. So put the daffodils in a separate vase for about a day, then rinse off their stems, and you can safely add them to the tulips.

Anchor vase with sand. Most flower arrangements are top-heavy. To keep a vase from toppling, funnel a layer of sand or small stones into it before starting your arrangement.

Immortalize your summer blooms. Why pay hothouse prices for a winter bouquet when you can enjoy one from your own garden? In the summer, trim the buds off your favorite daisies and violets and flatten them carefully between two paper towels. Choose a variety of small blooms and greenery, making sure they are fairly flat and not wet with dew.

Dry them for six to 10 weeks between the pages of a large book. Come winter, you can spend many a cozy hour creating cards, bookmarks, and framed posies from your dried treasures. You can even use them to decorate candles and lampshades in true Victorian style.

Get a second life from drying packets. Save the silica gel packets from boxes of new shoes and pill bottles. You can use them to dry cut flowers without losing the beautiful natural colors of the blooms. Simply pour them into a container, place the flowers inside, then sprinkle more gel on top. Drying can take anywhere from two to six days. Make sure the silica gel is not coarse or it can damage the flowers.

Protect buds while they dry. Place daisies face down when you dry them in silica gel. Same thing goes for other flowers that are open and flat with strong petals. But place complex, three-dimensional buds like dahlias face up in the gel so they keep their shape. When drying flowers like roses or hydrangeas, be sure to support the blossoms so the petals aren't crushed.

Easy-to-make flower press

Cut two pieces of plywood about 10 inches by 12 inches, or whatever size you like. Drill holes in all four corners and attach the pieces together with screws and wing nuts. Next, find some cardboard and cut several pieces slightly smaller than your press. Trim the corners so nothing interferes with the screws.

Open the press and stack a few layers of cardboard on the bottom. Arrange your flowers on smooth paper towels, newspaper, or blotting paper. Cover with more paper and cardboard, close the press, and tighten the screws. Check on your flowers in two weeks. They should be dry.

Spritz on everlasting shine. Dried flowers tend to fall apart and grow dusty, but hair spray can keep your arrangement looking fresh. Give them a quick spray-down before you put them in a vase. Hairspray will seal in their color and help them keep their shape so your flowers look fresh longer.

Turn faulty flowers into potpourri. If your flowers don't look perfect when it's time to cut, skip the vase. Dry your blooms and make up a batch of fragrant potpourri. Place petals in a single layer on a cookie sheet in a 180-degree oven with the door ajar. Remove after a few hours, and let them stand overnight to finish drying. Mix with your favorite essential oil, and store in a cool, dark place for several weeks.

Fill the air with ferns. To lighten the effect of a hanging basket, mix maidenhair or asparagus ferns with more substantial plants. Both ferns have a beautiful lacy look that takes the edge off stiff arrangements. If you can't get your hands on one of these classics, just about any open, feathery plant will do.

Create a dirt-free hanging garden. Dirty pots driving you crazy? Grow air plants. These tiny, spider-like plants, called tillandsias, absorb all the nutrients they need from the air. Usually you see them hot-glued on pieces of driftwood. But if you are fortunate enough to find them loose, you can attach them to fishing line and suspend them from a ceiling. Water the plant about three times a week, more often in hot, dry weather. These conversation starters do especially well in bright, damp rooms like bathrooms and kitchens.

Force trees to bloom in winter. Many trees and shrubs form flowers in the fall. After eight weeks of cold weather, you can force them to flower inside. Cut several long branches of apple, cherry, quince, spirea, or forsythia that are heavy with buds. Make a 2-inch slit in the bottom of each stem and set it in warm water. Keep the branches in a cool, humid area, out of direct sun. Be patient. The branches will take several weeks to bloom.

Make outdoor greens indoor favorites. If you hate to lose your favorite sun-lovers to the coming frost, bring them in from the cold. Pot up garden plants and spray them with water to clean off any dirt. Check carefully for pests. Leave the plants outdoors in a shady corner for a few days before easing them into your home. Keep these guests separate from your regular houseplants until they adapt.

SPRING March April May

Flower and Vegetable Gardens

❀ Prepare new planting beds and gardens by mixing in one to three inches of compost.

❀ Pull weeds when they first start growing, while soil is moist and roots are short, before they go to seed.

❀ Buy plants that resist disease and use less water.

Tree and Shrub Beds

❀ Prepare new tree and shrub beds by mixing compost into the entire bed (not just planting holes).

Lawns

❀ Start mowing, about three inches high for most lawns in northern states; two inches for lawns in southern states. "Grasscycle" — leave the clippings for free fertilizer.

❀ For lawns in poor condition: aerate, overseed, and top-dress with a quarter inch to half inch of compost.

❀ Fertilize lawns if needed in May with "natural organic" or "slow-release" fertilizer.

Watering

❀ Check soil moisture at plant roots before watering — don't water until they need it.

❀ Lay out soaker hoses in beds and cover with mulch. Prepare sprinkler systems by testing, adjusting, and repairing leaks.

Composting

❀ Harvest compost from your bin. Throw any uncomposted sticks or stalks back in for another cycle.

Information adapted from EPA's GreenScapes Program

SUMMER  June July August

Flower and Vegetable Gardens

- Mulch flower and vegetable beds with compost or grass clippings to conserve water and control weeds.
- Use fabric row covers to keep pests off sensitive vegetables.
- Identify bugs before you spray, squash, or stomp — they may be "good bugs" that eat pests.

Tree and Shrub Beds

- Mulch shrub and tree beds with shredded wood, leaves, or bark once a year to conserve water, reduce weeds, and feed the soil.

Lawns

- Mow regularly and leave the clippings on the lawn.
- Keep mower blades sharp to reduce lawn damage and brown tips.
- Consider saving water by letting some lawn areas (ones that don't get heavy traffic) go brown and dormant until fall.

Watering

- Water at dawn to reduce evaporation.
- Water lawns one inch per week — if no rain — or let go brown and dormant (but water enough to moisten root zone once a month).
- Start and recheck watering systems and adjust for weather. (Don't water when it rains.)

Composting

- Add yard debris to compost pile; water pile to keep it moist. Place pile in shade or cover to hold moisture.

Information adapted from EPA's GreenScapes Program

FALL
September
October
November

Flower and Vegetable Gardens

- Pull emerging weeds in beds when ground is moist and before they develop deep roots.
- Mulch garden beds with leaves or compost to reduce winter weeds and feed the soil. Or plant winter cover crops in open beds.
- Prepare new planting areas by digging in compost.

Tree and Shrub Beds

- Mulch tree and shrub beds with leaves, shredded wood, or bark.
- Plant trees, shrubs, and many perennials in early fall to give them a good start.

Lawns

- Improve thin areas of lawn in September–October by aerating, overseeding, and top-dressing with compost.
- Fertilize lawns with "natural organic" or "slow-release" fertilizer in September to develop healthy roots and crowd out weeds.
- Plant new lawns to give them the best start before next summer.

Watering

- Reduce watering during cooler weather.
- Shut off and drain watering systems if you expect a freeze.
- Put away exposed soaker hoses, or re-cover with mulch if left out.

Composting

- Clear unwanted garden growth and compost it for spring. Keep pile as moist as a wrung-out sponge.

Information adapted from EPA's GreenScapes Program

WINTER December January February

Flower and Vegetable Gardens

❄ Rake winter leaf mulch back onto beds if winds blow it off.

❄ Weed beds once during winter to prevent weeds going to seed.

Tree and Shrub Beds

❄ Prune fruit trees and other woody trees and shrubs while they're dormant (December–February).

❄ If you have questions, check with your local Cooperative Extension office or a nursery.

Lawns

❄ Tune up yard equipment; sharpen mower blades. Plan drip irrigation or soaker hoses for beds and containers to conserve water.

❄ Winter is the time to plan for spring.

❄ Check storage areas for unwanted chemicals and dispose safely. Call your local solid waste agency for details. Plan to replace plants that have disease or pest problems.

Watering

❄ Let nature do the work.

Composting

❄ Continue to add fruit and vegetable scraps, coffee grounds, eggshells, nutshells, and houseplant leaves and stalks from inside your home to your compost pile year-round.

Information adapted from EPA's GreenScapes Program

Index

R